THE
KING'S
BED

THE
KING'S
BED

Sex, Power and
the Court of Charles II

DON JORDAN
AND MICHAEL WALSH

Little, Brown

LITTLE, BROWN

First published in Great Britain in 2015 by Little, Brown

1 3 5 7 9 10 8 6 4 2

A CIP catalogue record for this book
is available from the British Library.

Hardback ISBN 978-1-4087-0488-2
C format ISBN 978-1-4087-0489-9

Typeset in Electra by M Rules
Printed and bound in Great Britain by
Clays Ltd, St Ives plc

Papers used by Little, Brown are from well-managed forests
and other responsible sources.

MIX
Paper from
responsible sources
FSC www.fsc.org   FSC® C104740

Little, Brown
An imprint of
Little, Brown Book Group
100 Victoria Embankment
London EC4Y 0DY

An Hachette UK Company
www.hachette.co.uk

www.littlebrown.co.uk

To Dian and Eithne

An excellent prince doubtless had he been less addicted to women.

John Evelyn

CONTENTS

INTRODUCTION

The sexual revolution began in the sixties – the 1660s. When Charles II of England, Scotland and Ireland ascended to the throne in 1660 he became pivotal to a sexual upheaval at the top of English society. The newly reconstituted royal Court of St James blossomed into a seraglio of pleasure. The Puritans' emphasis on chastity was cast aside and the court threw itself into a vortex of giddy sensuality. At the heart of the revolution were Charles and his many lovers.

While writing our previous book on Charles II, *The King's Revenge*, we were aware of just how important the King's mistresses were in the life of both court and monarch. When the people of London came out in the autumn of 1660 to watch the executions of some of those responsible for beheading the King's father, Charles I, Charles II was cavorting with his current mistress, Barbara Palmer, the irresistibly sexy wife of one of his close supporters. From this contrasting tableau of torture and pleasure we began to consider to what extent Charles's mistresses had held power over his life. For example, had previous writers underplayed their importance? Contemporaries who wrote about their king certainly thought he spent too little time on affairs of state and too much time purely on affairs. This being so, we wondered if it might be possible to unravel something of Charles's character through these relationships. The result of these ruminations is the present book.

Charles not only loved the physical allure of women, he also adored their company – their society and gossip, the games, the rivalry, the coquetry. He surrounded himself with women, keeping former mistresses on his payroll in the royal seraglio at Westminster long after passion had abated. Some of his mistresses held such sway over him that they were in control of the relationship. This influence went beyond the bedroom to affect foreign and domestic policy. Barbara Palmer, who dominated the first decade of his reign, worked as a spy for France and connived successfully to persuade Charles to sack the most important statesman of the Restoration. His last great paramour, the Breton noblewoman Louise de Kérouaille, was a French agent who helped pave the way for England to become a puppet of the Sun King, Louis XIV.

We felt that if a king could allow his mistresses such power, then the way to the core of the man would surely be via his relationships. *The King's Bed* traces the impact of women on Charles in an attempt to understand his personality. So many contrasting views have been provided as to his character – ranging from 'essentially loveable', according to Antonia Fraser, to 'cold', according to Ronald Hutton – that we felt there was a case to reconsider this intriguing character in the light of the evidence provided by his private life.

Whitehall became a palace of fun, frequented by men and women who delighted in kicking over the sexual constraints of previous times. The libidinous king and his licentious court were the most potent symptoms of sudden and profound social change within the higher sections of English society. The years of the Restoration constituted an era of sexual liberation in the court of Charles II, albeit mostly for the men of the court. For those who wished, and who had sufficient social standing, it was a time of increasing freedom and experimentation.

The King's Bed also tells the story of this sexual revolution and the role of Charles II and his many women within it. Charles did not drive the revolution but he was its figurehead. Put together with current ideas about sexuality, including the belief that women had to have an orgasm to conceive, the new freedoms his reign brought in provided a sexual playground, albeit one in which men continued to hold most of the advantages. And no one had more advantages – and more sexual partners – than the King.

It became clear to us that Charles was not simply the randy king portrayed so often. It was more than that: women were an obsession with him. Among those he lusted after were some who became famous historical figures, such as Lucy Walter, Nell Gwyn and Barbara Palmer. There were many, many more we don't know about, one-nighters smuggled up from the river under darkness, then up a stairwell from a private jetty, for a quick fling in an anteroom kept specially for the purpose. The women varied from the rumbustious to the mild-mannered, from the brazen to the calculating, from common prostitutes to actresses and aristocrats. They all played their part in the King's sensuous dream world.

So this is not a book simply about Charles; it is also about his women. We cannot hope to tell the stories of all of them – the identity of many is simply not known. But we do know a good deal about many of them. The most important were the subject of constant gossip, appearing in bawdy ballads sold for sixpence a pop, in memoirs, diaries, letters and even – such was their prominence – official diplomatic reports. And all these and more were the sources for this work.

We decided we must recount what finally became of Charles's major mistresses and his numerous children. Without them, British life would be less varied and certainly less interesting. Together, the women and their offspring have created a surprising legacy that has come down to us today. Thanks to them, Charles's personal life is now more relevant than ever.

Britain is on the threshold of having its first monarch descended from Charles II's illegitimate line. At the time of writing, we have yet to experience the ascent of Charles III, yet it seems the nation can hardly wait for the coronation of King William V, descended from Charles II through his mother via two illegitimate blood lines.

In the meantime, the memory of Charles, the man, stays with us to amuse, infuriate or be venerated. We hope that this examination of his personal life will add something to the understanding of this most enigmatic of public men, while at the same time entertaining the reader. It is hard not to envisage him still, with his dark, knowing eyes evaluating how he might seduce a lady or escape a tedious meeting of council, anxious to be off, tearing out of the palace on his long legs as if the devil was at his tail, loping towards St James's Park or leaping onto a horse or into a coach to take him to Newmarket or his latest mistress. Whatever one thinks of him, Charles was never dull. In an age when there was much to fear, including the pox and the plague, what Charles feared more than anything was to be bored.

I

THE LAST SOIRÉE

It all unravelled so quickly. As on most evenings, he strolled through the palace after supper to visit his mistress.[1] Leaving his private apartments beside the river, he walked north through the maze of the old Tudor buildings and came to the entrance to another suite of rooms directly ahead of him. Behind this door lay the Queen's personal apartments.[2] There had been a time when he would have gone straight in, but a dozen or more years had passed since then. Their marriage had soured early on when it became clear that the Queen, though she could conceive, could not bear children that survived to full term. The Queen now spent an increasing amount of time at her other apartments in Somerset House, half a mile downstream. He turned away from her door and headed west towards the Privy Garden. As always, his spaniels ran ahead, knowing their way. They considered the palace to be theirs as much as the King's, even breeding in the King's apartments and permeating the palace with the sour perfume of their milk.[3]

It was the evening of Sunday, 31 January 1685. King Charles II of England, Scotland and Ireland was four months off his fifty-fifth birthday. He was a little the wrong side of his prime but still generally jovial and relaxed. For the last twenty-four years he had enjoyed life

in the old palace of Whitehall. The palace had grown in spontaneous fashion, his father and grandfather, and before them Elizabeth
I and Henry VIII, all adding to it until it became a sprawling collection of buildings of evolving styles along the banks of the Thames. It
was home to a vast array of residents: royal relatives, both near and
distant, mistresses current and passed-over, court favourites, amusing
confidants, tedious advisors, well-fed Beefeaters, bawdy laundresses,
gentle seamstresses and household and kitchen staff of all varieties,
along with the King's personal herbalist, his chemist, pimpmaster
and pox doctor. All these and more lived cheek by jowl, a whole city
crammed into a palace.

Zigzagging through the maze of interconnecting rooms, the King
passed through an ornate doorway and into the Long Gallery – a
grand sweep of two hundred and ten feet of faded grandeur. The
once-lovely Holbein ceiling was pockmarked with ad hoc repairs, but
the vista ahead of him was still one of graceful, even regal beauty.[4]
The gallery ran along the east side of the Privy Garden, whose austere Tudor formality Charles had enlivened with statuary and
ornaments, including one of his most prized objects, a fabulous
French sundial embellished with glass orbs and painted portraits of
himself, the Queen, several of his mistresses and all of his twelve
recognised illegitimate children.* It had been a monument to his
love of science and women, and to his pride in his progeny. The sundial was missing now, destroyed by that mischief-maker, the Earl of
Rochester. Returning from a drunken night on the town, Rochester
had taken exception to the dial's unfortunate phallic shape, or perhaps to the portrait it bore of the King. Shouting, 'What, doest thou

---

* The sundial, designed by the priest-philosopher Francis Line, is described as
'rising tree-like from its stone pedestal. Comprising altogether more than 250 units,
there were six main pieces of the dial in the form of stacked circular tables and large
globes supported by iron branches ... Round the tables were dials showing time
according to various historical and foreign forms of reckoning, above them glass
plates bearing portraits of the royal family.' (Anita McConnell, *Dictionary of
National Biography*).

stand here to fuck time?' he laid into the offending dial with his sword, reducing it to splinters.[5] The next day, the Earl fled from London, but he was eventually forgiven and returned to court. Five years later, syphilis and alcohol took him away for good. Charles would never need to banish or pardon his infuriating friend again.

On the other side of the garden lay the rooms of another intoxicating personality the King had at one time or another banished and pardoned. This was the most sensational of his many lovers, Barbara Palmer, Duchess of Cleveland, whose voracious sexual appetites had once thrilled him with all the 'tricks of Aretin', alluding to an Italian writer of bawdy poetry.* Some said Charles had starved his fleet of resources to lavish money upon her, leading to a humiliating military defeat in 1667 when the Dutch navy sailed up the River Medway and surprised the English fleet at anchor.[6] Despite past difficulties, including amorous indiscretions, the Duchess was now back in the palace but no longer in the royal bed. The woman who held that honour had rooms at the southern end of the Long Gallery, towards which the royal spaniels were leading the way.

As the King made his elaborate progress, an older, more austere figure was also heading for the same suite of rooms: John Evelyn, the polymath and diarist, a man of Renaissance abilities who managed to be both a trusted ally of the King and a stern critic of his rule by the simple expedient of confiding his censures solely to his diary. Evelyn was one of the founders of the Royal Society and had made his name as a horticulturalist. He wrote on many scientific and religious topics and was trusted with important work for the government. A strongly religious man, Evelyn did not like the profane life in Whitehall.[7] In a court filled with vice and licentiousness, he cut an incongruous figure.

By this time of the evening, Evelyn would have preferred to be seven miles away down the river at Deptford, where he lived at Saye

---

* Pietro Aretino, a sixteenth-century Italian writer credited with inventing literary pornography with his sonnets, Sonetti Lussurioso.

Court surrounded by his books and two hundred acres of gardens. This evening, business had detained him at Whitehall, requiring him, as it so often did, to stay on and attend the court soirées. If Evelyn had a fault, it was that he had a saint's delight in seeing how sinners lived and in recording the scenes for posterity.[8]

The King's progress through the Long Gallery was slow. Years of over-indulgence had taken their toll and he was no longer as vigorous as before. An attack of gout clung on tenaciously and he had an abscess on his heel that refused to mend.[9] Nor were the contents of the gallery what they had once been. In his father's day it had held more than a hundred paintings, including the finest works by Correggio, Titian and Raphael. Following his father's execution the paintings were sold and scattered across Europe. With limited resources he had attempted to restore the collection. Though the best were gone for ever, he rescued some favourites. One was a family portrait by Van Dyck, depicting his father and mother, his sister Mary, aged one, and himself at the age of two. He had been Prince of Wales then, heir to three thrones. Of the family group and its painter he was the sole survivor. His father had gone first in 1649, dying at the age of forty-eight on a scaffold scarcely two hundred feet from the entrance to the gallery. His mother died in 1669, possibly of an accidental overdose of the opiates she took for her bronchitis. His sister Henrietta Anne, to whom he was very close, died next in 1670, at the age of twenty-six, possibly poisoned by her husband Philippe, the openly homosexual brother of Louis XIV of France. Charles had been king now for twenty-five years and for all of those he had sought consolation for his family's calamities in the pursuit of sexual pleasure.[10]

In the apartment at the end of the gallery a sociable crowd had gathered. *She* was at its centre – Louise de Kérouaille, Duchess of Portsmouth, his mistress-in-chief, holding sway over a court within a court. From the moment she awoke in the morning her role was to be beautiful and available. More than that, she had to be on display. Before dressing, she would sit before her mirror and pose, her nightclothes artfully arranged to show off her beauty – including a good deal of flesh – to advantage. Courtiers and young gallants came to her boudoir as if to a *tableau vivant*, to gaze upon her. Maids fussed around, brushing her lustrous dark hair, discussing her selection of clothes and jewellery and her appointments for the day ahead.[11] Her sexual power irradiated the room. Once, another woman had held this position, that of chief courtesan, the King's consort in everything but title. This woman, the beautiful and voluptuous Barbara Villiers, whose marriage to Roger Palmer had resulted in his being cuckolded by the King and given an earldom in return for his wife, had ultimately been dropped from favour, but not before she had given the King five children. Well over a decade had passed since Louise had replaced Barbara, causing a sensation across the country, as she was notoriously both Catholic and French.

Most mornings, *he* was among her admiring visitors, basking in the flattering remarks – for to flatter her was to flatter him. Her morning ritual was a piece of theatre reinforcing her position as the most alluring, the most desirable, the most radiant woman in the land. As the King's mistress she was an object of greater desire and envy than the Queen, wielding power and influence over the King and with access to his wealth. For those who had hoped that the King's return from exile would mark a return of the monarch as a living symbol of divine rule, here was the all too fleshy refutation of the myth. If anything was a symbol of the human appetites and mortality of the King, it was the image of his mistress in her palace within a palace, an emissary from the powerful court of Louis XIV, the Sun King, who bankrolled his cousin's inferior court in London. In all her pomp and display, Louise was the embodiment of the failure of Charles's reign to allay the religious fears of his subjects, to reconcile the divided aspirations of those he ruled over, or to become a viable symbol of the national self-image.

With his short but painful journey at an end, footmen bowed and swung open the doors, and King Charles II entered his own earthly paradise. Its perfection had been achieved at huge expense – he had paid for these rooms to be torn down and rebuilt three times before *she* had been satisfied. The Queen had to make do with rooms on which little or nothing had been spent in twenty years.[12] The grand salon was decorated in the style of a French palace, which was hardly surprising, as its furnishings had largely been donated by Louise's other benefactor, Louis XIV. The apartment was described by John Evelyn as 'ten times' more magnificent than that of the Queen. Rich tapestries covered the walls, depicting landscapes in which sat French royal palaces including Versailles and the Louvre. Each tapestry was ten feet high and nearly seventeen feet long. Hanging in a room beside the flat banks of the Thames, the tapestries provided a window onto a rolling Arcadian, and very French, dreamland. One tapestry even depicted the Sun King himself hunting boar in parkland in front of the incomparable Château de Monceau.[13]

There could be no doubt on the part of a visitor that these tapestries adorned the walls of a woman of power – a woman sponsored by not one but two kings. Solid silver tables and Japanese lacquered cabinets stood about, containing vases of gold and silver. Behind all this lavish decoration lay the cold fact that the French king had encouraged the liaison between Charles and this woman in order to cement treaties between the two nations in 1670 – parts of those treaties still remained secret, including Charles's pledge to convert to Roman Catholicism.

The King was greeted by a relaxed and opulent scene. Music played while many of the indulged and indulgent guests played cards. The huge sum of £2000 in gold coins lay wagered on the table.[14] Apart from Louise herself, at least two of the King's former mistresses were present, the Duchesses of Mazarin and Cleveland. The sexual relationships between many of those in the room were so deliberately intertwined and exaggerated that they could best be described – like the décor itself – as baroque. It was no different for Charles himself. At one time or another he had thrown aside both Mazarin and Cleveland for their sexual infidelities, only to forgive them and allow their return to court. Such was the aura of sexual liberation for both sexes in the court that many of those present would have known one another in the most intimate manner. It was a time of freedom and sexual experimentation. Mazarin was infamous for her multiple affairs with both men and women, including, it was rumoured, Anne Lennard, the King's daughter by the Duchess of Cleveland herself (though some said Anne's father was really the Earl of Chesterfield). No one went so far as to claim Barbara's husband Roger Palmer was the father. As a French boy sang love songs and gallants paid extravagant compliments to ladies, gold coins clattered brightly across the gaming table and an aura of relaxed and luxurious decadence flooded the room. Charles felt at home.

John Evelyn, on his arrival, felt the exact opposite. He looked around, taking everything in with the eye of a recording angel, or at least of a disapproving intellectual. He observed every detail: the King's mistresses – those 'abandoned and prophane wretches' – and the courtiers who had wheedled their way into the King's confidence – those 'crafty men'.[15] Evelyn was no late convert to attacking the way the royal court was run. As early as 1662 he had recorded reckless levels of gambling with dice, with the King playing his part and women losing heavily. Evelyn described such scenes as 'wicked folly', suggesting that the court should be 'an example of Virtue to the rest of the kingdome'.[16] Twenty-three years later, little had changed. Evelyn expressed his dismay:

> I can never forget the inexpressible profaneness and luxury, gaming and all manner of dissoluteness and as it were total forgetfulness of God (it being Sunday evening) ... the King sitting and toying with his concubines ... It being a scene of utmost vanity; and surely as they thought would never have an end.[17]

But it would have an end – and soon enough if they all but knew it. The gathering that shocked Evelyn was to prove the King's last night of pleasure in a life full of sensual gratification. When it was late and he was sated with enjoyment, Charles made his way back to his chambers and to bed. Courtiers remarked they had rarely seen him in better spirits.[18] In the morning, he rose early as usual. He went to relieve himself and staggered out of the water closet confused and incapable of speech. He rallied a little but at eight o'clock, as he was about to be shaved, he cried out in pain and fell back in his chair in convulsions.[19] Before the week was out he would be dead.

2

THE MAKING OF A PRINCE

Charles's early years were marked by a struggle over his soul. While his mother, Henrietta Maria, was initially disappointed over his looks, she decided that at least his soul should be unblemished. She became determined that he should be brought up not in the religion of his father but in that of her native France, Roman Catholicism.

Charles was born on 29 May 1630, in a palace located on the site of an old leper hospital. This was St James's Palace, built to the orders of Henry VIII on the confiscated lands of an abbey whose monks had run the hospital dedicated to St James, the patron saint of lepers.* To begin with, Charles did not look as if he had the makings of a lothario. He was a large, sullen child and not at all good looking. The Queen complained about his dark complexion and wrote to her sister, 'He is so ugly that I am ashamed of him.'[1]

As was the custom for royal princes, Charles was brought up in his own household, first at St James's Palace and later at Richmond, where he had a retinue several hundred strong. It included some

---

* St James's Palace was built between 1531 and 1536. The British court continues to this day to be known as the Court of St James, despite Queen Victoria having moved the official royal residence to Buckingham Palace.

suitable boys of rank to play with, including George Villiers, 2nd Duke of Buckingham, who was brought up in the royal household after his father's assassination by a renegade soldier. Villiers and the Prince became great friends, but in later life their friendship would turn to enmity, and Buckingham would even threaten the security of the throne.

Charles spent a great deal of his childhood separated from his mother and father, though by all accounts they were loving parents. During his infancy, Mrs Christabella Wyndham, the daughter of a Cornish landowner and wife of Sir Edmund Wyndham, a career soldier, was appointed as one of his nurses. She held this position until Charles was five, when she left the royal entourage. Ten years later she would reappear in the Prince's life in a most sensational fashion.

Charles's schooling was haphazard. The capable Earl of Newcastle became his governor, responsible for running the Prince's household and for his education. Though he could have taught Charles much, his visits to the boy were sporadic. To make up for his absences he wrote excellent letters that must have been music to the ears of a small boy. Newcastle was of the opinion that the Prince should not be too studious, for 'contemplation spoils action.' He also felt that 'I would rather have you study things than words, matter than language.'[2] The Prince took his mentor's words to heart, developing grace and style rather than any great learning. While charm would become one of Charles's abiding characteristics, so too would a phobia of reading. Here at the outset was formed the young man's habit of not thinking too deeply about any subject or issue, a practice that would bedevil his adult life and drive his more serious-minded ministers to distraction.

When Charles was eleven, Newcastle resigned as governor. He had spent £4000 on his duties, a sum he felt was quite enough, especially as it was the tip of a financial iceberg he had expended on trying (and failing) to gain a major position at court. With Newcastle's departure as governor, Charles was tucked under the wing of his mother. Henrietta Maria was to have a great influence upon her son. She took him to her private Roman Catholic chapel at Somerset House. The chapel was a 'lavish setting for the mass' designed by Inigo Jones. Among its adornments was a large painting of the royal family by Peter Paul Rubens. No finer setting could have been imagined for the introduction to the Catholic religion of the heir to a Protestant throne.

Inevitably word got out and a public storm erupted over rumours of the Prince's possible apostasy. The King, who had complacently facilitated the debacle by encouraging his Queen to build a Catholic chapel in a royal palace, ensured that his heir was again given a suitable Anglican guardian. The task fell to the bookish but aged Earl of Hertford, who kept the Prince at Hampton Court, away from his mother's supposedly corrosive influence.

The matter of the Prince's religion did not go away and it was debated in Parliament. Concern over his mother's influence continued, with Parliament stipulating that the boy should be prevented from having contact with her. Here lay a problem that was to persist throughout Charles's life and his future as a king: the differences between Protestantism and Catholicism were enmeshed within his own family, between the faiths of his father and his mother and between those of their native countries.

Gradually, Charles grew into an agreeable youth, quick to see a joke and eager to learn about life. He began to take on his adult form, with a sallow complexion, black wavy hair and tall, athletic frame. The well-known portrait by Peter Lely from the 1660s captures his likeness well – the heavy lower eyelids and pronounced lower lip, and the early downward movement of the cheeks into jowls. Even on a canvas, Charles was no oil painting. But his quizzical good humour and restlessness shine through. He sits in his royal regalia, with his left hand clutching the arm of his gilded chair as if he might at any moment raise himself to be off. The pose, together with the fact that Lely never quite resolves the gaudy regal robes into a viable colour scheme, makes the painting appear initially ungainly. Longer inspection reveals that the painter has captured a great deal of the spirit of the man. If one forgets the regal clothes and setting, Charles looks for all the world like a canny gypsy horse breeder, anxious to be up and away from the painter's gaze and about his business, buying or selling a horse or seducing the owner's daughter.

Once Charles entered his teens, his parents began to think of suitable marriage partners. Two possible candidates were considered. The Queen favoured a match with Louise Henrietta, the daughter of Frederick Henry, the Dutch Prince of Orange, though Louise was three years older than the Prince. When this was turned down by Frederick, the Queen turned her ambitions to a prize of much greater value, Anne-Marie Louise d'Orléans, Duchess of Monpensier, the phenomenally rich French heiress who was closely related to the French royal line. While Henrietta Maria harboured dreams of this paragon of position and wealth marrying her boy, the Duchess, also three years Charles's senior, had her own dreams of marrying the child king Louis XIV. She even called him 'my little king'. In the event, neither marriage would come to pass. Another possibility was a marriage to the eight-year-old Infanta Joana of Portugal, the daughter of King John IV, but this idea too came to nothing. Joana was the younger sister of Princess Catherine, who would decisively enter Charles's life at a later date.

As the Prince grew up, the fractious relationship between King and Parliament was rapidly deteriorating, taking with it any chance of reconciliation on taxes and control of the military. Relations had broken down irreconcilably by 1642 and war broke out. Charles was by then a spirited youngster who loved action rather than learning and was already an accomplished horseman. That October, at the first set-piece battle of the war, near the village of Edgehill in Warwickshire, the twelve-year-old Prince exhibited bravery in the face of danger. When an enemy force unexpectedly broke through the royalist lines near the spot where Charles and his younger brother James were stationed, the Prince drew his pistol and shouted, 'I fear them not!' and made ready to charge before a cavalier grabbed the reins of his horse and led him away from danger.

Neither the Parliamentarians nor the King were to gain the quick victory both expected. The war fragmented into several theatres of battle spread across the country. By the spring of 1645, when the conflict had lasted two and a half years, the King became worried about the future both for himself and for his immediate family. The Queen had already left for France, taking with her Henrietta Anne, her youngest child. The next youngest royal children, Elizabeth and Henry, were in London where they were held virtual captives on the order of Parliament. The Prince of Wales and brother James were with their father at his headquarters in the royalist city of Oxford. For reasons of military strategy and for safety's sake, the King decided the Prince should no longer reside at Oxford, but should instead move to Bristol.[3]

In the south-west, the war was not going well for the royalist cause and the various local commanders were arguing over the best way forward. Seeing a means both to unite the forces in the west and to detach his eldest son from his side, King Charles appointed the Prince commander-in-chief of his Western Army. Although the title was largely honorary, the Prince was expected to act as a rallying point for deteriorating royalist efforts, allowing the King to concentrate on prosecuting the war elsewhere.

Aged a little less than fifteen, Charles left his father's headquarters at Oxford and for the first time in his life was expected to strike out in an autonomous role of importance. He was instructed to set up his flag in the royalist stronghold of Bristol where he had the military title of Captain-General, with his own royal court and council to make policy, with the Prince as a participant but without any veto. He left Oxford on 4 March.

At Bristol, the Prince entered a viper's nest. The local royalist grandees had failed to raise sufficient troops for the task at hand and quarrelled endlessly over who should defer to whom in military command. To make matters worse, Charles's flamboyant cousin Prince Rupert of the Rhine was in the West Country recruiting forces. Since Rupert was one of the royalists' best commanders, where did this place his much younger royal cousin in the pecking order? With forces raised by the local gentry, the idea of control going to a foreign commander, no matter how brilliant, was difficult to accept. In the circumstances, the Prince's advisory council found it equally difficult to assert its authority, even with the political heavyweight Edward Hyde, the Chancellor of the Exchequer, as one of its members. The local grandees saw Hyde and the council as being peripheral to their efforts and a threat to their authority.

Hyde was the foremost royalist statesman of the time. He had come to politics after an academic career in which he had developed a strong liking for historical research into the nature of English political life. Though immersed for so much of his life in the maelstrom of contemporary affairs, Hyde was by temperament never happier than when surrounded by his books in quiet study and reflection. He believed strongly that the ancient constitution of England was essentially sound and could, with judicious negotiation and compromise, provide a framework in which both sides in the argument could be brought together. He thought the war unnecessary and felt negotiations should be undertaken with the Parliamentarians. While Hyde believed the Stuarts had not been the wisest monarchs, they were nevertheless kings by right and with the best advice (i.e. his advice) could continue to rule a broadly united nation. Hyde believed he was the man to lead these wrongheaded sovereigns towards wise and peaceful rule.

While Hyde's analysis of the situation was generally accurate, there were two particular difficulties: first, a general political crisis which was not about to be cured by absolute monarchy of the type believed in by the Stuarts, and secondly, Charles I's inclination to listen to his French Queen and the belligerent cavalier elements in his court rather than to appeasers like Hyde. While the statesman and former parliamentarian theorised as to how the two elements of the state might be brought back together, the Queen and the cavaliers supported war to crush the rebels.[4] It was natural therefore that Hyde should have enemies in the King's court. When the idea of

Prince Charles being dispatched to head the Western Alliance came up, his enemies seized upon it to have Hyde sent off with him, along with other like-minded privy councillors such as Lord Culpepper. The person who stood to gain most from this was Hyde's rival, Lord Digby, a clever but often misguided man who wielded much influence over the King.

Despite their differences, the King recognised in Hyde the steadfast, unwavering qualities necessary to advise a prince not yet schooled in statecraft, let alone war. Unfortunately, Hyde's stern and schoolmasterish demeanour could make him appear a pompous and hectoring older man. Although still only in his thirties, to a fourteen-year-old boy Hyde would have seemed antediluvian. Nevertheless, Hyde was at the head of the council that accompanied the Prince to the West Country.

In April, Hyde and his fellow advisors recommended that the Prince should hold a general meeting in order to iron out disagreements between the various local grandees who ran the war in the western counties. None of them had anything but optimism that the royalist cause would prevail. After all, the rebels were thought of as being in 'some disorder and confusion' having removed their commander-in-chief, the Earl of Essex, and replaced him with a man of lesser rank, Sir Thomas Fairfax.[5] Prince Rupert advocated striking while the royalists' opponents were still in a state of disarray but his advice went unheeded.

What the royalists didn't know was that their opponents were pausing to reorganise themselves into the most efficient army of the age, one that was the forerunner of today's forces organised under a unified command. This was Cromwell's New Model Army. The Parliamentary leaders sacked ineffective officers, appointed new ones, and used their economic power to put their new forces on a centralised stipend. By the spring of 1645, this reorganisation was all but complete and the fortunes of the Crown would change for ever.

The young Prince and his council, oblivious to this vital shift in military power, met in Bridgwater, situated on the River Parrett in the lee of the Quantock Hills, a few miles from the Bristol Channel. A vast red sandstone fort dominated the town. Built around 1200 on the orders of King John, the castle had a moat fed from the river and made an excellent command post for a royalist garrison led by Sir Edmund Wyndham, who was also the local MP. The Bridgwater summit was to have an outcome unforeseen by the watchful Hyde, marking his young charge's evolution into manhood.

The summit was interrupted by a startling change in the Prince's behaviour. Charles was expected to sit in on at least some meetings of the council, to apply himself to participating and use his powers of judgement. He did his best, until he was reacquainted with his former nurse, Christabella Wyndham, the garrison commander's much younger wife. Christabella, vivacious and beautiful, was a marvellous distraction from the frustrations and anxieties of adolescence.

Christabella's father had been a notorious critic of the King, so she had been a surprising choice as the Prince's nurse. In 1628, two years before the Prince was born, Christabella's father, Hugh Pyne, a Somerset landowner, barrister and Puritan, criticised Charles I for being as 'unwise a king as ever was' and suggesting his own shepherd was as fit to rule.[6] Pyne was imprisoned and charged with treason. He was reprieved, thanks to arguing that the Treason Act contained nothing about being rude about a king.* Despite this awkward family history, Christabella was viewed as having redeemed herself by marrying a royalist.

It has been said that war can act as an aphrodisiac; if so, it certainly worked its spell on the young Prince and his former nurse. When they were reintroduced, sparks flew. This scandalous liaison was to set the tone for much of Charles's future life – a desire to please himself, allied to a total disregard for propriety, rather than the expected interest in tedious activities and duties. Hyde was outraged; being a

---

* The Treason Act, brought in by Edward II in 1351, codified acts of treason, making it an offence to 'compass or imagine' the death of the king or to wage war against him.

loyal servant of the Crown he was unable to criticise the Prince's character, so he vented his spleen by recording a far from glowing assessment of that of Christabella Wyndham:

> she being a woman of no good breeding, and of a country pride, *Nihil muliebre praetor corpus gerens,** valued herself much upon the power and familiarity which her neighbours might see she had with the Prince of Wales; and therefore, upon all occasions, in company, and when the concourse of the people was greatest, would use great boldness towards him ...[7]

Worse was to come. It became clear that the Prince and his former nurse had developed a secret world in which they shared private jokes. The Prince encouraged Christabella's disparaging views about his advisors, Hyde recalled:

> coming to Bridgewater, and having an extraordinary kindness for Mrs Windham, who had been his nurse, he was not only diverted by her folly and petulancy from applying himself to the serious consideration of his business, but accustomed to hearing her speak negligently and scornfully of the Council; which, though at first it made no impression in him of disrespect towards them, encouraged other people who heard it, to take the like liberty; and from hence grew an irreverence towards them; which reflected upon himself, and served to bring prejudice of their councils throughout the whole course.[8]

What Hyde was describing was adolescent rebellion and defiance of authority, allied to a strongly emergent interest in sex. This adolescent behaviour would become a pattern throughout his life. In the fourteen-year-old boy frolicking with a woman, mocking those in

---

* Literally, 'women wearing nothing but a body', meaning women without education or reasoning.

authority, we have a perfect picture of the man he would become. The image in the Lely portrait was already coming to life.

From the public display of affection for her former charge, some of those present reached the conclusion that Christabella had deflowered the Prince. Charles was a month off his fifteenth birthday. Among the aristocracy it was considered quite normal for an older woman to show a young man the way in sexual matters. In the seventeenth century, royal princes and princesses could be married before their teens and live together from the age of twelve. Charles's own younger sister Mary had been married at the age of nine to the Prince of Orange. Therefore, the fact that the Prince's former wet nurse assumed the role of sexual educator was not in itself unusual. What caused comment was the open show of affection between the two. Hyde was particularly outraged.[9] In his memoirs, he fulminated at the manner in which Christabella ran across a room packed with courtiers and members of the council, flinging herself at the Prince, showering kisses on his face and head.

According to contemporary accounts, Charles was 'diverted by her folly and petulancy'.[10] Hyde, always watchful, felt Christabella showered the Prince with affection so that he might award grants of money or lands to her husband. When it became clear that the Prince was in no position to do any such thing without the agreement of his council, Christabella became even more disruptive, fomenting 'jealousies and dislikes' between members of the council and the Prince's household. Clarendon and his fellow councillors couldn't wait to get away and to sever contact between the Prince and his temptress. Business was hastily concluded and the court returned to Bristol.

Christabella's feisty spirit gave rise to a story, probably apocryphal, that when Bridgwater was besieged by Fairfax and Cromwell three months after Charles and his council had decamped for Bristol, she ran to the castle ramparts, bared one of her breasts to signify her closeness to the royal heir, grabbed a musket and fired a shot that missed either Fairfax or Cromwell (depending on the version) by a whisker, to plug a nearby adjutant or sergeant-at-arms. In truth, what seems to have happened was that when a messenger was sent by Fairfax demanding a surrender, Mrs Wyndham placed her hand on her breast and said, 'These breasts gave suck to Prince Charles, they shall never be at your mercy. We shall hold it to the last.'[11] She may not have bared a breast, but she had pluck all the same.

The fling with the beautiful Christabella would not be the last time that the Prince's attention would be diverted by a pretty woman when he should be dealing with more important matters. The pattern was to continue throughout his life and have a crucial effect upon his reign. Another pattern to emerge from this period was of Hyde's lifelong disapproval of the frivolous side of Charles's character. Many years later, it would drive a wedge between them.

Charles was back at Bristol for only a brief time before plague hit the city. His council recommended moving to Barnstaple. By now Charles, as a young man who loved outdoor sports and craved action over inactivity, was finding that his position as heir to the throne forced him into a life removed from the excitement of war. He whiled away his days riding in the open countryside and enjoying the new sport of sailing. There was some good news. The Parliamentary expeditionary force to the West Country led by Sir William Waller was brilliantly routed by the best of Charles's squabbling commanders, George Goring, the son of the 1st Earl of Norwich, and a professional soldier known as much for his drunkenness as for his ability as a commander. Despite this success, the royalist situation in the West of England was deteriorating much as it was in the rest of the country thanks to the New Model Army's superior fighting capability. Royalist armies were routed and strongholds besieged. Stuck out of the way in the west, Hyde could bring no pressure to bear upon the King to negotiate an end to the war. Prince Rupert could see which way the wind was blowing, but by adding his voice to the call for an agreed settlement, he was branded by some as a traitor.

On 14 June, at the advice of Lord Digby, the King risked his forces against the New Model Army at the Northamptonshire village of

Naseby, fifty miles north of Oxford. It was the decisive battle of the war. Parliament's war machine crushed the King's army. By July, the situation looked precarious for the royal family and the King ordered the Queen to leave for France. Henrietta Maria went into exile, taking her youngest child, Henrietta Anne, who was barely a toddler.

Under orders from his council, the Prince moved further west to the fortress of Pendennis in Cornwall. It was obvious to Hyde that arrangements had to be made for the safety of the heir to the throne. Orders were given for a ship to lie off the coast, ready to take Charles away. A discussion took place among his advisors about his possible destination.* He could go to France, which was friendly towards the Stuarts, and where his mother Henrietta Maria was now living off the charity of her royal relatives; or he could go to Scotland, where the lairds had often complained about the Stuarts not making enough of their ancient connection, or to Denmark, where the family had relatives on the throne. There was even Ireland to consider, though this was the most risky due to friction among those leaders supportive of the King and a fluctuating military situation.

Despite the efforts of the better royalist commanders in the west, by the autumn the situation was lost. The dashing George Goring gave up and left for France. The situation deteriorated further as winter approached and in December the embattled King issued his eldest son with an ultimatum to leave the country so he would be at liberty to ensure a future for the Stuart dynasty. For two months, the Prince ignored his father's orders. It was a fine display of youthful folly and stubbornness, perhaps even bravado, but it also exhibited something of the young man's determination to suit only himself and no one else, a characteristic much in evidence in his mature years.

Finally, on 2 March 1646, Prince Charles sailed away from England and into a life of adventure and myth. On 4 March, he

---

* Charles's advisors included Edward Hyde (later Lord Clarendon), the Earl of Southampton, the Earl of Berkshire, the Duke of Richmond, Lord Culpepper and Sir Ralph Hopton.

arrived on the Isles of Scilly, an archipelago lying twenty-eight miles off south-west Cornwall. It was one year to the day since he had left his father at Oxford. The Scillies were beautiful but badly provisioned. The arrival of the Prince and his court of nearly three hundred put an extra burden on the islands' meagre resources. News of his flight quickly reached the Parliamentarian forces and soon a flotilla of warships encircled the isles. But luck was with the Prince and a storm blew up, scattering his pursuers' fleet. Charles and his advisors debated what to do. To the surprise of his council, the Prince produced a letter from his father, which he had kept secret until then. The King had written to his eldest son the previous June, shortly after the Battle of Naseby, instructing the Prince to ensure his own safety even if his father's life was in danger: 'I command you (upon my blessing) never to yield to any conditions, that are dishonourable, unsafe for your Person, or Derogatory to Regal Authority, upon any considerations whatsoever, though it were for the saving of my Life.'[12]

Charles remained remarkably self-possessed and calm. Together with his council, he decided they must make for safer shores. On 16 April, with the enemy fleet still scattered, it was decided to seize the advantage and sail for Jersey, a more robust royalist stronghold 180 miles to the east. His luck held and, with favourable winds, Charles's ship reached Jersey without incident.

The Prince arrived in Jersey on 18 April, to be greeted by the governor Sir George Carteret, who ruled over the island from his fortress, the Elizabeth Castle, built on the site of the medieval abbey of St Helier on a rocky tidal island off the island's major port. Sir George, who was a member of Jersey's most prominent family, was pursuing a successful campaign of privateering, carrying out raids against Parliamentary shipping. In contrast to the Scillies, Jersey was an island of plenty. Produce was abundant and Sir George was able to lay on banquets the like of which Charles had not encountered since his days with his father at Oxford. The governor even welcomed his royal guest with a present of £1500 in cash.

While Jersey celebrated the arrival of the Prince, the New Model Army advanced on Oxford. Nine days after the Prince arrived at St Helier, his father disguised himself as a servant and left the city. On 5 May, he surrendered to the Scottish army at Newark in Nottinghamshire, gambling that he could do a deal with the Scots and perhaps regain his throne with their help. The King had long been in dispute with the Scots over the imposition of bishops and Anglican liturgy on the Scottish Church. Largely due to this disagreement, the Scots sided with the forces of the New Model Army. But a schism had also opened between the Scots and King Charles on the issue of the establishment of Presbyterianism in England – one that he hoped to exploit.

While the King parlayed with the Scots, his eldest son found himself facing enforced inaction inside the grim walls of Elizabeth Castle. Having been introduced to adult pleasures only the previous summer, Charles now found them replaced by eight months of abstinence. In the largely male environment of the garrison, it looked as if he would have to endure without female company.

However, Sir George Carteret had a daughter, Marguerite. According to a story promoted by the eminent nineteenth-century historian Lord Acton, the Prince had an affair with the girl – and even fathered a boy by her. Marguerite, aged about seventeen, was alleged to have given birth to an illegitimate son, who was named James de la Cloche after her husband, Jean de la Cloche, a member of another established Jersey family.[13] As we shall see, the story of the birth of a boy fathered by Charles would lead to one of the most enduring myths that surround the life of the future Charles II – that the child would grow up to convert to Roman Catholicism with his father's blessing, so proving Charles's early conversion to that faith. Unfortunately for the story, no contemporary sources allude to the birth of such a child.

While the Prince weighed up whether to remain on Jersey or proceed to France, where he was sure of the protection of his cousin, Louis XIV, several of his advisors, Hyde among them, wished him to stay on the island. They were anxious that he should not fall under the Catholic influence of the Queen. Hyde also worried that the French would promise much in terms of support but deliver little. The King advised his son to go to France. The Queen added her voice to her husband's, saying, 'make all haste you can to show yourself a dutiful son.'[14]

Despite the misgivings of his council, Charles decided to obey his father and sail for France. Hyde, with serious misgivings about the French Catholic court, decided not to accompany him. Charles would leave without the only man who could have attempted to keep him on the Protestant straight and narrow – and who would have been a downright nuisance to a red-blooded young blue blood. Charles set sail towards the determined arms of his mother and into a licentious court where sexual temptations awaited a young prince open to adventure.

3

EXILE AND FIRST LOVE

In the early summer of 1646 it appeared as if the Prince of Wales was leading a charmed life. Though a flotilla of Parliamentary warships had blockaded the Isles of Scilly, he had slipped through the net; next, on his way to Jersey, he had again evaded patrolling Parliamentary flotillas; and finally he had arrived in Calais without interception. For the action-loving Prince, the entire period must have been a marvellous escapade. In France, his love of action would be thwarted by the realities of a court in exile.

The Prince arrived in late June 1646. By then, royal expectations that the Scots would help restore his father to the throne had been dashed, and the King was held by the Scottish army in semi-captivity at Newcastle. While Parliament and the New Model Army engaged in a power struggle, King and Parliament held a series of negotiations aimed at finding a settlement, during which the King dragged his feet. Charles I was temperamentally incapable of negotiating in good faith but was not clever enough to play all sides against one another. Always one who preferred deals with well-born outsiders to negotiating with commoners from his own kingdom, Charles sent an emissary to the French in May, begging for military assistance. The man he approached was France's first minister,

Cardinal Mazarin. Now, both father and son – Charles I and the Prince of Wales – had placed their destiny in the hands of one man.

The hereditary king, Louis XIV, was seven years old, so it fell to his chief minister, forty-four-year-old, Italian-born Cardinal Jules Mazarin, to run the country. While little Louis was the embodiment of the French crown, Mazarin was its moving spirit. Louis had inherited the throne three years previously upon the death of his father, Louis XIII. Upon being widowed, Queen Anne had appointed Mazarin, her husband's first minister, to continue to run the government and, given the new king's age, with vastly increased power.

Mazarin was born Giulio Mazzarino in Pescina, east of Rome. His ambition took him from the Jesuit School in Rome to service in the papal army, before he became nuncio, or papal envoy, in Paris. There he came to the attention of Cardinal Richelieu, Louis XIII's chief minister, and this led to service for the French crown. When Richelieu died, Mazarin took over his duties, and at the death of Louis XIII in 1643 Mazarin became the most powerful man in France. He continued Louis's expansionist foreign policy and championed the crown against the ambitions of the country's powerful regional aristocracy. Mazarin was at the heart of the most culturally magnificent royal court in Europe. The underlying cracks in the French state were covered over by opulent silk hangings. Charles, now further away than ever from his father's side, arrived with little except marvellous French royal connections, thanks to his mother.

The English prince had sailed away from the stern presence of Edward Hyde – but he would discover he was now under the uncompromising thumb of the Cardinal. As for the French court, it was a dazzling inner hub of wealth and excess surrounded by a land in which the peasantry were as poor as they had ever been, due to backward economic practices, disease and over-population.[1]

The French court exhibited such wealth, such spending as the English prince could only long for. Charles's own purse was empty and he had a retinue to feed, composed of servants, gentlemen-in-waiting and cavaliers. Mazarin ensured he was given no money directly, though he cleverly increased Henrietta Maria's allowance so that she might support her son and his followers. Her allowance was nevertheless deliberately ungenerous; hence the amount she spent on her son was trifling, keeping him totally beholden to her while she tried to woo him away from Anglicanism into the arms of Rome. Charles joined his mother at the palace of St Germain-en-Laye, to the west of Paris, in time to celebrate the second birthday of his sister, Henrietta Anne. She would grow up to be clever, beautiful and ill-fated – and his one true confidante and ally.

To begin with, Cardinal Mazarin ensured the Prince was kept well away from the centre of the court. He had his reasons; chief among them was his desire not to alienate the leaders of the New Model Army whom he had correctly identified as the most potent power in England.[2] Charles I's entreaties went unheeded. With the outward display of indifference established, in private the French court was able to show a more welcoming stance towards its young guest.

Life in exile had its compensations. The grand and ancient royal palace of St Germain-en-Laye was the birthplace of Louis XIV, and it would remain the official centre of the French court until the Palace of Versailles was ready many years later. St Germain became a magnet for royalist generals and commanders, including Charles's cousin, Prince Rupert. Even the Earl of Newcastle, Charles's old governor, turned up. Life for the cavalier young-bloods could be dull. Duels broke out as they quarrelled over past slights, military blunders and, of course, women.

Charles soon received invitations to dine with Louis XIV. This was the signal for him to be invited into the vortex of aristocratic Parisian society. For a boy who had been on the run just a few weeks before, this was more like it. He became a novel figure in the palaces around the capital. The ladies discussed him and wrote about him. His manners were compared to those of the finest French aristocrats and found wanting. His looks were gone over, compared to his Bourbon ancestors, and found to be more or less acceptable.

His mother went to work to find him a wife. She renewed her

attempts to have him betrothed to Anne-Marie Louise d'Orléans, 'La Grande Mademoiselle' as she was known. Henrietta Maria believed she had the backing of Mazarin and the French Queen Mother for her plan. Such a match would bring a satisfactory link to the grandest of Bourbon royalty, since Anne-Marie was a cousin of the king and was satisfactorily both rich and Catholic. The Queen saw her wealth as a means of raising an army and restoring her husband to his throne. But there were several impediments, the major one being the Cardinal. Mazarin had no intention of allowing so much money to flow out of France and end up in England. Worst of all, from the French point of view, it might be used to strengthen England as a power at a time when France was already fighting a very expensive war with Spain.

Mademoiselle herself did not encourage the Prince, though she did at least entertain the notion of the marriage. She was a tall, stocky girl who suffered no lack of self-esteem. Hyde was very dismissive, describing the Duchess as 'Not at all handsome, being a lady of very low stature and that stature in no degree straight.'[3] He was incorrect, as Anne-Marie was a large, blue-eyed creature, not at all small or ill-shapen. In her memoirs, the Duchess recorded how she paraded through the extravagant interiors of her world, stopping at each and every gilt-hung mirror to ensure no self-reflection went unacknowledged by the assembled admirers.[4] Such self-love did not leave much room for an impecunious heir to a rocky English throne. Besides, she had wanted to marry Louis, her 'little king', before moving on to set her sights at the Emperor of the Holy Roman Empire. Charles is not recorded as having pursued Mademoiselle with any great diligence. From what little is known, he refused to speak to Anne-Marie even when he accompanied her to balls. He claimed this was because he could not speak French, though Mademoiselle noticed he could understand her well enough. Apart from Anne-Marie, Charles was also connected with another possible suitor, the Duchesse de Châtillon. This, too, seems to have fizzled out.

Nothing, however, could deter Henrietta Maria from her desire to see her son wed to the haughty Mademoiselle; in truth it was she who wooed Anne-Marie rather than her sullen, sex-starved son. In February 1647, a grand entertainment was held at the Palais Royal. Henrietta Maria pulled out all the stops to get her son into Mademoiselle's good books. She lent Anne-Marie diamonds to sew on her dress. Anne-Marie wore her favourite colours of black, white and rose, with the English diamonds on her frock. There were more diamonds and pearls in a fascinator, in the centre of which were three feathers, one in each of her favourite colours. Henrietta Maria could not have been more pleased with her strategy of helping the fabulous creature shine in the glittering gathering in front of the two kings of France and England.

'Nothing could have been seen better or more magnificently arrayed than I was that day,' recalled Mademoiselle modestly. 'I did not fail to find many people who assured me that my fine figure, my good looks, my pale complexion, and the splendour of my fair hair became me better than all the riches that shone upon my person.'[5]

The dancing took place on a large stage, brilliantly lighted by crystal chandeliers, with the spectators seated around the amphitheatre. In the centre of the stage was a throne, covered with cloth of gold, but the little King refused to mount it, out of courtesy to the Prince of Wales. Charles being equally polite, the throne remained empty until Mademoiselle ascended it without scruple. She felt – and was assured that she looked – born to a throne, and thoroughly enjoyed her position, having both the King and the Prince of Wales seated at her feet. If Charles had hoped his humble attitude would go down well with his cousin and placate his mother, he was mistaken. Temporary possession of the throne only served to increase Mademoiselle's self-esteem. She wrote:

While I was there, and the Prince of Wales was at my feet, my heart, as much as my eyes, regarded him de haut-en-bas; I had then taken into my head to marry the Emperor, of which there was much probability if the Court had only acted in good faith . . .

The thought of the Empire so entirely occupied my mind that I only regarded the Prince of Wales as an object of pity.[6]

Fortunately, respite was on its way. The Duke of Buckingham – Charles's close childhood companion – arrived at St Germain in late 1646, together with his brother. The young aristocrats were en route back to England on the last leg of their grand tour. Buckingham and his brother were exceptionally rich. Buckingham was an irreverent and mischievous boy who poked fun at authority figures, including the Prince's father. If, as Hyde discerned, Christabella had exercised a bad influence over the Prince, Buckingham was ten times worse. The disapproving Bishop Gilbert Burnet wrote that Buckingham corrupted Charles.[7] It is likely that he was already on his own path to perdition; if not exactly seeing the world through Buckingham's eyes, then at least searching for amusing antidotes to the starchy, self-important world of Louis XIV, who was as yet far too young to embark on his own ambitious sexual career.

The Prince spent his time partying. He sold his silver to pay his debts and failed to pay his servants. His father's situation meanwhile was much worse, and was rapidly deteriorating. Following a period of negotiation with the Scots, who found him as inflexible as the English, the Scots sold Charles to the English Parliament in a deal that included reparation for their part in the war. Before the King could return south and take up a settlement with the more amenable members of Parliament, the army kidnapped him and brought him to Hampton Court Palace, where he was placed under house arrest. There the King remained until he heard rumours of a plot to assassinate him. Believing this to be a strong possibility, he escaped by night and headed for the south coast. He put himself in the care of Colonel Hammond, the governor of the Isle of Wight, a Parliamentarian soldier whom Charles believed was sympathetic to his cause. Unfortunately for the King, Hammond saw his first duty as being to Parliament and locked him up in Carisbrooke Castle. From here, Charles plotted a new civil war. At the end of 1647 he made a secret pact with the Scots for Presbyterianism to be imposed in England in return for the supply of an invading army that would free him and restore him to the throne.

By the spring of 1648, the Scots were making their own overtures to the Prince of Wales to come to Scotland and take command of an invading army. To the hyperactive Prince, this was irresistible. For him, as for the King and the Queen, it was an exercise in the art of the possible – what today is known as realpolitik. The Anglican (and Catholic) House of Stuart would throw in its lot with the Presbyterian Scots. To the Queen, who had been politicking so hard for so long, it was also a welcome release from wheedling for money and military aid from her French relatives. The Prince left St Germain and headed to Calais, then to Holland, accompanied by many of the military men who had passed their idle months as guests of the French by quarrelling and duelling.

In England, a royalist uprising began in the spring of 1648 but came to very little. Royalists launched small-scale operations around the country but the hoped-for swell of widespread approval did not materialise and Parliamentary forces easily crushed the small bands who took up arms. Thanks to this, any invading Scottish army would be faced with the undivided attention of the New Model Army. But it was the royalists' only hope.

At The Hague, Charles was warmly welcomed by his sister Mary, who was married to William, Prince of Orange, and by his younger brother James, Duke of York. James had been held captive by Parliament in St James's Palace, but was sprung in an audacious move by an Irish officer, Colonel Bampfield, who disguised him as a washerwoman and spirited him to Holland. Seeing how often royalty and the aristocracy dressed as women in the seventeenth century, one could be forgiven for thinking it was not the theatre but the cavaliers who gave rise to the pantomime dame.

Then came an unexpected stroke of good fortune. A great portion of the Parliamentary fleet mutinied and sailed to the Netherlands,

arriving at the port of Helvoetsluys, south of The Hague. The possession of a fleet filled the young Prince with fresh hope. He seized
the moment and set sail to rally support in the towns along England's
eastern seaboard. There was even a plan to use the fleet to rescue his
father from the Isle of Wight. Of all the options open to Charles, this
was possibly the best, but he chose not to take it. Instead, he
attempted to establish a bridgehead at Yarmouth, where the locals
declined to join him and opted only to provide him with supplies.
The fleet then took to the sea with the intention of harrying
Parliamentary shipping and supply routes. In the event, the fleet
accomplished little and a small royalist uprising on land fizzled out
or was soon extinguished by superior Parliamentary forces. Better
news came in August with word that a Scottish army led by the Duke
of Hamilton was heading into England. As the moment surely
arrived for the Prince to reclaim his position as heir to the battered
English crown, he met a girl and became infatuated.

Lucy Walter was the daughter of a Welsh nobleman and was
about the same age as the Prince, possibly born in the same year,
1630.[8] In the summer of 1648 they became lovers in The Hague.
Lucy was one of at least seventeen lovers taken by Charles during his
exile. Among the others was Lady Eleanor Byron, wife of the first
Lord Byron and ancestor of the famous poet.[9] Lucy, however, meant
much more than any of the others, no matter how exalted, rich or
beautiful. Much has been written about Lucy and her character,
most of it bad. Whatever her true nature, she became a fixture in the
young Prince's life for at least two years, and was to continue to have
significance for many years after.

Lucy's parents were William Walter and his wife Elizabeth, the
daughter of John Prothero and the niece of the 1st Earl of Carbery.
The Walters, who were royalists, lived at Roche Castle near
Haverfordwest in Pembrokeshire. In 1644 Parliamentary forces
destroyed their home. Some time before this, Lucy's father and
mother had separated and Lucy moved between the two parents,
staying at various times in Wales, the West Country and London. It

has been suggested that Lucy accompanied her father to The Hague when he travelled to join forces with the Prince's court-in-exile.

Eighteen-year-old Lucy was, according to all who met her, physically and in character everything Anne-Marie, La Grande Mademoiselle, was not. She had beautiful dark looks and was full of fun. According to one version of her story, once she reached The Hague she became the mistress of a number of rich men. This account originated from James, Duke of York, who claimed that Algernon Sidney, the acclaimed Parliamentarian cavalry officer and political theorist, paid fifty gold pieces for Lucy to become his mistress. Apparently Sidney had to join his regiment in a hurry and so was unable to seal his bargain, which was taken up by his elder brother Robert, another cavalier officer and later Earl of Leicester.

This all makes for a good story of bad behaviour, but its factual basis is slight.[10] It was out of character for Sidney, who was studious and not at all of a wild disposition. The sum of fifty guineas, moreover, was well outside his spending power, for although he was the son of an earl, his father believed in keeping his sons on a tight financial rein.[11] There remains the possibility that Lucy arrived on the Continent due to her aunt, with whom she lived for a time in London and who was married to a Dutch merchant. And if there was any connection with the Sidney family, it was Robert whom she met up with and who fathered her child.[12]

A much more credible account of how she met up with the Prince is that she travelled to France in the entourage of her relative John Barlow in 1648, when he joined the growing military force collecting around the exiled Stuart court at St Germain.[13] This theory is supported by the fact that rather than go by her maiden name, Walter, she adopted that of her relative and was widely known as Mrs Barlow, possibly to make her less vulnerable while travelling alone.*

---

* In the seventeenth century, single women widely used the title Mrs to indicate they were of good character and to distinguish themselves from those using the prefix Miss, which, confusingly, could denote a prostitute.

Everyone who met Lucy agreed on one thing: she was beautiful. Charles's brother James, writing later with the intent of defaming Lucy, admitted she was lovely, with little wit but a great deal of the cunning 'her profession usually have', his words indicating that he regarded her as a whore.[14] John Evelyn described her as 'a brown, beautiful, bold but insipid creature' (insipid here meaning she had no education).[15] Clarendon said she was 'of no good fame, but handsome'.[16] In a portrait attributed to Peter Lely, Lucy stares at the viewer through almond-shaped brown eyes, with a half smile on her red lips, the lower of which is especially full. Her dark hair is fashionably piled up in ringlets and curls.[17] In an unusual head and shoulders portrait now in the Pembrokeshire County Council collection, also attributed to Lely, she is even better looking. Lucy was a young beauty who could capture any prince. Delirious days of lovemaking followed. The young Prince's enjoyment was enhanced by having at his command a fleet and a plan to restore his father to the throne. Then everything fell apart; through superior tactics and strength, Cromwell crushed Hamilton's army.

What followed was worse. The King was taken to London and put on trial for treason against his people. On 30 January 1649, he was beheaded outside his grandfather's stately Banqueting House in Whitehall. Whether or not the affair between the Prince and his young lover continued throughout this time is unknown. A few days after the execution of the King, a messenger arrived at the royal palace at The Hague with the news. The Prince learned from his father's former chaplain that his father was dead and he was now king. He fled from the room in tears. Was Lucy there to comfort him? We don't know.

On 5 February 1649, Charles was declared King in Edinburgh. Nine weeks later, on 9 April, Lucy gave birth to a baby boy at Rotterdam. Charles immediately declared the child his own and he was christened James Scott, in recognition of Charles's grandfather and his Scottish ancestry. He was now in the odd position of having a son but, since the child was illegitimate, no heir – and no throne.

His life was out of kilter. Lucy Walter and the new King of England faced their joint exile with a young child. Charles would later confer the title of Duke of Monmouth upon his son, whom he would continue to love dearly despite the trouble the boy would create throughout his eventful life.

Charles had to work out what his next political move might be. Scottish emissaries arrived to offer their support. In Scotland, the outrage caused by an English Parliament executing the King of the Scots without doing his subjects the courtesy of enquiring what they thought of the matter, led to the agreement that Charles was now their king. But this brought the old problem of religion: how far would Charles go in supporting the Scottish Covenanters' goal of cementing Presbyterianism as the religion of Scotland *and* of England?[18] In the event, during discussions at The Hague, it proved that the answer was, not far enough. The two parties did not even agree to differ; Covenanters of every ilk stoutly expected everyone – even their king – simply to agree with them. Charles proved to be a chip off the old block and dissembled as well as his father ever did. He possibly had little option, though his lack of sincerity did not go unnoticed. But relations were not completely broken off. Among Charles's circle, it was recognised that it was important not to forget Ireland. To rally the royalist forces under the Lord Lieutenant of Ireland the Duke of Ormond, Charles himself should sail for Ireland.

While preparations were made, Charles returned to Paris, bringing his child and Lucy. In Parisian courtly circles, Lucy became known as Charles's wife, giving rise to persistent rumours that the couple had secretly married in Holland. The fact that Lucy still used the name Mrs Barlow somehow helped stoke the rumours, and they would haunt Charles throughout his life. In later years the rumours were fanned when the legend of the black box was created. According to a host of third-hand accounts, Lucy is supposed to have secreted a copy of the marriage certificate and other documents in such a box. Like the Philosopher's Stone, it was to remain an unsolved mystery. No true witnesses, nor any other concrete evidence of the wedding, were ever produced.

In Paris, Charles renewed his acquaintance with La Grande Mademoiselle, for his mother was again promoting the match. Charles did little to support it but he did make one telling statement, which bore significance regarding his relationship with Lucy Walter. Without direct reference to Lucy, he said that whatever relationship he had as a bachelor would stop once he was married.[19] This was a clear intimation that Charles did not consider himself married to Lucy, whatever current or later gossip suggested.

Despite his relationship with Lucy and the birth of his son, Charles took another lover. This was a lady-in-waiting to his mother. Elizabeth Killigrew was some eight years older than Charles and had arrived in Paris with her husband Francis Boyle (who would later be ennobled by Charles as Viscount Shannon). Cuckolds could do well in the seventeenth century, providing their wife's lover was of royal blood. Boyle was the son of the Earl of Cork, the Lord Treasurer of Ireland, a colonial adventurer made good whose motto was 'God's Providence is my Inheritance'; he was also the brother of Robert, the notable polymath and alchemist later dubbed the father of modern chemistry.

On her own family's side, Elizabeth was the sister of Thomas Killigrew, the royalist playwright who had followed Charles into exile in 1647. Killigrew was famously lecherous, a character trait shared with his sister, who despite their age difference not only cuckolded her husband, but had a child by Charles. The child was born in 1650 and christened Charlotte Jemima Henrietta Maria FitzRoy, an appellation which recognised her as the offspring of the king.

In the same year another child was born who would have a great impact upon the King's later life. Like Lucy, she hailed from a Welsh family some of whose members had moved to England. The child's surname was Gwyn and she was christened Eleanor, known as Nell for short.

With his new love interest it was little wonder that Charles showed scant attentiveness to the various aristocrats his mother pushed his way. He preferred the company of the more bawdy young women in the English community swirling around St Germain and the Louvre. The French with their alien language and manners were not to his taste. Henrietta Maria, always anxious for her son to marry into the French nobility, must have been sorely vexed.

Then Charles received bad news. Cromwell had arrived in Ireland before him, and the Duke of Ormond's attack on Dublin was repelled. Despite the auguries, Charles sailed for Jersey, leaving Lucy behind, in order to be closer to Ireland and able to set sail at a moment's notice. Given the risky venture he was entering into, this made good sense, but it was not a wise move in regard to Lucy's vivacious temperament. She would find other lovers in his absence.

By the end of 1649, all royalist resistance in Ireland had been crushed. Charles now needed the Scots more than ever – and this meant the Scottish Presbyterian Covenanters. A conference was arranged at the Dutch city of Breda. An agreement between commissioners representing the Scottish parliament and Charles and his council was botched together on what one distinguished historian of the period, Ronald Hutton, has described as 'false expectations and mutual bad faith'.[20] The King's empty promise to ensure the future position of Presbyterianism as the premier religion in England was enough for the Scottish commissioners to invite him to Scotland.

On 23 June 1650, Charles's fleet anchored off Garmouth in the Moray Firth, and the Solemn League and Covenant was brought on board his flagship for him to sign. By signing, the King consented to Scotland's religious life being conducted without interference from England, and agreed that England would in effect take Presbyterianism as its official faith. It was obvious to all that he had no real intention of removing episcopal rule and that he himself remained outwardly Anglican. Debate has raged as to whether he was even that.

From the outset, the strait-laced, God-fearing Scots and the young King did not get along, though the Marquis of Argyll offered Charles the hand of his daughter Anne in marriage. Charles declined the offer. He was uninterested in marrying until he had fulfilled his primary goal. This did not mean that his attention was entirely given over to planning how to take back the English crown. The antics of his boisterous court – which included the irrepressible Buckingham – revolted the Scots, who asked several of the worst offenders to leave. The behaviour of the King himself scandalised his hosts. In one outrageous incident he was said to have forced himself upon a young female courtier. Whatever the exact circumstances, an interpretation of seigniorial rights extending to sexual congress held no sway in Calvinist Scotland. Lord Warriston, a judge who had helped draw up the Solemn League and Covenant, upbraided the King for what seems to have amounted to rape or attempted rape. Charles never forgave Warriston for his temerity.[21]

In 1650, Scotland was the launch pad for an ambitious plan. Charles intended not to rule in the ancestral home of the Stuarts but to use it as a means to invade England. In London, the Commonwealth government knew this too, and Cromwell had been recalled from Ireland to take an army north to defeat the Scots before they came, as they surely would. When Cromwell's army marched into Scotland in its pre-emptive strike towards Edinburgh, Charles was not at the head of the Scottish forces – the Scots did not want him there until he had definitively agreed to change his religion and confirm that the army had been raised to impose Presbyterianism on England. Charles had no such aim. He wanted to retake the throne of England by whatever means and with whatever allies were needed. It was all part of the old Stuart way – to seek foreign answers (in this case an army) to the problems of English government. For Charles it would prove as unreliable a strategy as it had for his father, a man who had always loved a scheme more than a solution.

Charles, anxious for action, joined the front lines without being invited. He was told to leave. The Scots at first did well against Cromwell – as well they might, for they were commanded by David

Leslie, a skilled commander and former comrade-in-arms of Cromwell, who therefore knew his former colleague's ability all too well. Leslie's defensive tactics wore the enemy down so effectively that the English had to retreat to Dunbar for supplies. The Scots advanced and through their superior numbers and better supplies had Cromwell at a disadvantage. Though Cromwell was famously circumspect during his campaigns, in a tight spot he could throw caution to the wind. Before the Scots could attack and deliver their intended *coup de grâce* on 3 September 1650, Cromwell launched a surprise counter-attack in the early hours of the morning, caught the Scots off guard and annihilated their army. Charles's ambition of regaining his crown by force began to look as unlikely as his conversion to Presbyterianism.

The following day, Commonwealth forces entered Edinburgh. The Scottish army withdrew to Stirling and within weeks Warriston denounced the House of Stuart as the cause of all their woes. He specifically had in mind the refusal of Charles I to embrace the Reformation. As for the new king, he was all too ready to embrace anything that would place him on the English throne, and the Covenanters knew that. The year ended with a standoff between Leslie in Stirling and Cromwell controlling the Scottish lowlands. Charles continued to try to build support through the difficult task of juggling the disparate loyalties of Scottish royalists and Covenanters, and across the sea, the Irish Catholics.

On 1 January 1651, Charles was crowned King of Scots at the ancient coronation site of Scone in the eastern Highlands. Importantly, this made him the supreme commander of the Scottish army, though it remained under the immediate military command of David Leslie. This change in the command structure was to have profound repercussions for Charles's campaign to retake the English throne.

In July, Cromwell decided to try to break the deadlock and advanced up the north-eastern side of Scotland. He won a battle at Inverkeithing against superior forces and soon took Perth. Cromwell knew that this advance would leave open a western corridor through which Leslie's army could leave its headquarters in Stirling and pour south to invade England. Cromwell reckoned that if it did so it would find little support and face defeat on foreign soil.

In Stirling, Charles and Leslie discussed what might be the best option. Ignoring Leslie's advice, Charles gave the order to invade. It was, after all, why he was in Scotland in the first place. He had spent too long among people with whom he had nothing in common, far away from his now banished friends and away from Lucy, Elizabeth, their children and – now that his wings had been clipped in Scotland – any other women that might take his fancy. Now he had both the titular power to enforce his will and an army with which to exercise it. As a man who craved action, it was surely the most exhilarating and vital moment of his life. For too long he had been pushed along by events, in exile without power or influence.

It was the moment foreseen by Cromwell, who was already withdrawing the majority of his forces southwards. Both men were moving towards the most important moment in the struggle for England since Charles I had hurled his army against the crushing machine of the New Model Army at Naseby six years before. In the years since then, Charles had had to put up with friends, gloaters and confidants telling him that his father had thrown away the crown. This was his moment to get it back.

4

THE FUGITIVE

Ten days later Leslie's warning against invasion proved right. Charles's gamble ended in calamitous defeat at Worcester. Outnumbered and out-generalled, his army was cut to pieces by republican troops outside the city walls. According to Oliver Cromwell, 3000 royalists were killed and 5000 made prisoner. Republican casualties were fewer than 300. On any score it was a royalist catastrophe. The one saving grace was Charles's escape after the battle. It was one of the great getaways in history, and royalist propagandists would seize on it to turn defeat on the battlefield into a personal triumph for the King. Charles would later lead the marvelling at his 'miracle escape', and make a royalist heroine out of Jane Lane, the woman who was said to have risked everything to help him. Inevitably, it was assumed in some quarters that Charles added Jane to his burgeoning list of mistresses. Be that as it may, Charles certainly added her to the story of his divine destiny.

Twenty years later, Charles dictated his own account of his escape to the diarist Samuel Pepys. It takes us into his mindset in the first bitterness of defeat as he decided against staying with the remnants of his troops as they limped northwards. Charles knew the vulnerability of a broken army and was desperate to put distance between himself and them. If he felt any sense of responsibility for men who had followed him half the length of England, he hid it. Rather he blamed them for not fighting on. 'I strove as soon as it was dark to get them from me,' he later confessed, 'and though I could not get them to stand by me against the enemy I could not get rid of them now.'[1]

Fifteen miles into their retreat, Charles managed to abandon his beaten army. Together with the Duke of Buckingham, the Earls of Lauderdale and Derby and another fifty or so 'gentlemen of quality', he quietly slipped ingloriously away and left the Scots to their fate.[2]

In the next six weeks nothing would be heard of him. While Scottish troops were captured in their hundreds, and leading English royalists arrested daily, Charles had vanished. Six days after the battle, Colonel Thomas Birch wrote from Manchester to the Speaker of the House of Commons: 'I think the Scots king came this way with Lieutenant-General Lesley and Lieutenant General Middleton, who were taken on Blackstone Edge in the moors betwixt Karsdale* and Halifax, and we believe that he escaped towards Yorkshire in some disguise.'[3] Ports were watched, highways patrolled, royalist houses ransacked. Charles wasn't found. There was speculation that he had been killed by peasants who had failed to recognise him. But the majority view was that Charles Stuart was back in Scotland or on his way to London.

In fact, Charles had gone to ground on the Boscobel estate in Brewood Forest, less than thirty miles north of Worcester. Owned by the Catholic Gifford family, the estate was suggested as a temporary hideaway by the Earl of Derby, who had hidden there when pursued by Parliamentary troops just three weeks earlier. It was remote and was tenanted by an extended family of ardent royalists, the Penderel brothers. Charles parted from Buckingham, Derby and the remnants of his retinue at Whiteladies, a former abbey on the Gifford estate, and put himself in the hands of the Penderels.

Charles was quickly disguised. The Penderels cut his hair 'very

---

* Probably modern-day Garsdale.

short' and threw his curls into the privy. Charles discarded his buff coat, richly laced doublet and embossed boots and exchanged them for the tattered clothes of a woodsman. Soot was rubbed into his face to make it grimy and he adopted a new name. Charles Stuart became Will Jackson, woodcutter. The King was ushered out of the abbey and for many hours lay concealed in the dense foliage of the forest, from where he glimpsed militiamen searching for fugitives from Worcester.

There followed a nerve-tingling week as a network of Catholic royalists smuggled Charles back and forth, from safe house to safe house, to keep a step ahead of the militia, and all within the radius of a dozen square miles. One day his six-foot-two frame was pushed into a priest's hole; another day he perched in the famous oak tree while troopers searched underneath; on yet another occasion he crouched stock still in an attic while a militia commander was bluffed out of opening the doors that would have revealed him; another time he hid on the forest floor during a day of endless rain, praying the downpour would persuade approaching ironsides to give up. Miraculously they did give up.

His main source of discomfort while at Boscobel was his feet. The woodsman's boots given him began to hurt during a failed foray across the Severn at night. Stupidly he threw them away and then had to stumble barefoot through miles of hedges, brambles and ditches to get back to Boscobel before dawn. Years later he made Pepys almost weep as he described the agony of his bloody, thorn-lacerated feet and the times he flung himself to the ground ready to give up.

The plan to get the King through the troops guarding the highways and out of England was conceived after the Lane family, leading lights in the Catholic royalist network, secured one of the travel warrants which Catholics needed for any journey of five miles or more. This one was to enable the Lanes' daughter Jane to visit a pregnant relative a few miles from Bristol. Jane was a spirited, unmarried girl of twenty-four, whose rather heavy features masked a lively, determined character. Charles was to pose as Jane's servant and to travel with her to Bristol where, it was assumed, a berth to the Continent should be possible to arrange.

Charles was brought to Bentley Hall, the Lanes' Staffordshire mansion, the night before the escape was to begin. Whatever manner of man Jane Lane expected him to be, it was certainly not the ragged peasant to whom she was presented. This was the antithesis of the dashing cavalier who just three weeks earlier had marched into the country and thrilled royalist hearts by having himself proclaimed King of England, Scotland and Ireland. The hand she kissed was dirty and cut, his face had a 'reeky' colour, he wore a greasy leather doublet and breeches and he clutched a sweat-stained old hat. Whether he smelled as rank as he looked we don't know.[4]

That night the Lanes gave him a bath, spruced him up and provided him with a different outfit. In his role of servant Charles had to be dressed in the grey-liveried serge of a Lane retainer. He was to be introduced as William not Will Jackson, the son of a valued tenant. He was also given a quick schooling in the do's and don'ts of being a servant.[5]

The plan had Charles and Jane riding pillion on the same horse, the 'servant' in front astride the animal and the mistress behind him, side saddle. 'Double horse', as this was called, was not uncommon and it would hopefully cause no comment in the days ahead. They would make for Bristol, around a hundred miles away.

The next morning Charles failed the first test. Once he mounted the horse he was supposed to pull his mistress up behind him. To giggles from Jane's mother, the King proffered the wrong hand and Jane couldn't mount.

The royal party consisted of Charles and Jane on their horse, her sister Withy Petre and husband John Petre also riding pillion on theirs and their cousin Henry Lascelles, a former royalist officer, riding solo. The Petres, who were only going part of the way, were not informed of the new servant's real identity and, surprisingly, seem to have remained in ignorance.

Just in sight, ahead of the party, rode Jane's brother Colonel John

Lane and the King's faithful Lord Wilmot, the latter of whom had appointed himself royal bodyguard and had tracked Charles from the day of the lost battle. The pugnacious Wilmot refused to be disguised. He would look too silly, he claimed. He and Lane made do with a hawk on their wrists as if they were out on a summer's day for sport and nothing to do with the riders behind them.

That same day, a hundred miles away, Parliament posted a reward for the capture of the royal fugitive. Below is a facsimile of part of the proclamation issued on 10 September.

By the Parliament.
A PROCLAMATION
FOR THE
Discovery and Apprehending of *CHARLS STUART*,
and other Traytors his Adherents and Abettors.
Whereas CHARLS STUART Son to the late Tyrant, with divers
of the English and Scotish Nation, have lately in a Trayterous
and Hostile maner with an Army invaded this Nation, which by
the Blessing of God upon the Forces of this Commonwealth
have been defeated, and many of the chief Actors therein slain
and taken prisoners; but the said Charls Stuart is escaped: For
the speedy Apprehending of such a Malicious and Dangerous
Traytor to the Peace of this Commonwealth, The Parliament
doth straightly Charge and Command all Officers, as well Civil
as Military, and all other the good People of this Nation, That
they make diligent Search and Enquiry for the said Charls
Stuart, and his Abettors and Adherents in this Invasion, and use
their best Endeavors for the Discovery and Arresting the Bodies

of them and every of them; and being apprehended, to bring or
cause to be brought forthwith and without delay, in safe Custody
before the Parliament or Councel of State, to be proceeded with
and ordered as Justice shall require; And if any person shall
knowingly Conceal the said Charls Stuart ... The Parliament
doth Declare, That they will hold them as partakers and Abettors
of their Trayterous and Wicked Practices and Designs: And ...
whosoever shall apprehend the person of the said Charls Stuart,
and shall bring or cause him to be brought to the Parliament
or Councel of State, shall have given and bestowed on him
or them as a Reward for such Service, the sum of One
thousand pounds ... Given at Westminster this Tenth day
of September, One thousand six hundred fifty one.

That afternoon 'the son to the late tyrant' and his party encountered their first brush with near disaster. Approaching Stratford upon
Avon they spotted a troop of cavalry stationary up ahead watering
their horses. Jane's brother-in-law John Petre wanted to avoid trouble
and turn off the road. Charles whispered in Jane's ear that it could be
fatal to turn back and after a row with Petre they rode straight on –
and the soldiers pulled their mounts aside to let the royal party
through. Later, in Stratford, they encountered the same cavalry
troopers, who saluted them, giving them 'hat for hat'.[6]

On the first night, spent at an inn in Cirencester, Henry Lascelles
surreptitiously gave up his room to the 'servant'.[7] On every subsequent night on and off the road Jane managed to secure a private
chamber for 'William', on the grounds that he was ill and needed a
separate room and better food. Judging from Lord Clarendon's
description she laid it on thick, and implied that Charles was more
charity case than servant:

She declared that he was a neighbour's son, whom his father had
lent her to ride before her, in hope that he would the sooner
recover from a quartan ague, with which he had been miserably

afflicted . . . by this artifice she caused a good bed to be provided for him, and the best meat to be sent, which she often carried herself, to hinder others from doing it.[8]

The subject that Jane and Charles most whispered about as they travelled in such intimate tandem that September was most probably not Worcester nor even sex, but the next meal. Every day Jane would ask him what he wanted and at every stop she set about providing it. Sometimes, in the privacy of his chamber, the king cooked it himself. He joked that he had become a master cook.

On the next evening they arrived at the grand three-storey manor house of Leigh Court, in Abbots Leigh, home of Jane's cousin Ellen Norton. Ellen was pregnant – a fact that would later present a heart-breaking dilemma to Jane. Abbots Leigh was geographically an ideal spot for a base while finding a ship to take Charles to France or Spain. Bristol, the busiest seaport in the country after London, was only three miles away. The task of finding the vessel was allocated to Wilmot, who was certain he would quickly succeed. Ellen and her husband were never told of William's identity but their butler, who had served in Charles I's household, recognised him. Luckily the man was a royalist who not only kept quiet but joined the search for a ship.

By now the wanted posters were going up, advertising the £1000 reward and describing Charles: 'a tall man, above two yards high, with dark brown hair scarcely to be distinguished from black.'

Understandably, the hunted twenty-one-year-old King showed the strain. One account describes his 'harassed appearance', enabling him to 'support consistently' the story that he was ill.[9] Charles himself recalled: 'My late fatigues and want of meat had indeed made me look a little pale.'[10] As for the impact on him psychologically, contemporary accounts give few clues. His habitual cheerfulness was remarked on but there were flashes of temper, too.

He remained a risk taker, and showed it in situations which must have given Jane the horrors. On the first day on the road, he asked a blacksmith shoeing his horse what the news was of Worcester and realised he had asked a fanatical republican. To cover himself, the King proclaimed his own king-killing republicanism. Charles Stuart, he asserted, was 'a rogue who deserved to be hanged'. The smith hailed him as a good man. Another time the royal party dismounted at an inn crowded with soldiers, and Charles almost invited a fight by using the horses to barge his way through the military drinkers. 'I alighted,' he said, 'and taking the horses, thought it the best way to go blundering in among them, and lead them [the horses] through the middle of the soldiers into the stable, which I did, and they were very angry with me for my rudeness.' The most suicidal moment came when Charles couldn't resist challenging a man who claimed to have fought at Worcester. What, the King asked, did Charles Stuart look like? The man stared him in the face and said 'three fingers taller than you'. Charles had the sense to leave the room at this point.

Thanks to Jane, his opportunities to betray himself with an unconsidered remark were limited. She persisted with the story that her servant was recovering from illness and needed special treatment. Unfortunately, Dr Gorges, a former chaplain of Charles I and well known to his son, was a neighbour of the Nortons and a guest at supper on the day the Lanes' royal party arrived. Charles spotted him immediately and skulked in the stables to hide until Jane secured him a separate room. At supper, the chaplain noticed food being taken to the sick servant. Without telling anyone, he slipped into William's room to give what help he could. Horrified, Charles shrank back into the shadows, saying as little as possible to Gorges and 'expressing great inclination to go to his bed' as the intruder tried to examine him. Gorges finally left, and went to Mistress Lane to inform her that he had seen William, and that 'he would do well.'[11]

Did Jane and Charles become lovers at this point? Jane was described as having 'no beauty' but it is easy to imagine some attraction between the sexually voracious young King and the adoring twenty-four-year-old. There was certainly opportunity for sex. They were in close physical proximity for at least nine days and at every stop Jane obtained a private room for Charles.

The search for a ship was proving fruitless. No vessel was due to leave Bristol for the Continent for more than a month. That, and unease at the proximity of a city with many people who could identify Charles, prompted the royal party to move south-east into safer territory. The new bolthole was to be Trent House on the Somerset–Dorset border, home of Colonel Francis Wyndham, brother of a former courtier and well known to Charles. Among its attributes, the mansion was yet another with a priest's hole. The party was to leave for Trent on 16 September. On that day, a hundred miles away in London, the Council of State decided to send all English rankers and junior officers who had fought for Charles to the plantations. Effectively that meant slavery. Those held at Chester, Worcester, Liverpool and Shrewsbury were consigned to Virginia and Bermuda. Three hundred were sent to New England, one thousand others were put to work digging drains in the Fenlands. The great majority of Scots prisoners, more than three thousand, simply did not return home, most dying of wounds, illness, ill treatment or hunger.

Were Charles to be caught he would have suffered the fate of his father. On the eve of the departure from Abbots Leigh, Ellen Norton miscarried and was gravely ill. Jane faced a dilemma. Should she stay and nurse her possibly dying cousin, so forcing Charles either to stay as well or break his cover? Or should she desert her cousin and leave with the King? For Jane, the decision was obvious. The King's escape was the more important. He and Lascelles concocted a letter reporting that Jane's father was on his deathbed and calling for her. On reading aloud what she knew was a forgery, Jane put in such a tearful performance that no one could doubt its genuineness. 'In the circumstances', wrote Clarendon, 'there could, of course, be no objection to her departure.'[12]

The party now set out for Trent House, which would serve as Charles's command post while Wilmot and others extended their search for a ship through Dorset and Hampshire. All told, Charles would spend nineteen frustrating days at Trent House. As he waited, he whiled the time away cooking for himself and boring holes in gold coins. The coins would be presented as mementoes to anyone who helped him.[13]

He had hardly settled in Trent when there was a reminder of the hostility with which he was regarded. He was awakened one morning by church bells, shouts of acclamation and the smell of bonfires. The village of Trent was celebrating a rumour that Charles had been captured. According to one report, he sighed and muttered 'poor people'. Another report has him 'petulant' at being awakened by the noise and 'angry' to discover the cause.

Jane Lane, who had risked her life for the King, now said her farewells and together with her brother returned home to Bentley Hall. Her departure did not fundamentally affect Charles's cover story of a servant travelling with his mistress. It had worked so well thus far that he persisted with it and a replacement for Jane was found. She was Juliana Coningsby, the niece of Colonel Wyndham's wife. She agreed to pose as an eloping bride, with Charles as her servant and Wilmot as her lover.

On 22 September, a skipper from Dorset named Stephen Limbre was finally found who was prepared to take royalists across the Channel to St Malo. For £60 his ship, a small coaster, was to land her longboat on the beach of the little coastal village of Charmouth and pick up two passengers. No one mentioned that one of them would be the King. Initially all went well. Rooms at the local inn were booked and the sympathy of the landlady secured by a story that she would be hosting two eloping lovers and their servants. On the evening of the appointed departure Juliana and Wilmot, the supposed lovers, arrived at the inn together with three 'servants', one of them Charles. They passed the time drinking and waited for a signal from the beach, but it never came. The longboat didn't appear. It would transpire that Limbre's wife suspected he was involved in something dangerous, got him drunk and locked him up for the night.

Unknown to the fugitives, the militia was on their trail. The mystery of Charles's whereabouts was on everyone's lips and a sharp-eyed ostler suspected that he was a member of the party at the inn. Luckily for Charles, the man was greedy and delayed reporting his suspicions until after the royal party had given him the customary tip. By the time he raised the alarm Charles and his company were on the highway, unaware that a pursuit had been ordered. They made the fortunate decision to turn off the highway to go cross-country, oblivious to the militia less than five minutes behind them. Had they not done so, capture would have been certain.

They returned to Trent House, while across Dorset and into Wiltshire royalist houses were ransacked as the ironsides combed the south-west for Charles. The house of Colonel Wyndham's uncle Sir Hugh Wyndham was one of those raided. Charles's pursuers realised that he was probably in disguise, though they thought he would be dressed not as a servant but as a woman. Claiming to suspect that one of Sir Hugh's daughters was the 6ft 2in Charles Stuart, they gave the unfortunate woman a very embarrassing time. The Trent branch of the family expected to be the Roundheads' next target.

The search for a vessel shifted still further east. Wilmot and his contacts switched their attention to the tiny fishing ports and villages along the Sussex coast. With Trent feeling less and less secure as the search for Charles intensified, he agreed to move eastwards too. On 5 October he finally quit Trent House and started out for Salisbury. Once more he played the servant, riding 'double horse' with Juliana. It has been suggested that had he played the lover he 'would probably have shown more zeal than discretion'.[14]

After reaching Salisbury, Charles learned that a ship had finally been found through a French merchant. It was a coal boat called the *Surprise*. He was to embark on it from the Sussex village of Shoreham on 15 October. En route eastwards, Charles and Juliana dodged from one royalist house to another, sometimes expected by the whole household, sometimes a stunning surprise. In one house the head of the family returned from the tavern to find what he took to be a Roundhead supping at his table. The man had to be restrained from booting Charles out.

The double horse ploy was discarded at Salisbury and Juliana Coningsby was sent back to Trent. It is not clear whether Charles was still playing a servant; but after Juliana's departure he contrived to be as inconspicuous as possible. He was described as dressed in the clothes of 'the meaner sort of country gentleman'.[15]

To the last, the chances of Charles completing his escape remained on a knife edge. The rendezvous with the captain of the Shoreham boat, Nicholas Tattersall, was at an inn still further east, in the village of Brighthelmstone. The royal party met him there after dusk on 14 October. Tattersall had not been told the identity of his passengers. But he had seen Charles three years earlier when the then Prince commanded a royal fleet, and he immediately identified the King. There are conflicting accounts of what happened in the inn after that but a lot of hard bargaining certainly followed, as well as a lot of hard drinking. The royalists were determined not to allow this captain to go home never to reappear, as had happened with Stephen Limbre, so they plied him with alcohol all night till it was time to leave. For his part, Captain Tattersall pushed and pushed for more money and eventually he forced them to buy the entire boat. Desperate, they agreed to pay a massive £400 for it and the final leg of Charles's escape was secured.

Charles finally left English soil for France aboard the coal boat at around 10 a.m. on 15 October.

Six weeks later, the roles the Lanes had played in Charles's escape became known, and Jane and her brother John were forced to leave Bentley Hall and follow Charles into exile. They too smuggled themselves out of England and were greeted as heroes in Paris. Charles, his mother, sister and two brothers received them with some pomp outside the city. As Jane approached the King, he held out his arms and exclaimed, 'Welcome, my life!'

A few weeks later he wrote to Jane:

I have hitherto deferred writing to you in hope to be able to send you somewhat else besides a letter ... The truth is that my necessities are greater than can be imagined but I am promised they shall shortly be supplied. If they are you can be sure to receive a share for it is impossible I can ever forget the great debt I owe you which I hope I will live to repay to a degree that is worthy of me.

True to this promise, Jane was well rewarded at the Restoration; so was everyone else who had aided his escape, but none so richly. Charles's gratitude was heartfelt. Jane was granted an annuity of £1000, twice or four times as much as the amounts granted to others, including Juliana Coningsby. Charles arranged for Jane to travel to Holland and become a lady-in-waiting for his sister, Mary of Orange. Was it simple gratitude or had she become one more in his lengthening line of conquests? We can only guess. Either way, he was now to embark upon the most demoralising period of his life.

5

THE LIFE OF AN EXILED KING

On the same day that Charles finally left English soil for France, the Earl of Derby, who had tipped him off about Boscobel, was beheaded for high treason. On the scaffold Derby announced:

> I confess I love monarchy and I love my master Charles the second of that name whom I myself proclaimed in this country to be king. The Lord bless him and preserve him. I assure you he is the most goodly, virtuous, valiant and most discreet king that I know today ... The Lord send us our king again, and our old laws again, and the Lord send us our religion again.[1]

Needless to say, the King did not live up to Lord Derby's eulogy. He quickly slid into an escapist world of sensuality and hedonism. Historians have damned him for it. He came back to France from Scotland, wrote one, 'reckless and hopeless, careless of religion, principle, and honour, and his subsequent wanderings on the Continent did nothing to restore his self-respect'.[2] Another described him as consoling himself 'in low debauchery for the kingdoms he had lost'.[3]

Charles's more conservative advisors, Sir Edward Hyde and Secretary of State Sir Edward Nicholas, feared for him. They worried over the impact on Charles of the endless whirl of partying and indulgence that was Paris in this, France's first decade under the rule of Louis XIV, the Sun King. Initially they reassured themselves that Charles was merely sowing youthful wild oats. In May 1652, Hyde wrote to Nicholas, 'there are and always will be some actions of appetite and affection committed which cannot be separated or banished from the age of twenty-one and which we must all labour by good counsel to prevent and divert . . . and must always remember that kings are of the same mould as other men and must be given some time to be made perfect'. But the following month Hyde was less complacent. 'It cannot be denied', he told Nicholas, 'that the King is exceedingly fallen in reputation . . . He is so much given to pleasure that if he stays here he will be undone . . . God send us quickly from this place.'[4]

When Charles returned to France in October 1651, the bewitching Lucy Walter was waiting for him in Paris. He found the high-spirited girl surrounded by gossip. During his absence she had borne a second child, a girl called Mary, who couldn't be his. There was talk about affairs with some of the most prominent gallants among the exiles, including several of Charles's friends. Theodore, Viscount Taaffe, Tom Howard and Sir Henry Bennet topped the list. According to the crusty Chancellor, Sir Edward Hyde, Lucy's immorality prompted Charles to dump her. 'She lived so loosely when he was in Scotland that when after Worcester fight he came to France and she came thither he would have no further commerce with her. She used in vain all her little arts.'[5]

Hyde may have been right that the physical affair was over, at least for the moment, but to the irritation of Charles's advisors, he didn't cut his mistress loose. Whether it was because she was the mother of his first-born son, or because she remained a sexual fascination for him or because he didn't wish to believe the worst of her, Charles would be entangled with Lucy in one way or another for much of her tragically short life.

In the three years after Charles's return, Lucy lodged in the splendour of the Louvre, in the apartments of the King's mother Henrietta Maria and his sister Henrietta Anne, whom he fondly called Minette. The three women lived in apparent harmony, if the lack of any evidence of friction can be relied upon. It is said that Charles was content with the arrangement because Theodore Taaffe, the Irish viscount and royalist diplomat, was picking up the bills for Lucy and the children. How long this domestic arrangement lasted is not known, but after 1654 everything changed. Under the terms of an Anglo-French treaty concluded by Cromwell and Mazarin, the Cardinal, among other things, agreed to expel Charles and his followers from France. Charles moved to Cologne, and Lucy's happy relationship with the Stuart womenfolk ended. She was vilified by Stuart agents and a tawdry struggle began for the possession of her son, James.

Over this period the men who had supposedly cuckolded Charles during his absence appear to have become, if anything, closer to the King. Viscount Taaffe, part roisterer and part trusted envoy – according to Charles, he was 'the best dancer in the country' – was the cavalier given the task of securing military aid from Spain. Later, Charles used Taaffe as an intermediary with Lucy. Another of her rumoured lovers, Henry Bennet, who was destined to be ennobled as Earl of Arlington, was the high-flying friend of everyone in the Stuart family. In 1654 the King wrote that Bennet 'is full of duty and integrity' and told his brother James, 'I shall trust him more than any other about you.'[6] Eight years later Bennet, still a favourite, would be made Secretary of State. Tom Howard, the brother of an earl, would be in the King's confidence too – until he was discovered to be in the pay of Cromwell's spymasters.

After Lucy, Charles's next genuine passion was Isabelle-Angelique de Montmorency, Duchess of Châtillon, who a decade or so before had been proposed as a possible royal marriage partner. The young widow was one more seventeenth-century beauty whose portraits belie enthusiastic contemporary descriptions of her looks. Angelique's portraits show her double-chinned and heavy-featured.

Yet judging from her admirers she must have been captivating. The Great Condé, France's most celebrated general, had been in love with her, as had the Duke of Nemour, and so too the flamboyant English exile George Digby, later Earl of Bristol. Even the disapproving Sir Edward Hyde was smitten. As for Charles, he had first been taken with Angelique during his previous sojourn in Paris but at the time she only had eyes for her husband. Now a widow, she happily entertained Charles's approaches. On the King's side, the affair that developed was so intense he talked of marriage. Angelique is said to have been intrigued enough at the prospect to enquire about the status of a queen in England. After hearing that even as Charles's consort she wouldn't take precedence over the queens of France she was not so keen. There was no marriage, but their liaison lasted several years, and a friendship followed.

Henrietta Maria's search to find Charles a good marriage resumed on his return, and with an all too familiar target. Before her son's cropped hair had time to grow, she arranged a new tryst with his Catholic cousin Anne-Marie Louise de Montpensier, La Grande Mademoiselle. Alarmed at the impact in England of a Catholic marriage, Charles's advisors Hyde and Ormond worked on him to put him off his narcissistic cousin. She was older than him 'by many years', they reminded him. She had been observed, in Hyde's words, 'not to be prosperous to Kings' and the advantages of her vast fortune would be outweighed by the anti-Catholic reaction to her among the English.

The penurious Charles ignored them. He needed money desperately and paid court to her at ball after ball over the winter months, but his efforts were wasted. Henry Jermyn, who was negotiating the marriage details on behalf of Henrietta Maria, is said to have let drop that once the marriage contract was signed 'we shall cut down her household and sell her property'. Suddenly, Mademoiselle's warmth evaporated and she insulted Charles. 'It pains me to observe you dancing the tricolet and amusing yourself', she said, 'when you ought to be there [in England] either risking your head or putting a crown on it.' These words brought an end to the prospects of a marriage.

During the 1650s, Charles's suit was pressed on many other women from the ruling families of Europe – the Duchess of Holstein, his cousin, Princess Sophia, the daughter of the Duke of Lorraine, and another cousin, Henrietta, granddaughter of the princess dowager of Orange. He was said to have become genuinely attached to Henrietta. An undated letter to her mother suggests that he had become desperate in the search:

> I beseech you to let me know whether your daughter the princess Henrietta be so far engaged that you cannot receive a proposition from me concerning her, and that if she be not you would think of a way with all possible secrecy I may convey my mind in that par-ticular to you. I know this is not the usual form in which such affairs are treated but as my present condition and yours are extraordinary so you may see is my value for you and your daugh-ter and my confidence in your honour. The messenger who carries this knows it is for you. You will be pleased to cause your answer to be returned as you think best.[7]

The plea fell on deaf ears. The girl's family considered his prospects were now too poor. They may also have been put off by Charles's philandering.[8]

The most politically explosive marriage scheme was to betroth him to the enemy. In 1654, a year after Cromwell made himself Lord Protector of the English Commonwealth, his close collaborator the Irish soldier and statesman Roger Boyle, proposed that Charles take Cromwell's daughter Frances as his bride. An outline of the project surfaced in a biography of Boyle written by his chaplain, Thomas Morrice. According to Morrice, Boyle put the marriage idea first to Charles and then to Cromwell. Charles was interested, but Cromwell laughed at the notion of Charles becoming his son-in-law and couldn't believe that Charles would go along with it.[9]

Morrice's book is sketchy on detail but it suggests that Charles was to be installed on the throne as titular king, with Cromwell commander-in-chief for life, 'with the whole power of the nation in his own hands'. The trade-off would have stuck in all their gullets. Given the bitterness existing between cavalier and Roundhead, the blood spilled, their fundamental political differences and Charles's implacable hatred for Cromwell, the project looks wildly implausible. However, Charles was in an increasingly weakened position, what with Cromwell consolidating his grip on power and the royalist failure to secure meaningful military aid. Just possibly Charles might be ready to think the unthinkable.

Boyle worked through contacts in Charles's court – 'some persons about the king' – to secure his agreement to the making of an approach to the Lord Protector. The proposal was approved and he proceeded to sound out Elizabeth Cromwell, the girl's mother. He also planted a rumour in the City of London that a marriage was in the offing. He then engineered a chance meeting with Cromwell during which he casually mentioned the rumour and talked up the benefits to Cromwell. Wisely he kept quiet about his contact with the King but asserted that Charles was so desperate that Cromwell would be able to dictate his own terms.

Cromwell told Boyle 'the king would never forgive him the death of his father'. Boyle, not caring to reveal that the King had already been asked, offered to find someone to act as mediator with Charles, or to do so himself. Cromwell would not consent and repeated, 'The king cannot and will not forgive the death of his father.' Boyle dared not attempt to disillusion the Lord Protector. It's doubtful whether the marriage would have occurred anyway. Time and again, the era of the civil war produced women prepared to outface even the most awesome of men. In this case, Frances Cromwell took on her terrifying father. She had fallen in love with Robert Rich, grandson of the Earl of Warwick, and against her father's wishes insisted on marrying him.[10]

The search for a royal bride went on right up until the Restoration and became increasingly desperate. Like Cromwell's daughter, the last two candidates were not even of royal blood. The first was Fatima

Lambert, the daughter of John Lambert, the republican general who was expected to succeed Cromwell. Lord Hatton, controller of the king's household, proposed tying Lambert to the royalist cause through his daughter. Hatton argued that by becoming Lambert's son-in-law Charles would have 'the most effectual means' of restoring the monarchy. 'No foreign aid will be so cheap nor leave our master at so much liberty as this way.' Knowing Charles, Hatton added some words about the beauty of the girl. 'The lady is pretty, of an extraordinary sweetness of disposition, and very virtuously and ingenuously disposed.'[11] An approach was then made to Lambert indirectly, through his wife, and she told Lambert. He turned out to be somewhat less Machiavellian than expected and promptly shared details of the approach with his republican colleagues – and rivals – thus ending all prospects of a marriage.[12]

The other non-royal candidate was Hortense Mancini, the thirteen-year-old niece of Jules, Cardinal Mazarin. The attractions for the Stuarts were the girl's wealth – she would inherit one of Europe's great fortunes – and the connection to the all-powerful Cardinal. Mazarin, however, didn't want to know. With the passage of time, Charles's reputation had grown worse not better. In diplomatic circles, one of the many rumours concerning his disreputable life in 1649 was that because of his behaviour the King of Spain had been 'obliged to put a guard over his house at Brussels and detain him there as a prisoner'.[13] After ten years, he was still the king without a kingdom, and too inconsequential to waste his niece on. The Cardinal replied to the Stuart approach with a barely disguised snub – an act he would live to regret.

Pleas for financial help were scarcely more successful than the match making. All Europe had flinched at the execution of Charles's father in 1649, and a number of powers on the Continent had reacted with promises of money for the Stuart cause. But by 1654 the states and statelets of Europe had one by one nearly all recognised the English protectorate set up by Cromwell; and very few had forked out anything like the money they pledged. Some never sent any.

These were lean years for the Stuart exiles. Cromwell brutally crushed their hopes in Ireland. The ex-royalist general George Monck snuffed out royalist resistance in Scotland, and in England a bruising system of fines and taxes on royalists seemed to have crushed the heart out of royalist resistance.

The relative penury of the exiled Stuarts continued throughout the 1650s. Charles and his mother subsisted on unreliable pensions from the French king and later a pension from Spain, plus what could be begged from the Holy Roman Emperor Leopold I and the other royals of Europe. The money didn't always arrive on time – indeed it failed to arrive at all during the years of the Fronde, France's own civil wars – and Charles was perennially claiming to be broke. The royal methods of saving money were striking. Charles dispensed with what he called 'the common luxury of a coach', his sister avoided the cost of a fire in winter by staying in bed all day, he omitted to pay his retainers and cut down on food. When not eating in a tavern where the meat was cheap, he kept 'plain table', which meant dining on one course only.[14]

His unpaid courtiers were even more hard-pressed and moaned constantly to one another. In March 1654, Sir Edward Nicholas told the corpulent Sir Edward Hyde 'that he had not received a shilling from the King for more than three years and was wasted even to nothing'. In July 1655 Hyde told the King, 'Lord Rochester has pawned his man Rose for his debts.' In 1657 Hyde told Lord Ormond, 'if some little sum be not speedily sent hither some men must literally starve, and many others be cast into prison'.

Further down the line, the wildest young elements at court, the so-called swordsmen, shared rooms and are thought to have made ends meet by the occasional robbery. In December 1656 an agent of the Protectorate reported from Holland that one of the richest churches in Bruges had been plundered and 'the people of Bruges were fully persuaded that Charles Stuart's followers had done it'.[15]

In all probability, it was money that brought the Lucy Walter story to a climax and then to its miserable end. This ugly little saga of deception, kidnap and blackmail was played out between 1656 and 1658. It centred on the financial support demanded by Lucy for herself and her children and the King's eventual determination to take possession of their son James.

The sequence of events began in 1654 when Charles effectively dropped Lucy. Having moved from Paris to Cologne, from then on he endeavoured to keep Lucy at arm's length. The most she would get from him in future were extravagant, usually empty, promises of support. She moved to Flanders and from man to man, sending out appeals for help to Charles and talking of the 'marriage' to him. Eventually, this gave way to threats that she would publish his letters to her. In 1655, perhaps in desperation, she found a wealthy man twice her age who wanted to marry her. This was the royal resident in The Hague, fifty-six-year-old Sir Henry de Vic.

De Vic and Lucy asked Charles's permission. Apparently he refused to give it. It would seem that the de Vic affair prompted a royal rethink about Lucy. In 1656 Charles's agents were negotiating with Spain for permission to form royalist regiments in the Spanish Netherlands preparatory to a strike against England. The last thing the Stuarts wanted at this delicate moment was a scandal concerning Charles. Mary, Princess of Orange, Charles's sister and confidante, decided that Lucy was an embarrassing encumbrance whose claims about marriage were damaging to the Stuart cause, and Charles was pressed to disown her. Throughout his life the King always tried to avoid confrontations with his lovers, current or former, and on this occasion too he passed the buck. He instructed Lucy's old protector Theodore Taaffe to contact her. 'Advise her both for her sake and mine', wrote Charles, 'that she goes to some place more private than the Hague for her stay there is very prejudicial to us both.' Lucy, a determined young woman, stayed put.

The next step was to discover what she was up to. This task was undertaken by another trusted courtier, Lieutenant-Colonel Daniel O'Neill, an Irish cavalier in Charles's inner circle who was frequently employed on delicate missions. He came back to the King with a dramatic report. Lucy was behaving like a common prostitute and her affair with Tom Howard had become a public scandal. Worse, her maid was ready to go public with the devastating claim that Lucy had twice had abortions – 'miscarrying of two children by phisic' – and she was ready to murder to keep the maid quiet. Aside from witchcraft, it is difficult to think of anything more damaging for a woman in the seventeenth century than the charge of abortion. O'Neill said that he had so far bribed and threatened the maid into silence, but warned the King that the dirt would come out and rub off on him if Lucy remained in The Hague.[16]

It is more than possible that O'Neill was fabricating incidents at the behest of Princess Mary or Sir Edward Hyde, both of whom were desperate for Charles to shake himself free of Lucy. Despite O'Neill's report, a meeting took place between Charles and his former mistress. According to Lucy's maid, they spent 'a day and a night' together. No details ever emerged of what happened but Lucy did as suggested and quit The Hague. She set off for England. Accompanied by her two children, her brother Justus and her current lover Howard, she landed in London in June 1656. They put up in rooms near Somerset House and let it be known that they were the family of a sea captain now dead. The fiction did not hold. Within two weeks the party was being interrogated in the Tower, their cover story blown and their real identities revealed. Among Lucy's belongings the authorities found a pearl necklace worth £1500 apparently given her by Charles the night before they embarked for England. There was also a pension warrant bearing the royal seal. It promised payment of an annuity of 5000 livres, 'with assurance to better the same when it shall please God to restore to us our Kingdoms'.[17]

The governor of the Tower – the forbidding Cromwellian general Sir John Barkstead – questioned Lucy about Charles and their son, and, loyally, she lied. She insisted that she had not seen the King for two years and maintained that the son he had fathered was dead. However, her maid contradicted her: the boy was Charles's and, indeed, Charles had spent that 'night and a day' with Lucy before they sailed. Barkstead believed the maid and reported as much to Cromwell. He in turn did maximum damage to Charles by shipping Lucy back to Flanders.

Lucy's affair with Howard ended after her London adventure and the money promised by Charles failed to materialise. In 1657, reportedly penniless and no doubt desperate, she again threatened to publish letters from Charles, together with other documents, which were said to prove her marriage claim. Courtiers known to her, including former lovers, were now employed to work on her, threatening or cajoling her into letting go of her son and the papers. One such was Theodore Taaffe, who attempted to mollify Lucy when the pension didn't come. Charles, he insisted to her, had everyone's best interests at heart, including hers. If she were patient, he would make up her unpaid pension immediately any money was available.

To get young James out of his mother's clutches, Charles finally resorted to kidnap. There were several attempts to snatch the boy in the winter of 1657–8, all of them foiled by Lucy. The most outrageous attempt took place in December 1657. It was masterminded by one of Charles's most trusted but giddy courtiers, George Digby, who by now had succeeded to the title of Earl of Bristol. Edward Hyde described Digby as 'having an ambition and vanity superior to all his other parts and a confidence peculiar to himself which sometimes intoxicated, transported and exposed him'.[18] Digby had his secretary Sir Arthur Slingsby provide accommodation for Lucy and then attempt to jail her for debt – unpaid rent. The idea was to get her out of the way in order to enable royal agents to seize both child and papers. The plan was scuppered because Lucy wouldn't go quietly. As she was being carried off by Slingsby's men, she clung to her son and let out such screams and protests that the entire neighbourhood turned out in her support and she was released. This bewitching beauty at bay must have made quite a spectacle, much to the embarrassment of Charles who had instructed his man 'to get the child in a quiet way if he could'.[19]

In the New Year, Lucy thwarted another kidnap attempt by again making a public scene, but she was ill and her resistance couldn't last. It finally crumbled in March 1658, when Charles took control of the boy. There are differing accounts of what happened. One has it that she was duped into leaving a visitor momentarily alone with her son while she searched out a document in another room and returned to find both visitor and boy had vanished. According to another account, she simply gave up after a threat that Charles would disown the boy and treat anyone who helped her as an enemy if she persisted in defying him. Charles would 'take any good office done to her as an injury to him', she was told.[20]

In the end, James was forcibly taken from Lucy at the age of nine, brought to France and placed first in the care of his grandmother, Henrietta Maria, and then in that of Thomas Ross, a Scots librarian, but more importantly, a Protestant. As soon as the child was separated from his mother, Charles severed relations with Lucy. It was a callous act. Abandoned in a foreign country, her child taken from her, and without any means of constant support, another woman might have sunk, but not Lucy. Being intelligent and resourceful, she made her way to Paris in the vain hope of regaining access to her son. There are various stories about what happened to Lucy after that. We will return to them later.

While his men were hounding Lucy, Charles comforted himself with other courtesans. The occupants of his bed after the mid-1650s, women such as Eleanor, Lady Byron and Catherine Pegge, tended to be much less volatile than Lucy – they certainly had less reason to be. Eleanor's affair with Charles had begun after her husband's death in 1652. To judge by what her friend Sir Peter Leycester wrote of her, she was yet another stunning beauty. Leycester described her as 'a person of such comely carriage and presence, handsomeness, sweet disposition, honour and general respect in the world that she hath scarce left her equal'.[21] However, judging from other sources she was no sweet innocent. John Evelyn dubbed her the King's 'seventeenth whore abroad' and one of the satires of the time has her 'hurting' one of the King's gentlemen of the bedchamber, i.e. infecting him with the pox.

It was rumoured that Eleanor did very well financially from the affair. She is alleged to have 'extorted' from the hard-pressed Charles upwards of £15,000 in money and jewels. How this exile in his tattered clothes could have afforded anything like such a sum is a mystery.

Catherine Pegge, Charles's main mistress in the late 1650s, seems to have prompted none of the spiteful venom usually directed at the King's women. The daughter of an exiled cavalier family from Derbyshire, Catherine was the King's regular lover for at least two years, possibly much longer. She bore Charles a son and a daughter, christened Charles and Catherine FitzCharles. Charles happily acknowledged both the children as his and when the boy reached the age of eighteen made him Earl of Plymouth. Very little is known about the mother. Given Charles's taste in his women one would expect her to have been another spectacular beauty. But she apparently inspired little comment. Perhaps, unlike Lucy and Barbara Villiers, she led the King a quiet life. Barbara, Catherine's successor, would be the stuff of dreams and nightmares.

6

RESTORATION

Oliver Cromwell died in September 1658. His death led to eighteen months of bewildering political upheaval. Richard Cromwell, Oliver's son, was smoothly installed as Lord Protector, only to be brutally unseated in an army coup seven months later, which was itself followed by a second coup that left the republic on the verge of another civil war. Charles watched from Brussels, at one moment brimming with hope, pushing to land in England, the next moment plunged into despair when told he had no support in England.

His prospects were transformed on 3 February 1660 when General George Monck, commander-in-chief of the army of Scotland, marched into London at the head of four companies of ironsides. Ostensibly Monck had come to save the republic, and on arrival he pledged to uphold it and never let the Stuarts return. However, at heart the general was a royalist who had come to feel that England needed monarchical rule to avoid chaos. It was a belief buttressed by the offer of a massive personal reward if he would defect to the Stuart cause. Just two months after reaching London he went down on his knees to a royal emissary and pledged allegiance to Charles; a month later he effectively gift-wrapped the throne for the exiled monarch.

On the same momentous day that Monck arrived in the capital, fate was paving the way for Charles to meet the nineteen-year-old woman who would dazzle and dominate him for nearly half his reign. She was the volcanic and intoxicatingly attractive Barbara Palmer. A letter to Charles penned that day, 3 February, by a royalist agent in London announced that Barbara's husband of ten months, Roger Palmer, had donated £1000 to the royalist cause and that he and his wife had agreed to become undercover couriers. They would be putting their lives in peril by smuggling money and letters to Charles in Brussels.

Palmer's wife was expected to be especially useful because Flanders had been hit by a virulent smallpox epidemic and Barbara was immune. Like Charles, she'd had smallpox and, like the King, she had survived unblemished by its ravages and could come and go in Flanders without fear.[1]

Barbara was a poor relation in the fanatically royalist Villiers clan. She had seen her immediate family all but ruin itself in the royal cause. She was the only child of William Villiers, Viscount Grandison, who perished fighting for the King after mortgaging everything he owned to fund his royalist cavalry regiment. Her mother married again, only to see her new husband's lands confiscated for his royalist involvement. Despite everything, the Villiers' commitment to the Stuarts remained undimmed. Barbara would recall how on every 29 May, Charles's birthday, she would be taken down into the unlit cellar to drink the King's health in secrecy.

At the age of fifteen, Barbara was brought to London by her mother to find a husband, suitably rich and ideally aristocratic. She was already tall and voluptuous, with blue-violet eyes, alabaster skin, full sulky lips and a mass of auburn hair. Soon after arriving in London Barbara threw reputation to the winds in pursuit of men. Her first lover was probably Philip Stanhope, Earl of Chesterfield. A dissipated rake,* seven years her senior, whose first wife had died, he

---

* Rake is short for rakehell, an archaic English word of uncertain origin meaning a dissolute person, particularly of fashionable circles.

had many lovers and bragged of regularly having six women in bed at a time. Barbara was besotted with him. She poured out teenage professions of passion. 'The joy I had of being with you last night has made me do nothing but dream of you,' she wrote. Chesterfield would not entertain the idea of marrying Barbara – she wasn't rich. His letters show him as rather offhand and Barbara as rather clinging, certainly not yet the virago she would become.

In April 1659, she married the royalist Roger Palmer. Physically, he was as unprepossessing as she was gorgeous, with a lantern jaw and sunken eyes. But he was rich. Before the wedding, her future father-in-law warned his son that Barbara would make him 'one of the most miserable men in the world'. Palmer quickly discovered what his father meant. He learned of the affair with Chesterfield, and that it was still going on. Palmer whisked his bride away to the imagined safety of his brother's home near Windsor, deep in the country. She reacted by smuggling out a letter to Chesterfield pleading to elope. 'I am ready to go all over the world with you,' she told him.[2]

In January 1660, Chesterfield dropped out of her life and Charles entered it. Chesterfield killed a man in a duel over the price of a mare and fled the country, while Barbara and husband Roger became underground couriers for the King and were received by him in Brussels. Sir Edward Hyde noted the King's unusual interest in the woman: 'He told me this day that she had had the small-pox ... Of what interest could that person's immunity be to anyone but her husband?'

No one knows how quickly the King took the beautiful new courier to bed. She became an anonymous presence after arriving in Brussels with her husband midway through February. There is no record of her first meeting with Charles there, nor of where she went or what information or money she couriered on his behalf. What is certain is that Charles could ill afford scandal at what was a delicate juncture politically. These were the momentous weeks in which George Monck purged the army of 'fanatics' (republicans), cleared the way for a pro-monarchist House of Commons and persuaded the country to see Charles not as an ogre but a saviour, the only hope of stability. A salacious story about the King and a newly married young bride would not have helped the new image. It is very probable that the affair began in Brussels, but very quietly.

On 1 May 1660 the new Parliament declared England a monarchy again. The House of Lords, abolished in 1649 but now re-established under Monck, announced: 'The Lords do own and declare that according to the ancient and fundamental laws of this kingdom, the government is, and ought to be, by King, Lords and Commons.' The House of Commons issued a parallel statement: 'This House doth agree with the Lords ...' On 8 May the absent Charles was officially proclaimed 'the most potent, mighty and undoubted King of England, Scotland and Wales'. Thanks to Monck no conditions were attached by Parliament, not even those his father had once agreed to accept. The general insisted that there was no need for conditions because Charles could be trusted. Hurrying Parliament into allowing the King carte blanche, Monck warned that 'blood or mischief' might follow if there was any delay over terms.[3]

Historians have judged the failure to tie Charles to any commitments to have been a disaster, though it would suit very well those close to the throne who would seek to manipulate the King over the next quarter of a century, not least the friends of Barbara Palmer and Barbara herself. William Cobbett wrote: 'To the King's coming in without conditions may be well imputed all the errors of his reign.'[4] According to Edmund Burke, 'the man given us by Monck was a man without any sense of his duty as a prince; without any regard as to the dignity of his crown; without any love to his people, dissolute, false, venal, and destitute of any positive good quality whatsoever except a pleasant temper and the manners of a gentleman.'[5]

Charles delayed his landing in England till 26 May so as to arrive in London on his birthday three days later. A huge crowd gathered under the cliffs of Dover to greet and goggle, cheer and fawn before the royal prodigal son. One assumes that most among them would have invested high hopes in the tall, swarthy figure springing athletically onto his home soil. George Monck was at their forefront. He sank to his knees as the King approached, to be swept up to his feet in a royal embrace of gratitude. Charles reportedly greeted Monck as 'father'. Courtiers and would-be courtiers came next, jostling to kneel and kiss the hem of the King's robe and be recognised. Charles smiled on all save George Villiers, Duke of Buckingham, his friend since boyhood and once 'his inseparable boon companion in his life of sensuality'.[6] The two had fallen out three years earlier after Buckingham quit Charles's exiled court and returned to England to make his peace with Cromwell. The King's attitude to the Duke at Dover was described as 'cold'. Nevertheless, when the first formalities on the seashore were over, the ebullient Buckingham placed himself in a position of honour in the King's cavalcade. He rode just behind Charles, his two brothers and Monck, as they struck inland on the road to Canterbury before heading to London.

Bishop Gilbert Burnet, a contemporary observer, reported a 'springtime of joy in all people's hearts' at Charles's restoration, and at Canterbury more crowds awaited. The Venetian ambassador was among them. He managed to grab a quick word of congratulation with the King, who replied in Italian. The ambassador reported: 'At great personal inconvenience he remained standing many hours to receive the respect and submission of the great numbers who came on purpose to kneel and kiss his hand, according to the custom of the country.' Underneath his suave exterior Charles was bemused at the welcome he was receiving. 'My head is so dreadfully stunned with the acclamation of the people and the vast amount of business that I know not whether I am writing sense or nonsense,' he wrote to his sister Minette the day after he reached England.[7]

After two nights in Canterbury and one in Rochester, Charles stopped at Blackheath where virtually the entire army was lined up to hail him. The uniforms sported all manner of regimental colours save one – the red of Cromwell's once all-conquering New Model Army. Then it was across the Thames and into London, arriving on his thirtieth birthday. 'The ways', wrote John Evelyn, were 'strewn

with flowers, the bells ringing, the streets hung with tapestry, foun-
tains running with wine, the mayor, aldermen and all the companies
in their liveries, chains of gold, banners; lords and nobles clad in
both cloth of silver and gold and velvet, the windows all set with
ladies, trumpets, music and myriads of people flocking the streets.'[8]

The Venetian ambassador was bowled over by it all. His dispatch
to the Doge dated 11 June reported that Charles entered the city

> surrounded by a crowd of the nobility, with great pomp and tri-
> umph and in the most stately manner ever seen, amid the
> acclamations and blessings of the people, beyond all expression ...
> He passed from one end to the other of this very long city, between
> the foot soldiers who kept the streets open, raising his eyes to the
> windows looking at all, raising his hat to all and consoling all who
> with loud shouts and a tremendous noise acclaimed the return of
> this great prince so abounding in virtues and distinguished quali-
> ties of every sort. Through this great crowd he proceeded to
> Whitehall where he remains, and where so far he has been
> allowed no rest, showing himself at every moment to the people
> who press impetuously forward to offer their devotion to their sov-
> ereign.[9]

According to *Augustus Anglicus*, a hagiography of Charles published a year after he died, the King concluded his first day back in
London by enjoying 'a sweet and sedate repose'. It seems more likely
that the pumped-up young monarch completed his celebrations in
bed with his new mistress. Nine months later to the day Barbara
bore him their first child, a girl christened Anne. The king would
acknowledge her as his own and four more of her children after her.

The low profile kept by mistress and sovereign continued for five
weeks. During that time the Palmers moved into a house in King
Street that conveniently backed onto the palace orchard, within a
few minutes' walk of the King's apartments. Till the beginning of
May the house had been the home of Edward Whalley, one of

Parliament's most celebrated generals. Whalley was the third signa-
tory to King Charles I's death warrant and had also been his
custodian – a considerate one – during the King's imprisonment at
Hampton Court. He was now a wanted man and wisely did not wait
around. On 4 May he and his son-in-law, William Goffe, another
Cromwellian general, smuggled themselves out of England on a
ship bound for New England. They would spend twenty years there
on the run, including two years hiding in a cave.[10]

On 13 July there was a party at the house. The three Stuart brothers attended – Charles, the tall and obtuse James, Duke of York, and
the brightest of the trio, twenty-one-year-old Henry, Duke of
Gloucester. The inquisitive diarist Samuel Pepys, who worked
nearby, stopped to listen to the music. He picked up what he could
hear of the conversation. In his diary that night, he recorded 'great
doings of music at the next house, which was Whalley's, the King
and dukes there with Madam Palmer, a pretty woman that they have
a fancy to, to make her husband a cuckold'. Pepys had no idea that
the pretty woman was already the King's mistress, and would turn
into a mistress like none before her.

Over the summer months and into autumn, the character of the
court of Charles II was shaped. It emerged in the image of its king,
amoral, carefree and high-spirited, lewd and enthusiastically licentious, with sex the dominant and sometimes ruinous preoccupation.
One of the consequences was noted by Samuel Pepys a year later:
'The pox is so common there ... as common as eating and swearing.'
However, the court would be dubbed 'the most brilliant the nation
had ever known'.[11]

The hedonistic pace was set by a group of iconoclastic young aristocrats close to the throne. George Villiers, the multi-gifted and
utterly unprincipled Duke of Buckingham, was the glittering star
among them, 'the wildest rioter, the coarsest reveller'. He easily
beguiled Charles into forgiving him for deserting to Cromwell three
years earlier and within two months of being cold-shouldered at
Dover was the King's boon companion again.

The wickedly witty Thomas Killigrew, appointed by Charles as groom of the bedchamber and master of the revels, Charles Sackville, Earl of Dorset and the playwright Sir George Etherege were other vibrant personalities in this inner circle. There were sometime hell-raisers, too, like George Digby, Earl of Bristol, who had tried to imprison Lucy Walter, and numerous hangers-on like Sir Charles Berkeley. The latter was said to be 'without any visible merit unless it was the managing of the King's amours'.[12]

The high-flying young courtiers soon got to know of Barbara's affair with the King; there were too many watchers to keep it secret for long. As early as August 1660 the young bloods took to gathering daily at the Palmer house in King Street; and more often than not from early afternoon onwards the King was there too. In some weeks he dined there four or five times. His passion for the twenty-year-old must have been obvious to his intimates. But it was not to be obvious to the outside world for many more months. Indeed it was a long time before Roger Palmer, blinded with love of his dazzling wife, had his eyes opened to what was going on.

Two other matters close to the King's heart concentrated attention during the rest of 1660 and for much of the following year. One was Charles's visceral need to avenge his father's 'murder' (as he called it), the other his need to get married, have a queen and an heir.

When he returned to England in May, he radiated clemency and reconciliation, but his intention was to wreak vengeance on the men who had signed his father's death warrant, and he determined that it would be done quickly. During his first week back in England he launched a manhunt for the signatories as well as for the anonymous axeman and assistant who had actually beheaded his father. The following three months were occupied compiling death lists as Parliament debated which of fifty or more republicans to execute.

After a show trial, the first 'regicides' – killers of the king – were hanged, drawn and quartered in the Strand within sight of the Banqueting House where Charles's father had been beheaded eleven years earlier. It was a brutal punishment in which the victim was first hanged until choking, then his testicles were cut off and waved before his eyes before being thrown on a brazier. Next, his intestines were cut out and, if the victim was still conscious, shown to him on a platter and then thrown on the fire. Finally, the victim was beheaded and his body cut into four pieces. During most of the executions, Charles left London early in the morning to ensure that no one would be able to find him and petition for clemency. But he is believed to have watched the butchery at least once, most likely from a gallery window overlooking the gallows. Barbara would probably have been able to hear from the house in King Street the cheers or groans of the crowd. She might even have watched with Charles.

On 16 October, a week after the first executions, Pepys again saw Barbara in royal company, this time in the royal chapel in Whitehall. He still did not realise there was anything between the couple. 'An indifferent sermon,' he noted, 'and after it an anthem, ill sung, which made the King laugh ... Here I also observed how the Duke of York and Mrs Palmer did talk to one another very wantonly through the hangings that parts the King's closet and the closet where the ladies sit.'

The urgent need for a bride to safeguard the dynasty by producing another male in the line of succession had been brought home to Charles a month earlier by a scandal that was closely followed by tragedy. His brother James, the Duke of York and heir to the throne, appeared in tears before him, sank to his knees and revealed that he had been having an affair with Anne Hyde, the Chancellor's daughter, formerly a maid of honour to the Princess of Orange. James had signed some kind of marriage contract with her and now she was pregnant and expected him to honour it. A week later, Charles learned that his other brother, the much-admired Henry of Gloucester, who was second in line for the throne, had contracted smallpox. The initial prognosis was good and a full recovery was expected but Henry died on 17 September.

The attractive side of Charles emerges in his reactions to James's revelations about Anne Hyde. He ordered lawyers to examine the marriage contract, and when they verified it quietly encouraged James to marry his mistress. He told his brother 'he must drink as he brewed'. There followed a secret marriage ceremony in the Hyde household, attended by just two witnesses at the dead of night, while the Chancellor slept, unaware of what was going on. In the morning, Charles had the news broken to him as gently as possible. Hyde exploded in fury, denouncing his daughter, shouting for her to be dispatched to the Tower. It is impossible to know whether this was an old man's genuine outrage or an attempt to buttress himself against the inevitable suspicion that he had engineered the whole thing. Though it was not beyond the bounds of possibility that the gout-ridden Chancellor was plotting to make his daughter a princess and possibly a queen if Charles was suddenly to drop dead, the marriage seems to have been pushed by the bride rather than her more circumspect father. Whatever the truth, Hyde's enemies whispered that he aimed to found a Hyde dynasty.[13]

The thought of marriage to this commoner induced a state of haughty outrage among the royal womenfolk. Before the end of the month, Mary, Princess of Orange, for whom Anne had been a lady-in-waiting, arrived in Whitehall bent on invalidating the marriage. Seething with anger, she vowed never to yield precedence to a woman who had stood behind her as her servant. The Queen, Henrietta Maria, stormed in from Paris to stop 'so great a stain and dishonour to the crown'.

One of the many unsavoury episodes of Charles's reign was now played out as courtiers attempted to blacken Anne Hyde's name and invalidate the marriage contract. The effort was masterminded by Sir Charles Berkeley, one of James's closest friends at court, and was abetted by several friends of the Duke, all of them also enemies of Anne's father. They included the Earl of Arran, Harry Jermyn and Thomas Killigrew. Berkeley persuaded them to claim that Anne had allowed them all 'familiarities' with her. Killigrew agreed to say that Anne had allowed him to go further and described vividly how she had 'surrendered her honour' to him in a water closet.[14]

Sir Charles Berkeley relayed the details to James, who was probably in ignorance of the plot, and told the Duke that 'he was bound in
conscience to preserve him from taking to wife a woman so wholly
unworthy of him'. Berkeley himself had lain with her; and for James's
sake, he said, he was content to marry her. James promptly broke
contact with Anne.

In mind of the lies told about Anne, some historians have speculated about the reputation acquired by Lucy Walter when the
pressure was on Charles to get rid of her. Was her reputation too
blackened by courtiers until Charles finally rejected her, the great
love of his life, as a whore?

The Anne Hyde episode, however, was different in one respect
from Lucy's miserable story. It had a relatively happy ending for the
woman. In time for the birth of a son to Anne on 22 October, the
better side of the Duke of York asserted itself. With the King's backing James publicly announced the marriage and Anne automatically
became a duchess. Later she was even accepted by the harpies in the
royal family. It had a positive outcome for her father too. To show his
continued faith in his Lord Chancellor, the King ennobled Hyde as
Earl of Clarendon. It is possible that Charles perceived a bonus in
making his Chancellor a peer. As a member of the House of Lords,
Clarendon couldn't be questioned about royal scandals or indeed
about anything else by his enemies in the House of Commons.

As for Berkeley and his friends, they apologised profusely for the
lies they'd told and resumed the merry-making life of the courtier.

In the world outside, the transformation in Charles's status from
despised exile to king of a feared power was endorsed as the ruling
houses of Europe scrapped with each other to provide him with a
consort. In a race that lasted through the rest of 1660 and all of
1661, Brandenburg, Portugal, Saxony, Denmark, Parma, France,
Spain and Austria all pitched in at various times with candidates
to share Charles's throne. It was made brutally clear to them that
the only determinants would be money – the size of the dowry –

and attractiveness. If there were any doubts about the primacy of sex in Charles's life, they would be banished by a glance through the reasons he rejected princess after princess in these eighteen months.

He said no to Eleanor of Mantua, widow of the Emperor Ferdinand, on grounds of age – she was 'poor in money but rich in years', it was said. In fact she was the same age as Charles. He turned down at least three German princesses on grounds of weight: 'I could not marry one of them,' he remarked, 'they are all foggy' (i.e. flabby, physically or mentally). He then sent his friend the Earl of Bristol hundreds of miles to check out two Italian princesses, whose names came up very late in the day. Maria Magdalena and Caterina were the sisters of the Duke of Parma. One at least was accounted to be 'most beautiful'. However, she turned out to be fat, and her sister ugly. Both were to die unmarried.

No such personal vetting appears to have occurred with the Portuguese princess, Catarina Henriqueta de Braganza, sister of Alfonso VI of Braganza, king of Portugal. Charles had to rely on portraiture in judging her. Painted by the Dutchman Dirk Stoop, who had painted Charles's triumphal return to England in May 1660, the portrait of Catarina, or Catherine as she would be known, shows her pretty, dark-haired and demure. Charles is said to have studied it and reported that its subject 'cannot be unhandsome'. That and the promise of a mouth-watering dowry made Catherine the favourite, but before the choice was made there was a prolonged diplomatic battle.

Alfonso was desperate to use the marriage to re-establish old ties with England, because he faced the threat of invasion from neighbouring Spain and there were no other potential protectors among the powers of Europe. Spain was equally desperate to sabotage the projected alliance by finding an alternative bride for Charles. The Spanish had no princesses of the blood of their own to offer him. Their two infantas had already been married off, one that same year to Louis XIV. So they came up with the idea of finding a princess from outside Spain, endowing her with the grand status of a Spanish infanta and offering her together with an appropriate dowry to Charles.

The leavings of war complicated things. England had been at war with Spain until just before the Restoration. She emerged from it occupying two Spanish possessions either side of the Atlantic, the island of Jamaica in the Caribbean and the port of Dunkirk in Flanders. Spain wanted them back. They would have to be part of any Spanish marriage deal.[15]

Further complications were introduced by Cardinal Mazarin, Louis XIV's first minister. Mazarin realised his mistake in vetoing Charles during his last year in exile in 1659 when he had bid for the hand of the Cardinal's bewitching little niece, Hortense Mancini. Then Mazarin had deployed a feeble excuse for rejecting Charles. Now that the king without a kingdom had three kingdoms, the man of God forgot his objection and offered a dowry of three million francs. He let it be known that if this was unacceptable he might obstruct another dynastic marriage also being negotiated, that between Charles's young sister Henrietta Anne and Louis XIV's brother, the Duke of Orléans.

One would imagine that Charles's personal preference at this stage was Hortense. He had known her as a thirteen-year-old, when she already promised to blossom into a truly beautiful woman. The libido in the man would have made him reluctant to close the door on such a prize. But it was not to be.

In 1661 a four-way diplomatic whirligig ensued, with Portugal apparently prepared to empty the bank to tempt the English, the Spanish searching Europe for an infanta and hinting at war if Charles said yes to Alfonso, Mazarin trying to sabotage other bids and Charles's ministers rubbing their hands hoping the offers would get bigger and bigger. Through the first quarter of 1661 they did.

In April everything was put on hold. Charles's coronation was scheduled for 23 April – St George's Day – and the whole machinery of government ground to a halt to enjoy what the Venetian ambassador called 'the pomp and magnificence' of it all. There were no meetings, no decisions for weeks while once again London let its hair down to celebrate the Stuarts. There were triumphal arches, glittering cavalcades, classical tableaux, ancient rituals and endless junketing. Night after night across London mansions banqueted and bonfires burned. Evelyn recorded sarcastically, 'King Crowned, great joy, much sin, the Lord pardon.' He added that it would have been worse but for the weather. 'Twas a very wett evening, which prevented something of God's Dishonour.'

By now there was no secrecy about the King's mistress and she accompanied him openly. Two days before the coronation Pepys spotted her with the King at the Cockpit theatre watching a Beaumont and Fletcher play, *The Humorous Lieutenant*. Pepys noted how the King displayed 'a good deal of familiarity' to his companion. She didn't, of course, accompany him to the coronation, indeed she may have missed it altogether, for there is no mention anywhere of her.

Two weeks later on 8 May the choice of queen was announced. The return of Jamaica and Dunkirk and the size of the dowry had proved the final sticking points that ruled out Spain, and Hortense was ruled out too. The decision was to go with Portugal. Her winning offer included the transfer to British sovereignty of Bombay and Tangier, special trading rights in Brazil and £500,000 in cash. Until then, contacts with the Portuguese had been described as being about trade. Now, addressing the nation during the full pomp of a state opening of Parliament, Charles revealed the truth. After speaking briefly about not becoming an old bachelor and the impossibility of finding a suitable Protestant, he announced that he was marrying 'a daughter of Portugal'. He ended with a commitment to 'make all the haste I can to fetch you a Queen hither, who, I doubt not, will bring great Blessings with her, to me and you'.[16]

Under the marriage articles the new Queen was guaranteed the free exercise of her faith and £30,000 a year for life, while the King was assured possession of her magnificent dowry, together with the territories and trade treaties promised. He penned a letter of welcome to Catherine, 'my lady and wife'. It declared his hope that he would soon see 'the beloved person of Your Majesty in these kingdoms, already your own'. He signed it 'the very faithful husband of Your Majesty, whose hand he kisses'. However, he was not to set eyes on her for almost another year. The wedding was to be in May 1662.

The impending wedding, and the choice of queen, concentrated the minds of Barbara Palmer and the group of courtiers associated with her. In the year after the Restoration Barbara had acquired a hold on the King that horrified the old guard on the Privy Council. The King began lavishing cash and presents on her, and listening to her and her friends over whom to reward in the scramble for government preferment. 'In the disposal of offices and places there was little regard had to men's merits or services,' complained Bishop Burnet. 'The King was determined to most of these by the cabal that met at Mistress Palmer's lodgings.' An ambitious and tough-minded queen could put an end to all that.

The main impediment to Barbara and company was the veteran Chancellor, Edward Hyde, now ennobled as the Earl of Clarendon. He was a man who enjoyed his reputation for rectitude. In March 1661 he told the King and the Duke of York that he was unable to deal with the new French minister Fouquet because the latter was corrupt. He had offered Clarendon a massive bribe – £10,000 – which Clarendon had indignantly refused. The brothers laughed out loud and the King remarked that the French always did business that way. Charles advised a now choleric Chancellor to take the money, which he refused to do.

A state of vitriolic war now existed between Barbara and the Chancellor. Barbara found him blocking her at every turn. He and his fellow privy councillor, the treasurer Thomas Wriothesley, Earl of Southampton, refused to touch any piece of government business associated with her. Land grants, subsidies and appointments promised by Barbara in return for cash either went unprocessed or were withdrawn by Charles under the Chancellor's persuasion. What made Barbara's behaviour unforgivable for Hyde was that he had almost worshipped her father, who had been his best friend. Hyde said of him, 'the court or camp could not show a more faultless person'. His hatred for his friend's daughter ran so deep that he could not bring himself to utter her name. Years later when writing his histories he would refer to her only as 'the lady'. The sneer almost jumps out of the page.

Barbara raged against Hyde. Whether in her King Street salon or in the royal presence chamber in Whitehall Palace, she spat and cursed and yelled for Clarendon's head. One wonders how much of her fury was fed by the money that he cost her and how much by the male chauvinism of the pompous, tactless fifty-year-old Chancellor who never bothered to disguise his disdain for the female intellect.

Not surprisingly she sought allies against Clarendon and found them in some of the men closest to the King – the flamboyant sycophant Sir Henry Bennet, who wore a patch across his nose to draw attention to a civil war scar, the wild Papist George Digby, who'd fruitlessly vetted the looks of princesses for Charles and later pimped lesser ladies for him, and the glittering George Villiers, whose return to favour was marked in April 1662 by Charles endowing him with the Order of the Garter and appointing him to carry the orb at his coronation. All hated Clarendon. They formed a faction around Barbara bent on the Chancellor's downfall.

Barbara's foes at court called her a whore but all had to acknowledge her intoxicating beauty. Reresby called her 'the finest woman of her age' and the contemporary historian Abel Boyer wrote that she was 'perhaps the finest woman in England in her time'. Samuel Pepys was almost orgasmic at every sighting of her: 'there with much pleasure [I] gazed upon her ... I went away, not weary with alooking at her ... strange it is how for her beauty I am willing to construe all this to the best ... I filled my eyes with her.' Perhaps the greatest tribute was from Peter Lely, whom Charles had appointed as court painter in 1661. Lely was to say he adored her and apologised that none of his portraits did her justice. Her beauty was 'beyond the power of art', the painter claimed.

She was supposed to have no wit yet was quick with the pithy put-down. Dealing with a property granted to her by the King which she intended to sell on immediately, the Chancellor remarked disparagingly that 'the woman would sell everything.' When this was reported to her she sent word to Hyde that he was right, because she'd be selling his place too before long.

Her other great characteristic was her volcanic, foot-stamping temper. Whether this was a Villiers inheritance or whether she deliberately employed it as a weapon, it worked on Charles. She appears to have unleashed it on him regularly, brow-beating and even humiliating him to get her way. Bishop Burnet's description of Charles emerging from a fierce argument with Barbara is of a man looking poleaxed. Her behaviour 'did so disorder him that often he was not master of himself nor capable of minding business'. One can conceive of only one other English monarch in two thousand years suffering such treatment – the barely functioning King Henry VI.

The build-up to Catherine's arrival in May 1662 began six or seven months earlier, in the winter of 1661–2 when Barbara discovered that she was pregnant for a second time and the King took steps to buttress her future status and that of her offspring. He bowed to her pleas to make her a lady of the bedchamber and raised her near the top of the aristocratic pecking order, bestowing an Irish earldom on her husband, thus automatically giving Barbara a title. Roger became Earl and Barbara Countess of Castlemaine.

Until then Roger had acted as if blind to his wife's infidelity. That was no longer possible given the wording of the royal warrant ennobling him. It restricted inheritance of the title to descendants of those 'gotten on Barbara Palmer, his now wife', which left no doubt that the honour was for her, and as Pepys put it 'the reason whereof everybody knows'. Humiliated, Roger Palmer tried to refuse the honour but eventually accepted it. He made a point, however, of never occupying his seat in the Irish House of Lords and in the years ahead spent the bulk of his time abroad.

It galled the new duchess that the title was not an English one. It had to be Irish because the warrant for an English title would require the stamp of the Great Seal of England, which Clarendon would not easily have allowed.

As Catherine's arrival loomed ever nearer, Barbara became more obviously agitated and aggressive and her enemies more confident. In January 1662 Pepys overheard snatches of gossip concerning 'private factions at court about Madame Palmer'. He was unable to fathom what that meant, only that they involved 'something about the king's favour to her now that the queen is coming'. The diarist learned nothing more about Barbara until April, when he heard of a row between Barbara and her Villiers cousin, Mary, Duchess of Richmond and Lennox. Pepys recorded that Lady Richmond and Lady Castlemaine 'had a falling out the other day', with the Duchess of Richmond calling Barbara a 'Jane Shaw'* and then telling her she hoped 'to see her come to the same end'.

Barbara was evidently in no mood to be put down. Far from retiring to the sidelines once the new Queen arrived, she threatened to go centre stage. Well into her pregnancy, she declared that she would have the child in the most embarrassing place possible – the palace of Hampton Court where Charles and Catherine were due to spend their honeymoon.

---

* Jane Shaw or Shore was the beautiful mistress of King Edward IV, who as a penance after his death was forced to walk semi-clothed through the streets and died in poverty.

7

THE BRIDE'S PRICE

In April 1662, an English fleet put into the Portuguese port of Lisbon under the command of Edward Montagu, 1st Earl of Sandwich. Montagu was a professional survivor, a man so adept at reading the political weather that he perennially sailed with the breeze. During the British civil wars he had fought on the Parliamentary side and sat as an MP during Cromwell's Protectorate, before executing a dazzling tack before a changing wind to become admiral of the fleet that carried King Charles II home from exile. Now, two years later, on his flagship the *Royal Charles*, he had another royal mission – to carry the Portuguese princess to England. As befitted his rank, Montagu was invited to take part in a grand parade in which Princess Catherine processed before adoring crowds in Lisbon before sailing away to her new life as queen to a foreign king.

In an engraving made of the occasion, we see Catherine resplendent in a gilded coach, preceded by an equally ornate coach containing her brother, King Alfonso VI, and followed by another containing Montagu and the English ambassador. The procession looks suitably grand, with many carriages carrying assorted royals, aristocrats and dignitaries, accompanied by hundreds of foot soldiers and cavalry, all wheeling around through triumphal arches erected in front of the huge Renaissance Ribeira Palace while the English fleet waits at anchor. In another engraving, the artist shows the princess embarking from a canopied pier onto a richly decorated barge that will carry her out to Montagu's flagship. The whole scene is so full of gaiety and colour that it seems the most auspicious of all days.

The artist who captured these scenes was Dutchman Dirk Stoop, who had studied painting at Utrecht. Having accompanied Charles (and therefore his admiral) on his voyage to England in 1660, Stoop was already acquainted with Montagu. Since painting Charles's triumphant entry into London, Stoop had chiefly been employed in the Portuguese royal household. His portrait of Catherine, sent to England in the spring of 1661 to show Charles what he was getting in his bargain with the Portuguese, is the best record we have of what she was like as a young woman just grown into her maturity.

The young princess is depicted three-quarter length, seated beside a red curtain and with a brooding sky behind her. She looks young for her age (which was about twenty-one) with an oval face and hair arranged in long, crimped waves over her collar. She appears slim, even delicate, with small hands and a slight frame. Her dress is particularly interesting, being of a dark cloth, with slashed sleeves and a high, embroidered shawl collar which sits across her shoulders leaving no flesh visible below her neck. Her bodice is stiff and straight – the costume of a young and very devout Catholic woman of high status and, most crucially, a virgin. Her skirt juts on either side at an alarming angle, held out by a farthingale at right angles from her waist in a fashion that would never have been countenanced at the royal court in London. To an English eye, her style was antiquated, Elizabethan even, for the Virgin Queen had worn a farthingale, exploiting the geometric volume provided by the hoops under her skirts to add gravitas and presence. With Elizabeth's death the fashion had died too. Apart from the stuffy clothes, Catherine's portrait reveals a woman nearing the end of her shelf life. She has lived in the most secluded fashion, in her early years hardly ever leaving the convent where she was reared, except to visit her parents.

Catherine valued Stoop's work so highly that she was taking him along to become her court painter in England. He was well suited for the job, being able to rise to depicting the big, ceremonial event as well as a good but flattering likeness. For the Dutchman, it must have seemed the most enormous opportunity to become an official painter at the Court of St James. He was not to know that his ambitions were to be thwarted by another savvy Dutch painter, one whose beautiful muse had woven an erotic spell over the King.

On 23 April, the English fleet set sail from Lisbon, bearing away Catherine, her entourage (or family, as it was called) of a hundred attendants and servants and a thousand boxes of sugar. Presiding over the sugar, at Montagu's insistence, was a well-established merchant brought along to sell it in London at the best possible price.

Following a rough crossing of the infamously stormy Bay of Biscay, Montagu's fleet arrived off Portsmouth on 13 May. It did not carry Catherine's dowry – at least, not the entire two million crowns that the cash-strapped Charles had hoped for. The Portuguese did not have the cash to hand. Most of it had been spent on war with Spain. Montagu was informed that he would receive half the dowry now and the rest later. This put the Earl in a dilemma. If he insisted upon the letter of the treaty – that the entire dowry would be paid before the Infanta set sail for England – then the marriage and the treaty were off. If he agreed, he had the responsibility of allowing the Portuguese to get away with it and of breaking the news to a king who valued the money more than his new bride.

Montagu decided the only option was to go ahead. But worse was to come. He discovered that the half of the dowry being loaded into his ships was not made up of cruzados, solid gold and silver coins stamped with a cross. Instead, it consisted of sugar and spices. This was extremely awkward for Montagu. He had already sailed to the mouth of the Mediterranean and secured Tangier, which was ceded to the English as part of the treaty. Ships had sailed to ensure Bombay also passed into English hands. It would be impossible to undo the treaty now. Montagu saw that he could only take his hosts' word that the rest of the dowry would be paid within the year.

Charles sent the Duke of York to Portsmouth as head of the reception party to receive his new queen and oversee arrangements prior to his arrival. Along with the Duke, hordes of courtiers and their ladies went down to Portsmouth too. The arrival of Catherine on 14 May was turned into a fashionable event. A crowd dressed *à la mode* waited to set eyes on the new queen. When Catherine came ashore from the *Royal Charles*, what the crowd saw was a small, rather dainty woman dressed thoughtfully in the English fashion. The Duke of York greeted her on behalf of the King. When she smiled she displayed crooked, protruding teeth.

Those who came with her made no better an impression, for there followed a large company of servants dressed in clothes so reticent as to be dowdy, a large platoon of priests, and a small group of ladies-in-waiting dressed in the most severe Portuguese court style, with large farthingales holding their dresses stiffly out to the sides like wings. The weight and bulk of these dresses made movement difficult, forcing those who wore them to walk in a penguin's waddle, much to the delight of the English, who were far too fashionable to hide their amusement. The urbane Irish soldier and writer Anthony Hamilton christened the ladies-in-waiting 'the six frights'. He had no better word for their deaf duenna, saying she was 'another monster, who took the title of governess to these extraordinary beauties'.[1]

The Duke enquired whether Catherine would like refreshment after the voyage. She replied she would like a cup of tea. This caused embarrassment, for there was no tea available. Catherine was offered a glass of beer. The cultural differences between the two nations were clear to see. In a country where beer was the national drink, tea drinking was yet to take hold. Catherine would turn England into a land of ale drinkers *and* tea drinkers.

Catherine and her entourage were under intense scrutiny. She had to endure it for many days, staying first on board the *Royal Charles* in the Solent and then at the home of the governor of

Portsmouth, before Charles arrived and their wedding could at last take place. The Duke of York asked her to exchange her English clothes for native Portuguese dress and Catherine obliged, either thinking he was advising her on the best thing to do or intending to hold her up to ridicule – we just don't know. In her dowdy, strait-laced bodice and huge farthingale, the foreign princess was immediately in danger of appearing as strange to local eyes as her ladies-in-waiting. But despite her looks and solemn demeanour, Catherine was clever and quickly took the lesson to heart. She switched again to the English fashion, changing into a white dress trimmed in gold to come ashore.[2]

While Catherine waited passively, in a sort of limbo, Barbara was all action, plotting a reception the new woman in the King's life would live to remember: she went ahead with her threat to move into Hampton Court. The King and Queen would honeymoon in the same house as a heavily pregnant and domineering mistress. Charles was so much under his mistress's thumb that he allowed her to have her way. He had a more pressing issue on his mind: the dowry. By now, Montagu had no doubt informed his master of what had happened at Lisbon. Six days passed between the arrival of the Queen and Charles's departure for Portsmouth.

Just as Montagu had had to make a decision whether or not to agree to carry the Infanta to England, now Charles had to decide whether or not to proceed with marrying a woman whose family had shown such bad faith over the conditions of the treaty. As matters stood, the Portuguese were gaining a valuable ally in their fight against their old adversary Spain, while Charles found himself robbed of the huge cash dowry which had secured the treaty with Portugal in the first place. Sadly, we have no record of the King's reaction to Montagu's news but the delay in his departure for Portsmouth can at least partially be put down to his pondering what to do. The most extreme reaction would have been to send Catherine packing home to Lisbon. This might have made both parties the laughing stock of Europe and would have seriously decreased Charles's chances of finding a suitable alternative spouse. Whatever went through his mind, he decided to make the most of it.

But before greeting his new queen, Charles ensured he had his fill of his mistress. For four days running he dined and supped with Barbara. On the fourth night he sent for a set of scales so that he and his pregnant mistress could compare their weights. Appropriately, Barbara was the heavier.

The next morning, Charles set off in his finest coach to greet his queen. Pepys, who was clearly infatuated with Barbara, wrote in his diary in May of his erotic excitement at seeing her fine petticoats and other intimate garments hanging to dry on a washing line in the Privy Garden. He lusted after Barbara, calling her 'my lovely Lady Castlemaine'. He bought a copy of a portrait of her and put it up above the fireplace in his office at the Admiralty.[3] The ardent diarist does not record whether he realised Barbara's petticoats were hung out like flags of war.

When Charles arrived in Portsmouth, Catherine was unwell, having caught a cold during the stormy voyage. She was unable to greet her husband as she had hoped in fine English clothes but was in bed in her nightdress. The woman Charles saw propped up in bed was in most respects like the image in Dirk Stoop's portrait, except that for the first time he could see her unfortunate teeth. As he reported in a letter to Clarendon, he was underwhelmed: 'Her face was not so exact as to be called a beauty, though her eyes were excellent good, and there was nothing in her face that in the least degree can disgust one.'[4]

Charles must have thought himself the most cursed king in Europe. He had a new bride whose looks fell below the levels of feminine beauty and sexuality he favoured, and she brought very little of the promised fortune. Neither his purse nor his heart swelled up, but he had no alternative but to keep his side of the deal. The wedding went ahead, first in a secret Catholic ceremony carried out in Catherine's private chamber in the governor's house and then in a public Anglican ceremony in one of the reception rooms on 21 May.

Bishop Gilbert Sheldon (later the Archbishop of Canterbury) offici-
ated. According to one source, the ceremony was an awkward affair,
with Catherine resenting the Anglican rites and Charles ill at ease.
This seems unlikely, for Charles was a master of poise. Catherine
wore a dress she had commissioned expressly for the wedding in the
English style, covered with little blue bows which were later snipped
off and distributed to well-wishers after Portuguese tradition.

Following the marriage, the bride and groom processed to their
private chambers, where the merry throng accompanied them to
wish them well before finally leaving the couple in private. Neither
could speak the other's language and they had no other language in
common. The wedding night went badly, the marriage remaining
unconsummated. Apart from having a cold, Catherine was having
her period. Charles put a bold face on this early setback. After his first
meeting with his wife to be, he had written to Clarendon, saying, 'I
think myself very happy.'[5]

Immediately after the wedding, the King was attentive to his new
bride, and was as gallant as any husband might have been expected
to be. But as the days passed, some of the Whitehall coterie noticed
that he was not as happy as he pretended. One of those present, Sir
John Reresby, wrote about what he saw as the heart of the matter: 'the
King was not much enamoured of his bride. She was very little, not
handsome (though her face was indifferent) ... she had nothing visible about her to make the King forget his inclinations to the
Countess of Castlemaine.'[6]

Not only was Catherine on the plain side compared to the beautiful women with whom Charles was used to having sexual relations,
she was coy and modest in her behaviour and had been brought up
to be an obedient wife, traditional attributes taught in a strict convent
attached to the royal palace in Lisbon – where she had also learned
that no lady of quality, let alone a princess, would use her sexuality
openly. This was utterly unlike Barbara, who used sex as the key to
her whole life. Although Bishop Gilbert Burnet attempted in his
history to paint Catherine with a very rough brush, this seems to have

been little more than propaganda by the famously inaccurate bishop. Third hand, he reported that the King had told a confidant, 'They have brought me a bat to marry.'[7] The veracity of this remark is questionable but it seems uncharacteristically ungallant. What is beyond doubt is that Catherine was cut from very different stuff from the women whose looks and sexuality appealed to the King. But Catherine had her qualities – she was clever for a start – and Charles gradually began to appreciate them. Beneath the demure, religious surface there was a sharp wit and an ability to act and dance. Charles also appreciated Catherine's mellifluous voice and he began to teach her English. Given her new position, Catherine had few ways of using her intelligence except by trying her best to fit into her new surroundings and to mould herself into the life of a wife to a foreign king.

After sixteen days of celebrations, the King and Queen set off for Hampton Court, where they were to spend their honeymoon. The palace had lain unused since the death of Oliver Cromwell. In its Tudor heyday it had been the venue for three of Henry VIII's honeymoons and for that of Mary I when she married Philip II, the Spanish king who sent an armada in an attempt to invade England in 1588. It was at Hampton Court that Henry was told of Kathryn Howard's infidelity.

In readiness for its first royal honeymoon in more than a hundred years, the palace was given a facelift. The neglected gardens were replanted and the palace was swiftly redecorated and refurnished. As the couple settled in, Charles was gallant and paid great attention to his new wife. Not only did the couple appear happy, at least one of them genuinely was. Charles arranged recreations for himself and his queen. They went boating and fishing and tried their hand at archery. Catherine turned out to be a natural archer – she had coincidentally been born under the sign of Sagittarius. In the fine weather of the English spring the small Portuguese princess began to unwind. She cast off her drab, restricting Portuguese dress for good and took to wearing English clothes that allowed freer movement.

She even took to wearing men's clothes, which was something of a fad at the time. Charles seemed genuinely taken with his new wife.

Could Charles genuinely have fallen for his new queen and forsaken his old ways? Of course not; self-development was an alien concept in the seventeenth century, and the inability of men to toe the marital line was the stuff of the theatre of the time. However, Charles, though cynical enough, also had a soft spot that was touched by the company of women. He could not resist a woman's allure and appeared to be in love with whichever woman he happened to be with at the time. Perhaps he even felt he was – for is this not a secret of the success of the true Don Juan? This individual spell seemed to linger for a while after each encounter – long enough for him to write to his sister and others a series of letters including what seemed to be truthful representations of his feelings for Catherine – truthful at least at the time. Once he moved on to the company of another woman, Charles's attention became entirely focused anew. And so it went.

As the newlyweds walked in the palace gardens and strolled arm-in-arm by the banks of the Thames, a snake lurked in the grass, or at least within the palace itself, where the heavily pregnant Barbara, Countess Castlemaine, lay awaiting the birth of a second child by the King. While there can be no doubt that Barbara had insisted on giving birth at the palace to reinforce her pre-eminence over the new queen, there was a deeper symbolism at work. Barbara would have been aware that Jane Seymour had given birth at Hampton Court to the future Edward VI. If she were to give birth to a boy, it would be seen to be born in a royal palace, just as a previous king's son had been. The part of the story Barbara would not have been keen to dwell upon was that Jane had died in the palace from complications two weeks after the birth.

Around this time, Barbara's portrait was first painted by the King's court painter, Peter Lely. To be portrayed by Lely was a sign of acceptance at the heart of the royal court. Lely had a knack of painting his female sitters as dreamy, doe-eyed ladies of fashion *à la mode* or as denizens of a classical landscape, attired in loose robes of an antique form he himself invented. It was not the role the Dutchman had imagined for himself when he arrived in England in 1642, hoping to benefit from the vacuum created by the death a year before of his illustrious fellow countryman Antony van Dyck. Lely had hoped to make his name painting lyrical landscapes. Still, being the painter of the court paid him handsomely and he made sure his female sitters all looked suitably alluring. The Duchess of York suggested that Lely should paint portraits of the young beauties at court, a commission that cemented his position as portrait painter of choice, and the 'Lely look' – sultry and sexy – became the female style of the times. In the background, Lely almost invariably painted an idyllic landscape, a nod to his youthful dreams.

When one looks at Lely's portraits of these beautiful young women, it is easy to gain the wrong impression not only of how they looked – for he gave them all his special dreamy makeover – but of how they actually dressed. In real life, their clothes would not have been quite so free-flowing. Over the top of their shift, or smock, of fine silk, their torso was enclosed in a bodice that was both decorated and stiffened. Their skirts, however, were generally free of hoops and other shaping devices, the material itself being sufficiently lined and shaped to give the required outline. Underneath, unlike the men, they wore no drawers.[8] Not only did this make the wearer vulnerable to the attentions (wanted or otherwise) of men, it also adhered to the current thinking regarding hygiene, allowing air to circulate freely around the lower regions of the body. For the new queen, who had a love of movement and dance, taking on this looser form of dress must have been an enormous relief.

While Charles juggled his affections for his new wife and his determined mistress, there remained a constant fear that his political enemies might be plotting to overthrow him. Reports of plots, some real, some not, were often brought to him. Against this background, Charles had unfinished business with those who had put his father on trial. Continuing with his pledge to track down his father's regicides, three more were kidnapped in Holland and brought back to

stand trial for high treason. On 19 April, John Barkstead, John Okey
and Miles Corbet were executed by hanging, drawing and quartering. Charles's spies ranged across Europe in an attempt to find and
either repatriate or assassinate other regicides hiding out in Holland,
Germany and Switzerland.

Two major political enemies of the House of Stuart were already in
captivity for their support of the Parliamentary cause. John Lambert,
the brilliant Roundhead general and political reformer whose daughter had once been mooted as a wife for the King, was imprisoned in
the Channel Islands, and Sir Harry Vane, the influential Puritan
politician, was detained in the Isles of Scilly. Under pressure from
Parliament, both men were brought to London to stand trial for treason, on the understanding that if found guilty they would not be
beheaded. The King commuted Lambert's sentence to life imprisonment. With Vane, Charles had a difficulty due to the Puritan's
continuing anti-monarchist views. Having previously given his word
that Vane would be exempted from death, Charles changed his mind.

On 7 June, he wrote to Clarendon about Vane, 'Certainly he is too
dangerous a man to let live if we can honestly put him out of the
way.' Honesty did not come into it. The trial was a brief, slanted
farce, in which the definition of treason was stretched to breaking
point. Charles, perhaps mindful of his previous promise to allow
Vane to live, ordered he would be spared the disembowelling of a
traitor's death; he would instead be beheaded. By any standards, the
execution of Vane was a shameful affair.

As England moved into summer, life brightened for the King, but
became no less complicated. On 18 June, as she had hoped, Barbara
gave birth to a baby boy. In a rare moment of self-assertion, her
cuckolded husband Roger, who had recently converted to Roman
Catholicism, took the boy and had him christened in the rites of the
Catholic Church. By doing so, Palmer was putting up a hopeless
façade to the world that his marriage was intact, though it was
already torn apart. When the King heard about the christening he
was livid. He immediately issued orders for the boy to be christened

in an Anglican ceremony. Within six days the boy was rechristened. In a further move, Charles had the boy's surname changed. He was no longer Henry Palmer but Charles FitzRoy. Unlike his younger sister Anne, the boy would have a title, Lord Limerick. The tussle over the child spelled the end for the Palmer marriage and husband and wife split for good.

The tug-of-war over the child's spiritual wellbeing could hardly go on without news reaching the Queen. The most likely source was the Portuguese ambassador, who had been in London for some time and was known to be well informed. When she heard about it she was devastated, for here was direct evidence of her husband's infamous behaviour. Hence, when Catherine saw the Duchess's name on a list of English ladies of the bedchamber provided by the King, she firmly crossed it off. Charles, abiding by the promises he had made to Barbara before departing to meet his queen at Portsmouth, was not to be thwarted. He desired Barbara so much he was willing to risk the displeasure of the Queen. For her to be available to him, a position of lady of the bedchamber was a good way of ensuring her permanent presence at court and within the royal household. It was also a way of securing Barbara's position after the end of her marriage. Deserted by her husband, without the visible support of the King, she was potentially a figure of such notoriety that she might have been shunned by society. By giving her a position at court, Charles had a way to give her support *and* money.

After the Queen rejected the idea of the appointment, Charles ordered Clarendon to persuade her to allow Barbara to take up the position. The statesman, who was as much against Barbara as ever, had a difficult discussion with Catherine, telling her she could not reasonably expect the King not to have had sexual relations before his marriage. Catherine broke down in tears and said with equal reason that she could not have expected to find the king 'engaged in affection' to another.

On the same day that Barbara's son little Henry was christened, the Queen was somehow deceived into receiving Barbara at

Hampton Court. According to Clarendon, 'The Queen was no sooner sate in her chair but her colour changed, and tears gushed out of her eyes and her nose bled and she fainted.'

The Lord Chancellor sided with the Queen. It was intolerable that the King's mistress should be foisted upon her as one of her ladies-in-waiting so that she would be forced to have close contact on a daily basis with the cause of her humiliation. Clarendon felt it was his duty to inform the King of his views. That was a mistake. Clarendon never knew when to bite his tongue and Charles was becoming tired of hearing it wagging with advice and admonishments. It was time to put the worthy Clarendon in his place. During what should have been the high summer of his contentment, Charles wrote a withering letter to Clarendon. Charles generally much preferred to do his business verbally or in short, pithy notes. The fact that he set out his feeling so clearly and at length on this occasion indicates a seething anger:

> I wish I may be unhappy in this world, and the world to come, if I fail in the least degree of what I have resolved, which is, of making my Lady Castlemaine of my wife's bedchamber. And whosoever I find use any endeavour to hinder this resolution of mine ... I will be his enemy to the last moment of my life.

When Clarendon read the letter he must have realised that the relationship between King and Chancellor had entered a new phase; one in which the thirty-two-year-old Charles had had enough of the fifty-three-year-old Clarendon telling him what to do. Charles was already giving more power to younger men like Henry Bennet and Charles Berkeley. The letter betrayed more than the King's exasperation with his long-standing advisor. The languid and courtly glove was wrenched off to reveal a steely fist: 'If you desire to have the continuance of my friendship, meddle no more with this business.'

Despite this sharp disagreement between monarch and minister, their relationship for now remained strong. But Clarendon did not help by being excessively prissy about Barbara. He banned his wife from even speaking to her. The slight was taken to heart; in September, Barbara pronounced in public her desire to see Clarendon's head on a spike outside Westminster as if he were a common traitor.

By now, Barbara was living in official court lodgings by the cockpit in Whitehall Palace. Pepys remarked upon her public position as the King's mistress. As he watched the procession of the Queen from Hampton Court to take up residence in Whitehall, Pepys noticed it was also being observed by a couple standing on the roof of the Banqueting House. It was the King, accompanied by Barbara. 'I glutted myself with looking on her,' wrote the diarist.

Clarendon was not alone in his condemnation of the King's treatment of his Queen. Charles's favourite sister, Minette, was keeping up with the London tittle-tattle in her home near Paris. Minette was only eighteen but wise beyond her years. She and Charles were confidants and close allies in a world of intrigue. This did not prevent Minette registering alarm at what she heard about her brother's behaviour towards Catherine. 'It is said here she is grieved beyond measure,' she wrote, 'and to speak frankly I think it is with reason.'

The new Queen found her life much more constrained than her welcome new English clothes. She was surrounded by young women who were more beautiful than she was. Worse, her new husband decided that most of her entourage should go home. This cannot have done much for Catherine's ego, nor for her libido. By now she must have realised what she was up against; she was the spouse of a monarch who valued beautiful women above just about everything but his throne. She might even have realised he tolerated her only because it was his duty.

In his early treatment of Catherine, Charles displayed the selfishness that was to characterise his adult life. Genial and affable as so many declared him to be, he could turn with sudden coldness on anyone who stood in the way of his wishes. The relationship between the couple was not improved by the fact that the Queen seemed unable to give birth to a viable child. In a malicious comment during negotiations for the marriage in the previous year, the Spanish ambassador had claimed that Catherine was barren. Though he could not have known it, he was almost right. During the year, the King and Queen were intimate and, as far as is known, made love on a regular basis. As the new Queen, Catherine would have been concerned to do all in her power to please the King, and chief among her duties was to produce an heir. For his part, Charles was equally determined that it should happen. But by the end of the year, gossip was circulating about why the Queen had not produced an heir.

Catherine knew she had to make the best of her situation. Being clever, she realised that if she were to have any sort of life, she would have to make one for herself. She continued to adhere strongly to her Catholic faith. Rather than flaunting it, as her mother-in-law had done in the misguided belief that it was her duty as a Catholic to let the Protestant people see her rejection of their faith, she was private about it. In this, the English people were pleased. They had had Catholic queens before, but it was best if they kept their observance out of sight and out of public mind. Catherine entered into court life with vigour, dressing to show off her trim figure and fine ankles, and enjoying dancing and masques. She became, if not quite a hit, at least a good sport who was seen to be kind and decent and with a quiet wit when she chose to show it. In all this she won the King's approval and even his affection.

Charles had one more disagreeable surprise for his new queen. He brought his son James back from France, where the child had lived under the care of Lord Crofts, one of Charles's most trusted followers and a gentleman of the bedchamber. Charles's firstborn was now thirteen, with looks that some said resembled one of Lucy's other lovers but which others saw as having more resemblance to Charles in his adolescent portraits. Having shown little interest in the boy until now, Charles soon doted on him. Although not well schooled, James was handsome and had a way about him that reminded the King of his own youthful self. Charles arranged for James to have his own source of wealth and gave him the tax rights over all cloth exports, worth £8000 a year.

With this gift to his son, Charles set a trend that was to lead to the money troubles that would plague his life. More and more gifts would follow to his various mistresses, who had insatiable appetites for finery and lavish living. But like the eponymous hero in 'The Fable of the Man with the Golden Brain' by Alphonse Daudet, Charles just couldn't stop spending and giving money away, no matter what the consequences. Of course, he knew he should cut costs – Parliament had told him so – but cost cutting was not in his blood.

All in all, 1662 was a tumultuous year both in the court and in the country. Samuel Pepys summed it up:

> Public matters stand thus; the King is bringing as he said his family and navy and all his other charges to a less expense. In the meantime himself following his pleasures more than with good advice he would do; at least to be seen to all the world to do so. His dalliance with my Lady Castlemaine being public, every day, to his great reproach; and his favouring of none at court so much as those who are confidants of his pleasure, as Sir H. [Henry] Bennet and Sir Charles Barkeley; which Good God! Put it into his heart to mend before he makes himself too much condemned by his people for it.

It was not a good report card. Pepys was right about some things, wrong on others. As a senior admiralty official, he was well placed to know how much was being spent on the navy, but he was wrong if he thought the King was balancing his budget in other ways. Charles was ignoring the tight budget allowed by Parliament. In fact, he was overspending.* Pepys could not know that a great deal of this expenditure was being lavished on Barbara; nor could he know the King

---

* For example, from late 1661 to late 1662, the King's income from Parliament was £1.2 million. He spent £1.5 million.

had secretly decided to take radical action to bolster his finances: he would sell the English outpost of Dunkirk to the French.

The port had been wrested from the Spanish in 1657, during the Cromwellian era. In the new era, with Charles keen to restore relations with France, which had been on friendly terms with republican England, he saw a way to make an overture to Louis XIV while restoring his coffers. Clarendon was in favour of the sale and Montagu became the chief facilitator. After various sums were proposed by each side, a figure of £400,000 was agreed, half to be paid immediately and the rest in instalments. The sale was not widely admired. The Elector of Brandenburg's ambassador in London was among those to be critical, saying the English were making a mistake by thinking their land was a separate world.

As an arch-philanderer himself, Pepys knew that little good could come of the King's public display of his fabulous mistress. Pepys was astute in his criticism of Charles for giving so much power to the self-seeking, immoral Sir Henry Bennet, who was keeper of the King's Privy Seal, and to Berkeley, a boisterous, slightly Falstaffian cavalier. The court was turning into a freewheeling and licentious cockpit, egged on by the King himself, who encouraged outrageous and bawdy behaviour for his own amusement.

Outside the court, a major change was taking place in the nation's religious life. Acts of Parliament enforcing the Book of Common Prayer and the compliance of all clerics with the authority of bishops split the church into conformist and non-conformist branches that exist to this day. Charles found that his liberal views on religious observance were of little use when faced with the illiberal views of the parliamentarians. A form of reverse Puritanism would sweep all but the most conservative officials from public employment.

Before the year was out, Barbara and her supporters helped to oust one of the King's oldest advisors, Sir Edward Nicholas, a friend and ally of Clarendon. The King happily accepted the view that, at seventy, Nicholas was past it and a mere cypher for the Chancellor. Nicholas was replaced as Secretary of State for the South by Henry

Bennet, shortly to be awarded the title of Earl of Arlington. This position carried wide-ranging domestic and foreign remits. The two men could not have been more different, with Clarendon serious and outspoken and Arlington socially adept and circumspect.

There is an anecdote that not only displays this difference but also an important facet of the King's character. One day when Arlington and Clarendon were discussing Charles's lack of firm leadership and the general deficiency of seriousness at court, the King came in unexpectedly and asked what they were talking about. To Arlington's dismay, Clarendon waded into a lecture about the King's 'excess of pleasures' and how he had already lost 'much of the affection and reverence the nation had for him'.

According to Clarendon, the King listened politely to all he said before replying 'as if he thought much that had been said was with too much reason'.[9] At this point, Arlington jumped in and made fun of Clarendon's earnestness, so turning the conversation to merriment. Within moments, both secretary and monarch were mocking Clarendon for his solemnity. As on so many occasions, the King was able to revert to his default position of frivolity. And there in a nutshell was the curious dynamic of the early years of Charles's rule: a politician who spoke his mind, another who knew what his monarch wanted – and did not want – to hear, and a king who hated anything that stood between him and his natural preference for pleasure over duty. The scene rankled with Clarendon so much that many years after Charles had finally grown tired of his censorious badgering and sacked him, he related it in his memoir.[10]

The year ended with an event that would have made Clarendon's blood boil. This was the grand New Year's Eve ball at Whitehall Palace. From the very first dance, the assembled crowd of merrymakers was treated to a display of the unconventional nature of Charles's family arrangements. As was customary, a line formed for the first dance. As the music began, the line advanced into the middle of the floor, surrounded by admiring lords and ladies of the court, maids of honour and young blades. Naturally, the King and

Queen led the line, with the Duke of York in second place accompanied by his wife Anne who, embarrassingly, was not only a commoner but the daughter of the increasingly irritating Lord Chancellor. But the truly shocking pairing came in third place with the king's mistress, the Countess Castlemaine, partnering Charles's bastard son – now known as James Croft – by his early lover, Lucy Walter.

The procession formed a surreal tableau vivant, revealing how much the ruling house of England, Scotland and Ireland had changed from the court of Charles I. To those present, it was clear that the entity now inhabiting the throne of the three kingdoms was not the reincarnation of the mythic, divinely anointed king of old, but something altogether more earthy, knowing, worldly and, above all, *carnal*. They had wished for a semi-divine figurehead. What they got was a man. By this public display of his domestic arrangements, Charles marked his disdain for Puritanism and his desire for a new, more tolerant and broad-minded order.

8

THE DISSOLUTE COURT

With her husband gone for good, Barbara was able to consolidate King Street as not only the home of a society lady, but an alternative court. However, the absence of a husband made Barbara more vulnerable. Without her husband's protection and wealth, she would have to work harder to ensure her many enemies who felt there was no place for such a public whore in the life of their King did not undermine her position at court. Therefore Barbara worked hard at promoting the interests of her supporters and the attractions of her soirées. A French envoy reported that at the Countess's house one could rely on getting a good dinner. One would probably also meet the King and hear all the hottest gossip.

At the King Street house, Barbara used all her charms to entertain those with power and influence. She was too astute not to realise that her place in society should not rest purely on her being the King's whore. With a keen knowledge of the dynamics of high society, she saw it was important to place herself in a position where she would not be an object purely of gossip and ridicule. To that end, she set out to embrace that section of court life that could cause her reputation most damage: the court wits. These were well-bred and well-heeled young men who fancied themselves as exponents of the art of facetious humour and particularly the art of the put-down. Among them were the King's childhood friend George Villiers, Duke of Buckingham, his sybaritic friend from exile, Henry Bennet, the equally louche Sir Charles Berkeley, and Henry Killigrew, son of the theatre impresario Thomas Killigrew, who made himself a sort of unofficial court jester.

As a group, the Wits were generally of some learning, and many of them had literary ability. But they were, above all, high in humour and low in morals. They spent much of their time in debauchery and in debunking their peers, especially those they thought too serious or steeped in affairs of the state. When not cuckolding lax husbands and seducing young women, they made up bawdy and satirical rhymes and the more able among them even wrote plays. Their talents were put into playing a part, in being exemplars of wit and flair. What they were creating was life presented as artifice. In their plays, their lifestyle was presented on the stage. They rebelled against the violent and uncertain history through which they had grown up by hardening themselves against compassion and ethics. Clever conversation and heartlessness were their armour against what many of them saw as a meaningless world, although the critic and historian Vivian de Sola Pinto has suggested that in fact they lived their lives with an eye for posterity.[1] They *were* their art.

At King Street, the Wits were given free rein to show off their talents. Their drollery was matched by their 'smoking' (leg-pulling) those who could not match their banter. They would smoke anyone, including the most exalted in station or in learning, even favourites of the King. One of their targets was Thomas Hobbes the philosopher, who was himself no slouch when it came to amusing conversation. Hobbes became known as 'the Bear' as on the occasions he came to court, the King would exclaim, 'Here comes the bear to be baited.'[2] Hobbes enjoyed the raillery of the younger men and allowed them to co-opt him as a sort of demiurge who had helped create their world. Hobbes's view of humanity was well attuned to that of the Wits. He saw humanity as brutish, with each person out for himself or herself in a selfish scramble.[3]

Although the Wits' self-image was very much one of refined tastes and exalted behaviour clothed in impeccable manners, the reality could be very different. When not at court or at King Street, the Wits spent a good deal of their time in the taverns of Covent Garden, where they felt they could give full rein to their abilities. To see why, we need only consult the anonymous authority of *The Character of a Tavern*, published in 1675: 'A tavern is an Academy of Debauchery, where the Devil teaches the seven deadly sins instead of sciences, a Tipling-school, a degree above an ale house, where you may be drunk with more credit and Apology, 'tis the Rendezvous of Gallants, the Good Fellow's Paradise, and the Miser's Terrour.' Taverns were exciting places. A fight could break out, a combatant might assault another by breaking 'a Candlestick or Bottle over his crown' while in another corner, an habitué might repeat 'scraps of Old Plays or some Bawdy Song, all with loud hooting and laughing'.

Within Barbara's circle, there was sufficient wild behaviour to keep Restoration playwrights well stocked with plot lines for decades. According to the Wits' code, any woman married to an older man was entitled to take a lover. After all, the fun of cuckolding husbands had caused laughter since Chaucer's time and had been a staple on the London stage since the beginning of the century, when Thomas Middleton's *A Mad World My Masters* (1604) was performed to generous applause. Inevitably, philandering would give rise to jealousy and revenge. A notorious case involved the Earl of Carnegie, who suspected his wife of having an affair with the King's brother, the Duke of York. In revenge, he plotted to pass the clap to the Duke via his wife. According to Anthony Hamilton, only the first part of the plot went to plan:

He [the Earl] went to the most infamous places, to seek for the most infamous disease, which he met with, but his revenge was only half completed; for he had gone through every remedy to get quit of his disease, his lady did but return him his present, having no more connection with the person for whom it was so industriously prepared.[4]

Outside this rakish circle, older and more staid rules applied, especially for women. Society was being pushed too far, too fast. According to the etiquette of the time and beyond, a woman could not be seen to pursue a man. Only the man could make the running. If a woman was seen to be making overtures it revealed an immoral and corrupt nature. This was complicated by the fact that it was understood that a woman should experience the same degree of delight in sexual pleasure as a man – indeed, sexual pleasure was thought necessary for conception to take place – but despite this, for a woman to instigate a sexual relationship was an example of 'whorishness'.[5]

Barbara saw the circle of Wits as suitable allies in her exalted yet precarious station in life. She ensured the house in King Street was their headquarters.[6] Here they could gather in the evenings after spending the afternoon at nearby Whitehall or in other social pursuits in the fashionable houses of the area, or perhaps head back to after attending a performance at the theatres of Covent Garden, only a short coach ride away. At the theatre, they might meet up with the King and his brother, who were both keen theatregoers, before heading back for what Hyde contemptuously called 'a late congregation' at the Duchess's house which could include music, gambling and more intimate pursuits.[7] Often, the Wits' coaches would not drive away until dawn. George Villiers and his friends were not simply wastrels; they wielded influence and Villiers himself was, like his cousin Barbara, a sworn enemy of Clarendon.

Increasingly, the century's new ideas were to be found among educated, wealthy, tolerant men, not especially interested in religion, who felt that people should be free to live as they pleased. This was not entirely a new phenomenon thrown up by the Restoration. There had even been men like it among those who had opposed Charles's father and the monarchy.

And there were women like it, too. While women such as Barbara Palmer might choose to live as courtesans, others leading more conventional lives also felt the new tide of liberal thinking sweeping through the salons of the elite. Though barred from the universities, women were not prevented from reading about or discussing the latest thinking on philosophy, politics and the social order. The polymath Margaret Cavendish, Duchess of Newcastle, might have been a rare Renaissance figure among seventeenth-century women, but she was far from alone in her interests in literature and the natural sciences.* While the developments gave rise to what is today seen as the typical Restoration rake, women are often ignored in the sexual changes that were taking place, the incorrect assumption being that they were always merely pliant receptacles for the advances of philandering men. Women such as Lucy Walter, Barbara Palmer and others would give the lie to this, for they exhibited a healthy sexual desire allied to the ability to pursue their male quarry, rather than being passive creatures waiting to be chosen.

As for the men at court, there were three main types: the men of state, like Clarendon, Thomas Osborne (later the Earl of Danby) and the Earl of Southampton, who ran the machine of government; the Wits, those men of fashion known for their savoir-faire and intellectual ability to hold sustained entertaining conversation allied to the morals of an alley cat; and the fops, lesser men of fashion with little wit but who tried gamely to ape the Wits. Some could move from one group to another. There were Wits and rakes in the machinery of government, while some among the Wits, like Buckingham and Bennet, aspired to hold high office. Not all groups were solely from one social class. Among the Wits were not only men of independent means or high social status but also theatrical managers and playwrights who by dint of their abilities could join in the fun at court.

From these three groups, the King favoured men who fell into the second category. The men of state were generally far too solemn,

---

* Margaret Cavendish, Duchess of Newcastle, wrote some twenty plays, as well as numerous papers on politics, natural philosophy, and social and sexual issues, including *Observations upon Experimental Philosophy*, 1666, and the satirical work of proto-science fiction, *The Description of the New World, Called the Blazing-World*, 1666, republished together in 1668.

with some notable exceptions such as Arlington and Lord Halifax, while the fops were merely the chorus line or spear-carriers in front of whom the Wits could shine. The King was dismayed by earnest men: 'Serious men terrify him, merry and amusing ones make him laugh,' reported the French ambassador.[8] Opposite in temperament and in philosophy to the serious politicians, the Wits, or Merry Gang, had grown up and 'lived high under Oliver',[9] but had taken no part in the political disputes that had led to the breakdown of Charles I's rule, nor in the long hostilities which followed. By the time of the Restoration, they had developed a cynical, irreligious view of the world in which the only values were a ready wit and a studied indifference. With Charles's view of life hardened by exile and disappointment, it is little wonder that the King and these young men should find an affinity. They were those that the Duke of Ormond had complained about to Clarendon, declaring, 'The King spent most of his time with confident young men, who abhorred all discourse that was serious, and, in the liberty they assumed in drollery and raillery, preserved no reverence towards God or man, but laughed at all sober men, and even on religion itself.'[10]

The role the Wits fulfilled was that of jester or clown. They cavorted, joked and pricked the pompous in order to entertain the King. No one fulfilled this role better than Barbara's second cousin, George Villiers, 2nd Duke of Buckingham. When George was just seven months old, an assassin murdered his father, the famously handsome 1st Duke, at a Portsmouth inn. George was fostered by Charles I and raised among the royal children in the royal household. He was the chief bond between the Wits, the King and Barbara.

The trouble with Buckingham was that Buckingham was trouble. Though highly intelligent, he was born into such wealth and power that his self-assurance led him to make fantastic gaffes and misjudgements. He was a rumbustious and unruly child. As young boys, Charles and George were taught mathematics by Thomas Hobbes. George thought the lectures so tedious that he masturbated during geometry lessons.[11] His father, the 1st Duke, had been James I's lover – his 'sweet child and wife'.[12] Young George inherited his father's libidinous nature, though not his sexual orientation, nor indeed his good looks. But George grew to have style and was as congenial as his father had been handsome.

When the Commonwealth Parliament sequestered the enormous family estates, young Buckingham had left for the Continent. To support him, his advisors arranged for the family art collection to be sold in Antwerp. Luckily for Buckingham, his father had amassed one of the greatest collections ever seen. With revenues from the estates put at around £20,000 a year, he had collected a reputed nineteen paintings by Titian, seventeen by Tintoretto, two by Giorgione, thirteen by Veronese and three Leonardos, among many more. He had bought Rubens's own collection for £10,000.[13] With the cash liberated from this fabulous collection, Buckingham led a congenial life in Europe (much in contrast to the impoverished lifestyle of his boyhood friend Charles). He soaked up the more hedonistic traits of European society and with his natural propensity for pleasure, unsurprisingly grew up to be one of the greatest libertines of the Restoration. He was helped in this by having swagger, grace and wit. His contemporaries remarked on it.[14] Being two years older than Charles, he had fought in the second civil war and became a cavalier hero after an episode when he held off six Roundheads with his back to a tree. Later, he fought alongside Charles in the disastrous battle at Worcester.

Buckingham was the sempiternal rake, a man who drew the line at drawing the line. Nothing was off limits for George. In 1661, he had been entrusted with the delicate task of accompanying Charles's favourite sister, the seventeen-year-old Henrietta Anne, to Paris for her marriage to Louis XIV's brother, Philippe, Duc d'Orléans. Henrietta was the apple of her older brother's eye. She was young, sparky and very pretty. Inevitably, Buckingham was smitten by her. Rumours flew that they had an affair. Charles, who should have known better than to trust Buckingham with such a task, indignantly recalled the unruly gallant in disgrace.

Here was the Duke's problem in a nutshell: he was talented, he was witty, he was fun, he was a nuisance. Among his detractors was John Dryden, the future Poet Laureate. Dryden had reason to hate Buckingham, whose play *The Rehearsal*, first performed in 1671, satirised one of Dryden's heroic dramas in which characters spoke in a grandiloquent manner. *The Rehearsal* well and truly punctured Dryden's balloon and he later dropped his high-flown style. Years later Dryden took his revenge in a satire in which the Duke was likened to a biblical prince who was a womanising buffoon, 'stiff in opinions, always in the wrong'.[15]

Among the others regularly found at Barbara's soirées was one of Buckingham's protégés, George Savile, later Lord Halifax, clever in government and famed for writing *The Trimmer*, a bible for high office and the art of compromise (a word hardly understood by any of his friends and contemporaries, who were always galloping away on their high horses). As already mentioned, there was Henry Killigrew, one of the King's gentlemen of the bedchamber who could always be relied upon for a jolly quip, and Sir Charles Berkeley, soldier, keeper of the Privy Purse, an ardent plotter against Clarendon, and a close confidant of both Barbara and the King. According to Pepys, he not only pimped for the King but also for Barbara. Berkeley's subsequent death in the second Anglo-Dutch war, when his head was split open by gunshot, led to a tasteless quip that the injury 'gave the first proof that he had brains'.[16]

There was Baptist May, groom of the bedchamber. He became keeper of the Privy Purse after Berkeley's death, though he had no real control over payments. He was one of Charles's boyhood friends, always ready to divert him from matters of business, and also known to be one of his pimps. May had a truly unique relationship with the King. Not for him the sycophantic 'Yes, you are indeed correct, Your Majesty'. May openly differed with Charles on all the burning issues of the day – he was anti-French, hated Catholicism and opposed arbitrary government – but he was great fun. Then there was Fleetwood Shepherd, agreed by everyone to be a pleasant and clever man. He enjoyed good company and a good joke and lent his support to John Milton when the Puritan got into hot water because of his republican views.

Contemporary accounts tell us who all the men were, but we hear little or nothing of the women who must have been present at least at some of the soirées at King Street. Of course, Barbara would have wished to be the central figure in her own court, and so rival beauties were not to be encouraged. Even so, in general, contemporary accounts of court life only mention women when they are referred to as someone's daughter engaged to be married, who got married to so and so, or ran off with or was seduced by yet another so-and-so. Their absence from the drama indicates how they were viewed by their male chroniclers very much as secondary characters in the play. This was an age when, despite the example set by those such as Margaret Cavendish, women were struggling to exert their potential beyond the domestic sphere. The trouble was, the spheres into which they might expand were extremely limited. A society woman could not become an actress, but she could become a writer (though most likely to remain unpublished) or a mistress (though whether or not she had any greater control in the relationship than in her married life rather depended upon the personalities involved).

In 1664 a young man came to court who satirised everyone's behaviour. Not only that, he outdid everyone in debauchery. His name was John Wilmot, 2nd Earl of Rochester. He was the son of Henry Wilmot, who had helped Charles escape to the Continent in 1651. Like Buckingham, he was a cousin to Barbara, Lady Castlemaine.

Wilmot managed the rare feat of being the most insightful, amusing and hated man in English public life. He packed more into his short life than most men might do in living twice as long. By the age of fourteen he was addicted to alcohol and sex, and by seventeen had acquired a good knowledge of modern and classical European thought; he became a war hero by eighteen, at nineteen was appointed a gentleman of the bedchamber to the King on £1000 a year, and at twenty married Elizabeth Mallet, an heiress he had scandalously attempted to abduct two years before. Habitually drunk, he infamously had a taste for both heterosexual and homosexual sex; he was dead in his thirties.

Rochester and the King were close friends, spending days together at the races and occasional evenings at court where Rochester entertained with his brilliant conversation. Rochester was an intelligent man ruined by drinking. Here is Pepys on Rochester and his relationship with the King: 'This very morning the King did publicly walk up and down, and Rochester I saw with him as free as ever, to the King's everlasting shame, to have so idle a rogue as his companion.'[17] One evening, in a drunken brawl perhaps begun by Rochester himself, one of his companions was killed by a thrust from the pike of a night watchman. Rochester ran away and lay low at his country estate until the heat was off – one of his many enforced absences from the city.

Though a rogue, he was not so idle as the famous diarist supposed. He wrote large amounts of poetry of variable quality, some of which contained genuine insight into the nature of human relationships. This hell-raiser could write love poetry ranging from the dreadful – 'To this moment a rebel I throw down my arms/ Great Love, at first sight of Olinda's bright charms' – to the beguiling:

> Beauty does the heart invade
> Kindness only can persuade
> It gilds the lover's servile chain
> And makes the slave grow pleased again.

Alcohol and syphilis were to end Rochester's roller-coaster life at the age of thirty-three. The Bishop of Salisbury, Gilbert Burnet, was present at his deathbed and later recorded the rake's full and complete recantation of his debauched ways.[18] The *volte-face* is so extreme as to make one wonder at the veracity of the account. If the bishop did exaggerate the rake's deathbed confession, he was guilty of the rare offence of cynically exploiting the death of a cynic.

Rochester's death was but one example of the seventeenth-century scourge of sexually transmitted diseases. In London, syphilis and gonorrhoea were rife but looked upon as a natural hazard of love. All sections of society were at risk, from the lowliest labourer to London's social elite. In some ways, the elite had more to fear, having both the leisure to indulge in the promiscuous behaviour that created more chances of catching an infection and the money to pay for the most dangerous remedies.

The most feared scourge of the sexually active was syphilis, known as the pox or sometimes 'the French disease' – so-called due to the belief that it had come from France, even though it may originally have reached Europe from North America or Africa. Physicians referred to it as *lues venerea* (venereal plague). It spread rapidly through Europe in the sixteenth century and by the middle of the seventeenth had reached epidemic proportions in London. The pox was so ubiquitous that it was frequently alluded to in private correspondence, public newssheets, plays, ballads and satires. 'A pox on you!' was a common insult.

All this begs the question: if everyone knew sexual intercourse lay at the root of such terrible diseases, why did people not take precautions? The answer was that effective condoms, made from materials ranging from silk to animal intestines, would not become readily available until the early eighteenth century.

Like Rochester, Charles grew bored easily and craved novelty and excitement. Among their joint passions was the theatre, the newly revived entertainment that held up a mirror to the changing fashions and morals of the age. Rochester was a mentor to many engaged in the theatre and wrote at least one play, an adaptation of Fletcher's *The Tragedie of Vallentinian*. Like Charles, he loved the novel appearance of women on the stage, becoming their supporter and, when he could, their lover. One to whom he became lover, mentor and coach was the reportedly dreadfully bad teenage actress Elizabeth Barry, who in time conquered her awkwardness to become the most accomplished actress of the age. She gave birth to children by both Rochester and George Etherege, the playwright. Elizabeth was also the only woman that Rochester, despite his cynical Hobbesian public persona, really loved.

The King was not to be outdone in his patronage of willing young female talent. Plays were staged generally in the afternoon, so they could take advantage of natural lighting through roof-lights. In an era before gas lamps, artificial stage lighting was difficult and unsatisfactory. Charles and his brother James spent many an afternoon scouting out the talent on stage and in the pit during the flood of new plays that poured through London's playhouses to quench an insatiable capital's demand for entertainment and excitement. The theatre became the mirror to fashionable London's desire for entertainment and novelty. If Wilmot was the leader of the Merry Gang, as well as jester-in-chief and a sort of scatological poet laureate, then the leader of the revels was the King himself, who unlike even Rochester, genuinely and disconcertingly lived for pleasure alone. For Charles, there was no remorse, no 'agenbite of inwit'.

This did not mean he could not feel pain when his character was pierced or his behaviour dissected by a skilful practitioner such as Rochester. For good or ill, Rochester is chiefly remembered today as the writer of some unsurpassed scatological satire. Here he is, aged twenty, writing on the King's prodigious carnality and his reputedly above average amatory equipment:

> Nor are his high desires above his strength:
> His scepter and his prick are of a length,
> And she may sway the one who plays with th' other,
> And make him little wiser than his brother.
> Poor Prince! thy prick, like thy buffoons at Court,
> Will govern thee because it makes thee sport.
> Tis sure the sauciest prick that e'er did swive*
> The proudest, peremptorious prick alive.

---

* Swive = to have sexual intercourse.

Though safety, law, religion, life lay on 't,
'Twould break through all to make its way to cunt.
Restless he rolls about from whore to whore,
A merry monarch, scandalous and poor.[19]

Rochester drunkenly sent this rhyme to Charles in mistake for another. The King was outraged, not just because it was an assault on him, but because it contained an obvious attack on Barbara. Rochester had to flee to escape a spell in the Tower. But Charles was forgiving, feeling that even those with the most blaggardly reputations were fit company for at least this particular king. Rochester was allowed to return to London. We may deduce that Barbara did not read the poem.

9

MARRIED LIFE

On 14 February 1663, Charles made one of the great blunders of his reign. His pride in Lucy's son, James, led him to elevate the fourteen-year-old to the status of first prince of the blood. He proclaimed publicly that he was the boy's father and made him a duke – giving him the title Duke of Monmouth – with precedence over everyone bar the King himself and the Duke of York. Immediately the court began to ring with speculation that Charles would go a step further and legitimise the boy, so replacing York as heir to the throne.[1] That divisive possibility would come to haunt English politics – and threaten the throne – for the next two decades.

The Queen Mother, the Duke of York and the Chancellor all protested at the boy's elevation to royal status. So did Queen Catherine. Since her defeat in the bedchamber affair Catherine had borne humiliation silently. She not only accepted the presence – and snipes – of Barbara, she made a calculated attempt to become a friend of her husband's boisterous mistress. Even when Charles moved Barbara into lavish chambers in the Palace of Whitehall in September 1662, the Queen had made no fuss, at least publicly. But the elevation of her husband's illegitimate son was too much. It was an affront to her and to the children she expected to bear the King.

The Duke of York reported in a letter to Clarendon that Catherine had threatened to leave Charles when the King told her of his plans for the boy: 'My brother hath spoken to the queen ... concerning the owning of his son, and in much passion she told him that from the time he did any such thing she would never see his face more.'[2]

Catherine, of course, had nowhere to go and no option but to accept the situation. It was the same with the other member of the family most concerned at the boy's promotion. The Duke of York had to accept James as his brother's son. Indeed, he and his nephew would remain on the friendliest terms, among other things racing and hunting together. But they would end as bitter rivals for the throne.

The world took to Lucy's son and would continue to admire him into manhood. He had the King's charm and athleticism and his mother's looks, as well as both parents' absorption with sex. Pepys called him 'the most skittish, leaping gallant that ever I saw'. Another contemporary author, Madame D'Aulnoy, described him as the 'handsomest and most attractive man in the world, young, gallant, endowed with every grace'. It would emerge, however, that he was none too bright, which would prove a fatal flaw.

Charles the proud family man now emerged as he petted and fussed over his teenage son. According to the memoirs of French courtier the Comte de Gramont, the King's behaviour put Barbara 'quite out of humour', because the two children she'd had with Charles were made to look like 'little puppets compared with this new Adonis'. The teenage James was given an apartment in Whitehall plus a retinue and equipage suitable for an heir to the throne. If Barbara was upset by this reception for the boy, she wisely did not show it for long. Instead she almost outdid the King in demonstrating affection for the teenager – and continued to do so. Gramont speculated that this was to make Charles jealous – to 'give the King uneasiness' that his mistress showed his handsome son 'such marked affection' in public. Three months after recognising the boy, Charles had him married to the richest heiress in Scotland,

Anne Lennox. Gramont implied that the fourteen-year-old was married off so quickly to avert him being bedded by the twenty-two-year-old Barbara.

While Charles's extended family manoeuvred for position in the royal affections, a more significant battle was being fought on the national stage. Facing implacable insistence from the Anglican hierarchy, Charles signed the Act of Uniformity which sought to force the Anglican form of worship on everyone. The opening paragraphs of the Act stated that 'nothing conduceth more to the settling of the peace of this nation ... than an universal agreement in worship of Almighty God'. Charles, with his secret sympathy for Catholicism, was against the diktat, as was the Chancellor, but he bowed to the intransigence of the Anglicans, led by Archbishop Sheldon.[3]

Every minister was now required to give his unfeigned consent to Anglican worship and the Anglican prayer book. For many that was impossible. More than two thousand ministers, a fifth of the English clergy, refused and were driven from their parishes over the next year or so. This became known as the Great Ejection. In November 1663, partly in reaction to the diktat, the North blew up in rebellion while other plots bubbled to the surface as far afield as Dublin and London.

'In the streets the insolence of the mob is on the Increase,' reported the French ambassador, 'Fanatics swarm everywhere.' The Crown's fear of insurrection was reflected in the number of times that mass arrests were ordered, while ex-soldiers were banned from within twenty miles of the capital.[4]

Charles, generally so reluctant to undertake business, now took excursions downriver to the dungeons of the Tower to interrogate alleged plotters. Typically, Clarendon told Parliament how good his master was as an interrogator. According to the Chancellor, prisoners broke down and told everything they knew when confronted with the King. Fond as he was of stories about himself in action, one can imagine Charles regaling the Castlemaine salon with the details of his brushes with his would-be assassins.

Meanwhile, he continued to flaunt his relationship with Barbara, having her accompany him and the now subdued Queen at public occasions. At night he generally supped with her in her apartment or at a rumoured Thameside hideaway in Surrey. Pepys heard that Charles 'most often stays till the morning ... and goes home through the garden all alone privately ... the very sentries take notice of it and speak of it.' Besotted though he was with Barbara, the diarist penned his disgust at the King's 'public dalliance' with her.

There were mutterings inside the court too. Daniel O'Neill, who as groom of the bedchamber was one of the most senior courtiers, exploded about Barbara in a letter to his friend James Butler, the Earl of Ormond: 'The great tranquillity of our court is not like to continue,' he wrote. 'It is impossible for the Queen to endure the neglect of the king, & the insolence of the dame [Lady Castlemaine] ... We, that see it ... can hardly credit our eyes.'[5]

The resentment that Barbara provoked took a dangerous turn for her in the autumn of 1663 when three masked men confronted her as she walked home through the park after supping at St James's Palace. She was accompanied only by a tiny page and a lady-in-waiting. The men, noblemen judging by their attire, surrounded her and, in the French ambassador's words, 'addressed to her the harshest and bitterest reprimand'. This included a reference to Jane Shore. The trio didn't harm her physically, but after they released her and she reached her bedroom she fainted. Charles was informed, 'ran' to his mistress and called out the guard. A search produced seven or eight arrests but all those held were released. The order went out to conceal the incident, presumably so as not bring public attention to Barbara. Cominges, the French ambassador, told Louis, 'I believe the secret will not easily be kept.'[6]

Pepys, the silent spectator, had begun to lose his ardour for the lady in 1663. In June of that year he noted that Barbara was 'not so handsome as I have taken her for, and now she begins to decay. This was my wife's opinion also, for which I am sorry.' In July he was plunged into a confusion of feelings after hearing – prematurely as it turned out – that Lady Castlemaine had fallen from favour and had retired from court. He hailed it as 'great news . . . for which I am sorry: and yet if the King do it to leave off not only her but all other mistresses, I should be heartily glad of it, that he may fall to look after business.'[7]

Charles continued to combine business with pleasure. He took to holding court in his mistress's chambers before going to church. Ministers were summoned there to transact affairs of state. Bishop Burnet called this a 'great scandal to the world'. Neither Clarendon nor Southampton would attend. Charles's continued obsession with Barbara did not keep him from other women – nor did it keep her from other men.

From among the continually renewed supply of pretty hopefuls forming the queen's maids of honour Charles selected Winifred Wells. She was described in the Comte de Gramont's memoirs as 'a big splendidly handsome creature' and by Barbara as 'a goose'. Her name was on every courtier's lips after a bizarre, hardly believable incident at the palace in early 1663. At a winter ball the dancing was interrupted when news went round that one of the ladies had 'dropped a child' mid dance. It may have been a practical joke, perhaps a lady sticking a cushion under her dress, but the story circulated that it was a barely formed foetus and that someone had swooped to secrete it. The next morning every lady-in-waiting put in an early appearance in Whitehall to ensure that the finger didn't point at them. Winifred Wells, however, fell sick that afternoon, and wasn't seen in court for weeks. That set tongues wagging about her being the mother and Charles the father. The story developed that the King had secured the foetus and dissected it. According to gossip picked up by Pepys, he made 'great sport' of it, establishing that the gender was male, which had him lamenting that he was the sufferer in the affair because he had lost a subject.[8] Winifred returned to court before the month was out. Later she would be given a pension of over £1000 a year by the King.

Halifax, writing with the knowledge of a courtier, asserted that the King seldom picked his women himself: 'It was resolved generally by others whom he should have in his arms as well as whom he should have in his councils. Of a man who was so capable of choosing he chose as seldom as any man that ever lived.'

Various members of Charles's inner circle were said at some point or other to be pimping for him. This could mean chatting up a court lady on his behalf and smuggling her up the back stairs and into the royal presence, or doing the rounds of the brothels and theatres with the King in tow. Two men became the King's most trusted pimps for casual sex. The first was Baptist May, a close childhood friend; the second, William Chiffinch, keeper of the King's private closet, was effectively the gateman and guardian of the back-stairs entry into Charles's chambers – the wits of the day dubbed him the Pimpmaster General. He handled the women who were brought there, along with, later, the huge sums in bribes to the King that came from Louis XIV of France. Chiffinch was such an interesting individual that some background on the man and his duties will help explain how Whitehall Palace functioned to serve Charles's specific amatory needs.

William Chiffinch was born in 1602 in Salisbury, Wiltshire. He was two years younger than his brother Thomas, whom he succeeded as one of the King's closest and most trusted servants. Thomas had been spotted by the Bishop of Salisbury and introduced to Charles as a likely young page. The Bishop was right about the youngster's talents and he quickly rose to be Keeper of the King's Closet, then Keeper of the King's Jewels and finally receiver of revenues from the American colonies, a position which made him not only powerful but rich.

It is worth noting that when Thomas died in 1666, such was the esteem in which his employer held him that he was buried in Westminster Abbey, where his memorial states he was a man of great honesty and probity who was 'from his tenderest years a faithful servant, in good fortune and bad, to His Most Serene Majesty Charles II'. It was deemed natural that his brother William should step into his shoes. They fitted him well.

Chiffinch junior's apartments in Whitehall adjoined the King's rooms and provided secret access to the monarch. Foreign emissaries, sometimes carrying bribes, could alight from the river into Chiffinch's rooms and hence glide unseen to the King's chambers. Suitable young women could be brought there in secrecy, with the all-providing Chiffinch later dropping gold into their purses as the wherry took them away down the dark river after nightfall. According to contemporary historian Anthony Wood, Chiffinch was the chief provider of these so-called 'supper companions'. In reverse, if the King should wish to slip out of the palace for a little supper *à deux* in the city, the jetty by Chiffinch's rooms was the way to the river. Despite the secrecy, word got out, as it always did, and the King's evening frolics were lampooned in printed broadsheets:

> It happen'd, in the twilight of the day,
> As England's monarch in his closet lay,
> And Chiffinch stepp'd to fetch the female prey.

Barbara herself was not backward at procuring men. The number of her alleged lovers would become legion. Over her life she would take all kinds to her bed, all classes too. They ranged from the brutally ugly Henry Jermyn, Earl of St Albans – a diminutive figure with a large head who was supposedly as exciting a lover as Barbara herself – to the impossibly handsome eighteen-year old lieutenant, John Churchill, a distant cousin of Barbara's who was to become one of English history's greatest war heroes. The lovers whom the court gossiped about in 1663–4 were Jermyn and Sir Charles Berkeley, the courtier behind the attempt to discredit the Chancellor's daughter, Anne, who now of course was the accepted wife of the Duke of York. Two witnesses claimed to have often seen through her bedroom window Barbara go to bed while 'Berkeley [was] in the chamber all the while with her'.[9] Others to whom she was rumoured to be 'kind' included James Hamilton, another groom of the bedchamber, who was described in the Gramont memoirs 'as the liveliest wit, most polished courtier, most accomplished dancer, and most general lover', and the man who outshone Hamilton and everyone else in all these departments, her cousin, the Duke of Buckingham.[10] Her bit of rough, meanwhile, was the well-muscled and 'pretty' young rope dancer Jacob Hall, whose acrobatics drew crowds at London's annual St Bartholomew's fair.

Such antics provided strong ammunition for the satirists. Charles was anything but amused by the anonymous critiques of court life and determined to clamp down on 'seditious treasonable and unlicensed Bookes and Pamphlets'. His censor Roger L'Estrange was especially exercised by *Eniaytos terastios Mirabilis annus, or, The year of prodigies and wonders*, which interpreted certain signs and portents which had appeared in the sky in 1661 and 1662 as foretelling doom. The anonymous pamphlet featured a mythical king, who was quite obviously Charles. It declared:

> God by a prodigie doth sharply reprove the debauchery of this King and his concubines, with the rest of his Associates, and thereby also declares the sudden period and determination of his Kingdom ... amongst the Hellish rout of prophane and ungodly men, lest especially the Oppressors and Persecutors of the True Church look to themselves.

In 1662 Charles brought in a Licensing Act so tough that the publishers of *Mirabilis annus* faced possible execution and one distributor was hanged, drawn and quartered at Smithfield.

Barbara, the major target of much of the satire, can be said to have been well compensated for it. The King's support allowed her use of all manner of avenues to get cash via customs farming – the right to collect customs duties. This gave her a reported £10,000 a year; via the tax on beer another £10,000; and through the Post Office another £5000. She also handled the distribution of offices, spiritual and temporal, usually auctioning them off to the highest bidder. Meanwhile the King picked up her gambling debts, which were colossal. She was addicted to the table. Her usual stake was between £1000 and £1500. One night she reportedly lost £25,000 at play and Charles paid. Vast amounts also went on her clothes and jewels. She not only charged diamond rings to the privy purse, but borrowed from the Jewel House in the Tower, and allegedly always managed to turn the loan into a gift. No wonder that she was, in Pepys' words, 'much richer in Jewells than the Queen and Duchess (of York) put both together'.

Over the years, she was also to acquire a fortune in royal properties and estates in England and Ireland. Among them was the crumbling but still spectacular Nonsuch Palace in Surrey. Built by Henry VIII, this was a glittering Renaissance extravaganza designed to rival Francis I's Palais de Chambord. To pay yet more gambling debts, Barbara pulled the palace down, sold off the building materials and carved the estate into half a dozen farms which were auctioned off too. Charles also gave her Berkshire House, a mansion opposite St James's, which had once been occupied by her bitter enemy the Earl of Clarendon. And she almost got her hands on the Phoenix Park estate in Dublin, which included the summer residence of the Lord Lieutenant of Ireland. The Duke of Ormond put a stop to that, earning Barbara's undying hatred. She lost nothing, however; Charles decreed she be given £1000 a year in compensation for being denied the estate.

Barbara extended and refurbished Berkshire House. With the King's connivance, adjoining land which had been seized to help form the Green Park was instead transferred to Barbara's uncle and thus to her. This enabled her to build two new wings on to the house, which became a showpiece. The King's yacht was used to ship in furniture, tapestries, mirrors and tableware from Flanders and Paris to create what John Evelyn called 'a noble palace'. The staircase and gallery were 'sumptuous', wrote Evelyn in his diary. It was too good 'for that infamous—' he added, leaving a blank space after 'infamous'. He made no comment on a statue in the house that was presented by Barbara's first lover, the Earl of Chesterfield. The records describe it as 'a Cupid kneeling on a rock and shooting from his bow a stream of water up towards heaven'.

Until now none of Charles's liaisons had affected the dominance of his chief mistress. But in 1663 Barbara's preeminent position was to be threatened by the imminent arrival of an altogether more challenging enchantress. Her name was Frances Teresa Stuart. Charles first heard about her from his little sister Minette, Duchess of Orléans, in February 1663. In a letter that was sure to awaken her brother's predatory appetites, Minette informed Charles that one of the English ladies at her court was bringing her fifteen-year-old daughter to England to become a lady-in-waiting to Queen Catherine and that the teenager was something special. She was the 'prettiest girl in the world . . . one of the best fitted I know to adorn a court', wrote the Duchess.

Frances was tall and slender, a violet-eyed teenager who had entranced the court of Louis XIV, where her playfulness and looks made her every gallant's favourite girl-child. She and her parents were among the royalists who had sought shelter in France during the civil wars. After the Restoration her mother decided to bring her to England to seek a rich husband and place her on display by securing her appointment to Queen Catherine's household. She was known in the Sun King's court as 'La Belle Stuart' and Louis did not want to lose her. He pleaded with her mother to think again and is said to have promised to find the girl an important husband and a dowry if she stayed to ornament his court. At fourteen she was apparently even more stunning than twenty-two-year-old Barbara. She arrived in London early in 1663.

Frances was giggly, playful, beautifully mannered and an exquisite dancer. She also became inordinately vain. Once established at court she wouldn't let praise for another woman's face or figure go by without demonstrating her own superiority. The Comte de Gramont's memoirs quote the courtier George Hamilton as saying:

Miss Stuart is so fully acquainted with the advantages she possesses over all other women that it is hardly possible to praise any lady at court for a well turned arm and a fine leg but she is

ever ready to dispute the point by demonstration; and I really
believe that, with a little address, it would not be difficult to
induce her to strip naked, without ever reflecting upon what she
was doing.

According to most contemporaries, Frances was also not very
bright. Her favourite pastimes were hide and seek and constructing
houses out of playing cards. Her behaviour suggests a seventeenth-
century version of the dumb blonde. According to the Gramont
memoirs, 'It was hardly possible for a woman to have less wit or
more beauty.'

Pepys first noticed her – and a change in Barbara's demeanour –
one bright day in July when he encountered the royal entourage out
for a ride in the park:

> The Queen looked mighty pretty in a white laced waistcoat and a
> crimson short petticoat . . . her hair dressed a la negligence . . . the
> King rode hand in hand with her. Here was also my Lady
> Castlemaine. Riding amongst the rest of the ladies; but the King
> took methought no notice of her, nor when they alighted did any-
> body press as she seemed to expect . . . to take her down, but was
> taken down by her own gentlemen. She looked mighty out of
> humour . . . I followed them up into Whitehall, and into the
> Queen's presence, where all the ladies walked, talking and fiddling
> with their hats and feather . . . it was the finest sight to me . . .
> above all Mrs Stuart . . . with her hat cocked and a red plume, with
> her sweet eye, little Roman nose . . . is now the greatest beauty I
> ever saw, I think, in my life, and if ever a woman can, do exceed
> my lady Castlemaine at least in this dress nor do I wonder if the
> King changes, which I verily believe is the reason of his coldness
> to my lady Castlemaine.

In no time, the thirty-three-year-old King was smitten with the
ingénue. His ardour was attested by a love song he wrote to her:

I pass all my hours in a shady old grove,
But I live not the day when I see not my love;
I survey every walk now my Phillis is gone,
And I sigh when I think we were there all alone;
O then, tis O then, that I think there's no hell
Like loving, like loving too well.

Other rakes were similarly entranced, among them the embodiment of cynicism, George Villiers. He too is reported to have written
songs to Frances. Evidently he spent hours building card castles with
her and keeping her giggling with his stories and his mimicry of various courtiers. There is an unlikely story that 'Bucks' confessed his
love to her and she boxed his ears and told him not to be silly.

Barbara decided that the way to deal with the pretty new challenge
was to make a fuss of her and pose as her mentor before the King. As
the memoirs of the King's French friend, the Comte de Gramont,
put it, she was confident that 'whenever she thought fit, she could triumph over . . . Miss Stewart; but she was quite mistaken.'

The first mistake was one day to let loose her terrible temper on
her young friend; the second was to follow up the row by barring the
girl from her famous soirées. According to the French ambassador,
Charles riposted that he would never set foot in Barbara's apartments
again if he did not find the 'demoiselle' with her. At this Barbara did
what she'd done before – yelled for her carriage and drove off in high
dudgeon to her uncle's house in Richmond to sulk. It worked; the
next morning the King chose to go hunting near Richmond and
found himself near the uncle's house. He called in and made up. As
this was not the only episode when Charles knelt to ask Barbara's forgiveness, there was obviously still something about her he was unable
to resist.

Barbara never repeated the mistake. She met the King's threat to
boycott Barbara's salon if Frances wasn't there by including the girl
in every activity she laid on, down to bedroom games. In one famous
episode she set up a mock marriage with herself as the groom and

Frances as the bride. The pair went to the darkened marriage bed, dallying there a little before the groom was replaced in bed – by the King. Here too Charles was apparently allowed to go so far with Frances but no further. The royal frustration can be imagined.

Pepys was told that Buckingham and several others, including Edward Montagu and Sir Henry Bennet, had formed a committee in order 'to get' Frances for the King. After Buckingham had got nowhere with his flirtations and mimicry, Bennet, recently ennobled as Earl of Arlington, was next to try. The story did the rounds that the new earl had hardly begun to speak to her when she burst out laughing. A pompous man radiating self-importance, Bennet had been one of the butts of Buckingham's mimicry. Hearing and seeing the real thing, Frances couldn't contain herself. The Earl, who was described as 'serious, punctilious and proud', became enraged and stormed off.

All through the rest of 1663, the King was to chase the girl, who allowed him 'many liberties with her person' but not the ultimate liberty. Charles's frustration built and built. He became obsessed with her, and damn the outside world. Careless of the bustling court around them, he would pinion Frances into a corner and be 'half an hour together, kissing her to the observation of all the world'. Months of frustrating petting and pawing went by, until one day his customary good humour ran out, he lost his temper and burst out with the hope that he might live to see her grow old and become 'ugly and willing'.[11]

Charles soon recovered his temper. In 1664, against his council's advice, he allocated Frances a suite of rooms that were normally solely for the Queen's use. 'Some of the best parts of the Queen's jointure are, contrary to faith, and against the opinion of my Lord Treasurer and his council, bestowed or rented, I know not how, to my Lord Fitzharding [Charles Berkeley] and Mrs Stuart,' noted Pepys.

Despite such noblesse oblige, Frances was very much a prisoner in the palace. She had arrived when still a child and had nowhere else to go. Her outwardly superior status masked the fact that her presence in the palace was solely as a plaything for the King and that day-to-day she had to fend off a sexual predator. Somehow, Frances continued to rebuff Charles. Her modesty served to fuel court speculation on how the frustrated King might somehow be driven to divorce Queen Catherine and marry La Belle Stuart. Getting rid of the Queen would soon become a recurrent obsession in court circles.

10

ILLNESS, PLAGUE AND FIRE

Smallpox was one of the scourges of the age. It had threatened to kill Charles, who had contracted it just before the Restoration. It did kill two of his siblings almost immediately afterwards. His youngest brother Henry, Duke of Gloucester, died in September 1660, aged twenty. Two months later the King's sister Mary, the Princess Royal, died. In October 1663, Queen Catherine caught the 'spotted disease' and doctors despaired. She lay in her chamber 'as full of spots as a leopard' and was so ill that the last rites of the Roman Catholic Church were said over her. Charles was at her bedside every morning, and every morning he left in tears. On 1 December the French ambassador visited and reported to his King, Louis XIV: 'I am just come from Whitehall, where I have left the Queen in such a state that ... little room is left for hope.'[1]

Charles seemed to be genuinely moved by the suffering of the woman whom he had treated so shabbily. He watched by the bedside as she sank into delirium and raved about a baby son to whom she imagined she had just given birth, and he humoured her. The child was 'a very pretty boy', the King assured her. He humoured her again when she awoke evidently believing that she and Charles had three children. One looked very like himself, the King told her. During bouts of lucidity she begged him not to desert her poor little country and asked that she be buried there.[2]

How deeply the monarch really felt about his apparently dying wife is arguable. No one doubted his genuine concern, nor that the tears were unforced, but immediately after quitting the Queen's bed-side, it was on to laughter and sex. Charles invariably made straight for Frances Stuart's chambers and then for Lady Castlemaine's. 'He hath not missed one night since she was sick, of supping with my Lady Castlemaine,' noted Pepys.[3] Charles rarely allowed anything to disrupt his pleasures.

The King's tears were premature, for his diminutive consort sur-vived. She could not hear or walk for a time, but by New Year 1664 she was slowly recovering. She was and remained in love with Charles and characteristically attributed her survival to the King's prayers. As for the thirty-three-year-old monarch, Pepys picked up the first sign that dissipation was taking its toll. 'I never till this day observed that the King was mighty grey,'[4] noted the diarist. Around this time the King started to wear a periwig.

Several other changes surfaced in the year of Catherine's illness. One was Barbara's religion. She took the risky step of converting to Catholicism and attending mass openly in the Queen's chapel along with Catherine. One wonders what was going through the mind of the deeply religious Queen when her husband's statuesque 'whore', all outward innocence, followed her to the altar rail before blithely taking a sacrament that is supposed to be reserved for the repentant. The Queen's only known comment was that the conversion was 'not for conscience sake'. If she was right, and Barbara had not converted through faith, then one is left with the strong possibility that she did it for political reasons, there being a large Catholic contingent at court. Charles's comment was 'that he never interfered with the souls of ladies, but only with their bodies'. Later, Barbara's conversion was to cost her dearly, but in 1664 the anti-Catholic hysteria that would one day threaten the throne had only just begun to build.

Queen Catherine's illness began a terrible three years for

England. Calamity followed calamity as London was decimated by bubonic plague and then by fire, before the nation was humbled in the second Anglo-Dutch war, the greatest humiliation in English naval history.

The plague made surreptitious landfall in England shortly after Catherine's illness. It is thought to have arrived from Holland to claim its first two victims in November 1664. There followed a break of several months before the infection reached London in the spring of 1665. The death count in London went from hundreds a week in June, to thousands a week in July, to as many as ten thousand a week in August. The dead were thrown into plague pits, those not yet dead left to fester in their boarded-up houses, guards posted outside to keep them there.

Sir John Reresby told one of the more ghoulish stories that circulated:

> A bagpiper being excessively overcome with liquor, fell down in the Street and there lay asleep. In this condition he was taken up and thrown into a cart, betimes the next morning, and carried away with some dead bodies. Meanwhile he awoke from his sleep, it being now about daybreak, and rising up began to play a tune, which so surpriz'd the fellows that drove the cart . . . that in a fright they betook them to their heels, and would have it that they had taken up the Devil in the disguise of a dead man.[5]

In July the King, the Queen and the entire court fled the 'pestilence', decamping westward through the Middlesex countryside in an interminable caravan of coaches, hoping for safety at Hampton Court and in neighbouring villages. The stricken city which they left behind was described by Thomas Vincent, one of the non-conforming ministers, who stayed to brave the epidemic:

> Now people fall as thick as the leaves in autumn when they are shaken by a mighty wind . . . there is a dismal solitude in London

streets ... shops are shut in, people rare ... there is a deep silence in every place. No prancing horses. No rattling coaches. No calling in customers nor offering wares ... Now the nights are too short to bury the dead.[6]

Hampton Court proved to be no sanctuary for the royal party. A sentry guarding the palace keeled over at his post bearing tell-tale buboes, the hallmark of plague, and the caravan took off for Salisbury. Officers were sent ahead to mark with chalk the houses where they were to be billeted. Residents busily scrubbed out the chalk and many tried indignantly to resist the billeting. A French envoy evacuated with the rest commented that he now understood the saying 'an Englishman's home is his castle'. The court nevertheless retained its happy abandon during its flight, especially the young ladies led by La Belle Stuart wearing masculine clothes, in a popular style that allowed young ladies to show off their legs. Pepys watched the King and Queen depart the red brick palace and was charmed 'to see the pretty young ladies ... in velvet coats, caps with ribbons and with laced bands, just like men'.[7] They evidently didn't have a care in the world.

Plague reached Salisbury about the same time as the royal refugees, and there were rumours that the Duke of Buckingham and the Duchess of Richmond had died. This wasn't true but the court was quickly away again, this time to the spires of Oxford. There Charles hoped to celebrate two births, one by Barbara his mistress and, far more significant, the other by Catherine his wife. Both women were accommodated in Merton College, where Barbara was allotted lodgings in a fellow's rooms and the Queen in the Master's more expansive quarters. Twelve years earlier, Catherine's mother-in-law Henrietta Maria had been lodged in the same quarters at Merton when she conceived her youngest child, Henrietta Anne. It may have seemed to augur well for the young Queen, but nothing came of it.[8]

On 28 December, Lady Castlemaine gave birth to a boy, George, whom Charles acknowledged and later made Earl of

Northumberland. In contrast to that happy moment, the following month Queen Catherine delivered a stillborn child. The child's gender is not recorded. While the Queen mourned, so did Chancellor Clarendon. He had thrown his weight behind the Braganza marriage and for his own standing needed the union to provide his King with an heir. As well as bolstering the dynasty, the arrival of an heir would, it was hoped, induce in Charles a more responsible attitude to his role as monarch. The Chancellor was no doubt among those who prayed for it to happen, though his enemies put it about that he counted on the Queen remaining childless so his own son-in-law, James of York, would succeed to the throne.

Clarendon's hold on power had looked unshakeable during the first two years after the Restoration. The King was increasingly irritated by the Chancellor's nagging about his lifestyle, but he saw Clarendon as a master at handling Parliament and a brilliant administrator, and depended on him, so he stayed. Barbara and the clique around her were his most vehement opponents. She was a beacon to his enemies, who numbered some of the most ambitious and dissolute men in Whitehall. They included the Duke of Buckingham, the Earl of Bristol, the Earl of Lauderdale and Sir Charles Berkeley. The quieter but deadly Earl of Arlington must also be counted among the Castlemaine group. All of these men had various reasons for opposing Clarendon, some personal and some political. All too were cronies of the King, having mostly been so since his years in exile, and most of them regularly caroused with him now. All except Buckingham were regulars at the Castlemaine suppers. At one time or another at least three were Lady Castlemaine's lovers.

The likes of Bristol, Arlington and Lauderdale could also be counted in the so-called Somerset House junto, the malcontents and Francophiles grouped around Henrietta Maria, the Queen Mother, before she left England for good in 1665. No one was more vehemently opposed to Clarendon than the woman who had fought him for dominance over her son in the years of exile.

The power balance had begun to change in October 1662 with the dropping of Clarendon's fellow veteran, the first Secretary of State Sir Edward Nicholas. The appointment of Arlington as Secretary of State, and of Charles Berkeley as keeper of the Privy Purse, meant, as Pepys put it, that 'the old serious lords are out of favour' at court and 'the young men get uppermost'. The new appointees had the career-boosting advantage of being close to both the King and Barbara. In the words of William Cobbett, the two had 'the management of the mistress'.[9] There is no doubt that her voice in Charles's ear hastened their rise and, eventually, hastened Clarendon's fall.

The following year, the Earl of Bristol made a frontal attack on the Chancellor, attempting to impeach him. It was an ill-judged move. With no apparent sense of irony, Bristol accused the Chancellor of trying 'to alienate the affections of his majesty's subjects by venting in his own discourse ... opprobrious scandals against His majesty's person and course of life, such as are not fit to be mentioned'. At that stage Bristol's friends among the Wits were creating opprobrious scandals across London. This may explain why the House of Lords lost no time in throwing out the impeachment motion.

Buckingham found a more subtle way of getting at the Chancellor – mockery. He made him a continual target for his notorious mimicry. His take-off of Clarendon became legendary:

> Behold how he changes now. Villiers is no longer Villiers. He is Clarendon, walking solemnly to the Court of the Star Chamber: a pair of bellows is hanging before him for the purse; Colonel Titus is walking with a fire shovel on his shoulder, to represent a mace; the king, himself a capital mimic, is splitting his sides with laughter; the courtiers are fairly in a roar.[10]

Such performances caused royal laughter but also royal embarrassment, for the King was portrayed as taking orders from a buffoon – all of which sounds no more harmful than a bunch of schoolboys sniggering behind the teacher's back, except that it went on for years, helping bit by bit to undermine Clarendon in his patron's eyes.

Clarendon's Achilles heel turned out to be a war that he opposed – the violent struggle over trade that became known as the second Anglo-Dutch war. The Earl of Southampton was also against the war, and initially the King was lukewarm. However, most of those associated with Barbara smelled profit or glory and were in the pro-war camp. On his visits to her suppers Charles would have encountered a chorus of anti-Dutch aggression from the likes of Lauderdale, Berkeley and Ashley as well as from Arlington and Barbara. A biographer of Arlington writes that 'the war spirit reigned unchallenged at Lady Castlemaine's suppers'.[11]

However, for 'war spirit' read 'blind arrogance'. According to the French ambassador to England, the Marquis de Cominges, 'the coming contest was seen as a sport: there would be, of course, some important battles, but they would be won; besides this, most of the game would consist in chasing the Dutch merchantmen; there would be a fine sport indeed, and spoils worth the risk.' In March 1665, Charles declared war. He would come to regret it. So would Clarendon, of whom the King was to make a scapegoat after the country's defeat.

Not everything went well for Lady Castlemaine in the mid and late 1660s. These were the years when she became the great hate figure of the newssheets and ballads sold in the streets of London denouncing the dissolute court. A typical example was a note about her pinned to the door of her Merton College lodgings during the court's sojourn in Oxford. It ended:

> The reason she is not ducked?
> Because by Caesar she is fucked.

Unlike the waylaying of Barbara in St James's Park by three masked gentlemen, this apparently trivial incident wasn't kept quiet. The King offered a large reward for information leading to the capture of whoever wrote the Merton College verse. This produced nothing.

In London, the plague had abated sufficiently by February 1666 for King and court to return from Oxford. Pepys' diary suggests that, for a brief moment at least, some courtiers attending the King were chastened by the immensity of an epidemic that would leave one in five Londoners dead. Creel, one of the diarist's court informants, reported finding 'all things mighty dull at Court ... they now begin to lie long in bed; it being, as we suppose, not seemly for them to be found playing and gaming as they used to be.' If the Buckinghams and Digbies did pull in their horns, it didn't last. At the end of the year a despondent Pepys called it 'a sad, vicious, negligent Court, and all sober men there fearful of the ruin of the whole kingdom this next year'.

One great change was that the Queen who returned from Oxford was no longer the muted bystander of her first year in England. In the continued attempt to win her husband's heart, the once demure Portuguese girl presented as a different woman, wearing the latest, most daring décolleté fashions from Paris, covering herself in jewels, and revealing a passion for dancing and masques that attempted to rival Barbara's entertainments. 'She entered all the extravagance of the court,' wrote Burnet. Almost every afternoon she held receptions in her withdrawing rooms overlooking the Thames. Almost every evening there was another, more gripping function for favoured members of the court to go on to – Barbara's suppers. You were always assured of a good meal there, the French ambassador informed the Sun King.

But poor buck-toothed Catherine was no competition for Barbara, and Barbara would probably have been no competition for Frances Stuart had the girl slept with the King. Charles could not keep his hands off Frances, who remained unwilling, and the King's pursuit went on for months, stretching into years, his ardour continually fanned by her coquettish teasing. Frances still let Charles touch her, caress her and kiss her – anything but make love to her. He was driven wild with desire. It reached the point where the Queen felt inhibited from walking in certain parts of the palace, including her own quarters, lest she happen across the fondling couple. In Pepys' words, 'the good Queen will of herself stop before she goes sometimes into her dressing room, till she knows whether the King be there for fear he should be as she hath sometimes taken him, with Mrs Stuart.'[12]

Barbara's relationship with the King was attended by incessant rows, but despite these and his obsession with La Belle Stuart there were constant signs that Barbara's magic still worked for him. He had celebrated his thirty-fourth birthday dancing all night at a ball she threw in his honour. He refurbished her quarters in the palace extravagantly in the French fashion. He gave her the Christmas presents sent to him by peers in the Upper House. He continued to pick up the tabs for her jewellery and gambling debts. At a minimum he spent one night a week with her, but more usually four nights. Most striking of all, she could still insult him and have him, the King, apologise, perhaps self-mockingly but nevertheless on his knees.

Members of a high-powered French delegation sent to London in 1665 to try to stave off the looming Anglo-Dutch war learned first hand of Barbara's continued standing. They called her 'La Castlemaine' in dispatches to Louis XIV and in them described how Charles acted like the host at her establishment, how 'the most secret affairs of state [were] freely discussed' there and how one day when the French ambassador faced Charles and Clarendon in a last attempt to secure peace, the King brought negotiations to an abrupt end so as not to be late for supper at Lady Castlemaine's.[13] That illustration of the King's priorities must have had the watching Clarendon grinding his teeth.

Barbara's continuing power over Charles has been attributed to her sexual prowess but in large part also to her being the mother of his children. Indeed, had Queen Catherine presented him with a legitimate heir, his attitude to her and the whole balance of power between her, Barbara and Frances would have been transformed. As it was, the Queen's failure to deliver a live child was to undermine her throughout the rest of the decade and beyond. The malicious rumour the Spanish had put about years before in an attempt to scupper the royal marriage was turning out to have some substance.

The Queen made desperate efforts to conceive. 'Nothing will be left unattempted to give an heir to the British crown,' the French ambassador reported.[14] Catherine consulted soothsayers and doctors and was advised to take the spring waters at Bourbon in France. For some reason, perhaps financial but probably political, she went instead to the English springs at Bath and Tunbridge Wells; the waters of the latter were said to 'make a barren woman as fruitful as a coney-warren'.

On her subsequent regular excursions there, Catherine was some-times accompanied by the King, sometimes only by her ladies. At Tunbridge she dispensed with formalities and arranged dancing on the lawns lasting late into the night. The name of the town would one day be synonymous with staid Victorian sobriety, but not in the 1660s. Catherine's courtiers brought with them the habits and morals of Whitehall and Tunbridge Wells became, if it wasn't already, one of the raciest places in Europe. As one contemporary chronicler said, the spa town was not only a place to cure one's ailments, but to shop and find other amusements: 'Here is, likewise, deep play and no want of amorous intrigues.'[15] The memoirs of the Comte de Gramont describe it as 'the general rendezvous of all the gay and handsome of both sexes ... constraint is banished ... joy and pleas-ure are the joint sovereigns ... Never did love see his empire in a more flourishing condition than on this spot.' In his poem 'Tunbridge', Rochester was less effusive. He called the place 'the rendezvous of fools, buffoons and praters, cuckolds, whores'.

In Whitehall, the Queen's position became a loudly whispered issue after her illness. During the weeks when she had been at death's door, speculation had it that on her death the King would lose no time in marrying Frances Stuart. With Catherine's recovery and continued failure to bear a child, the gossip focused on how to get rid of her so Charles could marry again. George Villiers and George Digby pushed the idea of annulment or divorce, and over the next half dozen years various grounds for questioning the validity of her marriage to the King were explored. Had the marriage been fully consummated? Had Catherine taken a vow of chastity? Was it true that she was judged incapable of motherhood before she married? The Archbishop of Canterbury, Gilbert Sheldon, was approached but turned the subject to one Charles did not want to deal with: 'Sir,' he told the King, 'I wish you would put away the woman that you keep.'[16]

Charles reportedly accepted a scheme by which 'the queen's confessor persuade her to leave the world, and embrace a religious life'. The Pope, who was secretly consulted, was unsurprisingly anything but enamoured of the proposal to retire a Catholic queen. Strangely, Barbara was the main obstacle to the plan. Fearing that she might fall victim to any new queen, she is said to have opposed the proposal so fiercely that it was dropped.

The second major disaster of the 1660s was the Great Fire of London in September 1666. The King first heard details of the fire from the diarist Samuel Pepys, who was alerted to it before dawn by a fearful woman servant, and scaled the highest point in the Tower for a bird's eye view. He saw parts of the city already consumed in flames and no one fighting the fire. Instead everybody was endeavouring to remove their goods, and 'flinging into the river or bringing them into lighters that lay off shore' or 'staying in their houses as long as till the very fire touched them, and then running into boats, or clambering from one pair of stairs by the water-side to another'. Post haste, Pepys took the frightening news to Whitehall and was summoned before Charles. He told the King 'that unless his Majesty did command houses to be pulled down nothing could stop the fire'. The King told Pepys to find the Lord Mayor and 'command him to spare no houses, but to pull down before the fire every way'.

The Lord Mayor, Sir Thomas Bloodworth, had fatally delayed. 'Pish! A woman could piss it out,' was his reaction when first told of the fire at 2 a.m. that morning, and then he went back to bed. Thereafter the fire proved unstoppable. Strong winds, a tinder-dry summer and people resisting demolition of their houses saw it rage for three days. Another diarist, Pepys' friend John Evelyn, wrote of 'ten thousand houses all in one flame' and described the noise of 'crackling flames ... the shrieking of Women and children, the hurry of people, the fall of towers, houses and churches'. About 13,200 houses were destroyed and 87 of the city's 109 churches. Among them was the medieval cathedral of St Paul's, which was being propped up by wooden scaffolding. Melted lead from the cathedral roof covered the ground around the ruined church, glowing red from the heat. No one could get near for days.

Coincidentally, five days earlier a party of experts and officials, including Evelyn and Christopher Wren, had examined the building and decided that it had to be rebuilt. Evelyn set down their conclusion in his diary: 'We had a mind to build it with a noble cupola, a form of church-building not as yet known in England, but of wonderful grace. For this purpose, we offered to bring in a plan and estimate, which after much contest, was at last assented to.' Three weeks later Christopher Wren was given the task of planning the rebuilding of almost the whole city.

The fire claimed 436 acres, including four-fifths of the City. It would take fifty years to rebuild. Miraculously, only ten deaths were recorded, but many probably went unrecorded, with would-be lynch mobs gathered in the ruins looking for scapegoats to blame for their ruin. The hunt was on for 'incendiaries' among the large numbers of foreigners in London and anyone else who could be deemed suspicious. A woman concealing something under her smock was murdered after being accused of carrying fire bombs. Her breasts were hacked off and she was beaten to death. It transpired that she was actually concealing chickens. Later, a deluded French tailor named Robert Hubert laid claim to starting the fire and kept insisting that he was the culprit. Everyone involved with him knew that he was a fantasist. Nevertheless, Hubert was tried, found guilty on his own testimony and hanged at Tyburn. Charles moved to stop the lynch mobs by issuing a declaration that the fire had been caused by an accident at a Pudding Lane baker's shop that supplied the palace with its bread.

The fire presented a moment for the King to rebuild his popularity and he didn't let the opportunity pass. He helped to fight the blaze, memorably armed with a spade and bucket, getting dirty and wet through. He ordered action against looters, arranged for bread stalls for the homeless, and later ordered other cities and towns to allow in refugees from the capital and permit them to set up their trades. His brother James, charged with organising the front-line fire-fighting, performed still more gallantly, a constant presence near the worst of the blaze.

It was typical of the King's court that Baptist May was roundly applauded when he joked about the fire. Recalling how the City had always given the Stuarts a lot of trouble, May said that there was 'no way else to govern that rude multitude except by force', and the destruction of the city walls and gates left the city wide open for the King's troops. After the Restoration this made the Great Fire of London 'the greatest blessing that God had ever conferred' on the King. Evidently the King was not amused, but some courtiers were.[17]

Many in that superstitious age inevitably saw the fire as God's retribution for the sins of the country. It was certainly seen that way by the Dutch. What became known as 'Holmes' bonfire' had taken place the previous month. A fleet led by Vice-Admiral Robert Holmes raided the Vlie estuary, destroyed about 130 merchantmen and then sacked and plundered the town of West-Terschelling before setting it aflame. They burned all but thirty dwellings to the ground and carted off all that they could carry. The Dutch were outraged. Dutch leader Johan De Witt suggested some retaliatory 'light spoiling' along the east coast of England, but then accepted that such actions would be 'counter-productive and even somewhat unchristian'. But the next year the Dutch would take their revenge in the most humiliating fashion.

II

RIVALRY AND BETRAYAL

In March 1667 the machinations of Barbara Castlemaine were finally to bring about the downfall of the girl whose beauty had captivated and tantalised the King for upwards of four years, Frances Stuart.

Unknown to the King and most of the court, La Belle Stuart was being courted by a widowed cousin, the King's namesake, Charles Stuart, Duke of Richmond and Lennox. Richmond appears to have been desperately smitten and genuinely in love with Frances. He was no handsome saviour, however, but a raddled, diminutive drunk who came knocking on Frances' door in January 1667, only two weeks after burying his second wife. That, it would seem, didn't bother Frances. She would later explain that she had reached the point of desperation where she had to marry or prostitute herself to the King.

Barbara's spies in the palace got to know of the amour and informed her of a late-night tryst between Richmond and Frances in the latter's apartments. As usual the King had been with Frances earlier that evening, but had left her after she deployed the lover's great excuse, a headache. According to the Gramont memoirs, Barbara stopped the King as he returned to his own quarters and badgered him to go back, taunting him about Frances. It is possible that Charles had suspicions of Frances anyway, for she had been noticeably colder to him recently, so he did return to her chambers. Pushing past a maidservant who insisted that her mistress was asleep, the King found Frances in bed and the Duke, his namesake, 'sitting at her pillow'. Charles exploded. 'He testified his resentment to the Duke of Richmond in such terms as he had never before used.'[1] Richmond was petrified by the torrent of threats. He bowed, retreated from the chamber and fled from London. He had dared venture not a word to the raging monarch.

Left to face the royal wrath on her own, the supposedly docile Frances stood up to the King, insisting that the Duke had honourable intentions and that if she was not allowed to receive such as he, then she was a slave in a free country. She talked of quitting England and finding refuge in France. The King's response appears to have veered from bullying threats to pleas for forgiveness.

The next day the palace was alive with rumours. Charles issued an order banning the Duke from court, while Frances was said to have thrown herself at the feet of Queen Catherine, tearfully pleading for protection from the King and angling for support for her marriage to Richmond. Frances let it be known that she hadn't realised the hurt caused to the Queen by the King's attentions to her and had apologised for it to Catherine. The Queen reportedly cried along with her beautiful rival.

Charles refused to allow the marriage. In his desperation to keep Frances he offered to sever all ties with other women, courtesan or prostitute, and to make her a duchess. Frances was unmoved. Richmond was no great catch, despite the title – as well as being an alcoholic and a wastrel he lacked a huge fortune – but he was genuinely in love and Frances was determined to marry him. A few nights later she slipped out of the palace grounds to join the waiting Richmond.

A midnight marriage ceremony was held at a chapel on Richmond's estate with two servants the only witnesses. At the news of the marriage, the King banned Frances and her new husband from court and swore never to see her again.[2] Four months later he was finally to dismiss his mentor of twenty years, Lord Chancellor Clarendon, one of his prime reasons reportedly being the Chancellor's supposed role in the loss of Frances. Charles was thought to have accepted the allegation that the Chancellor had promoted the young beauty's elopement with Richmond so as to prevent the King from divorcing his wife and marrying Frances. As a result, the King's attitude to Clarendon hardened into 'a violent and irreconcilable aversion'.

La Belle Stuart's impact in court had been unique. Virginity never held such sway for so long in the history of British monarchy, let alone in the sexually charged court of the Stuarts. Charles's mood cannot have lightened when Frances sent back the jewels he had given her. Nevertheless, five months after her flight he was still obsessed with her. On 26 August he wrote to little sister Minette:

> I do assure you I am very much troubled that I cannot in every-thing give you the satisfaction I could wish, especially in this business of the duchess of Richmond [Frances' formal title through marriage], wherein you may think me ill natured, but if you consider how hard a thing 'tis to swallow an injury done by a person I had so much tenderness for, you will in some degree excuse the resentment I use towards her; you know my good nature enough to believe that I could not be so severe, if I had not great provocation, and I assure you her carriage towards me has been as bad as breach of friendship and faith can make it, there-fore I hope you will pardon me if I cannot so soon forget an injury which went so neere my hart.[3]

While Charles grieved over Frances, the country was involved in the second major conflict with the Dutch in a dozen years. The first had seen an English triumph under Cromwell. During those belli-cose suppers at Lady Castlemaine's in 1664, it had been taken for granted that a second sea war would be another triumph. It wasn't to be. The most recent major sea battle, in August 1666, had been an English victory but over the entire conflict more than 7000 Englishmen had been killed as against some 5000 Dutch, and at the turn of the year their fleet stood much less battered than the English.

The war was hitting trade and tax revenues badly. That, together with the financial costs of the great fire and the lavish spending at the palace, produced a new financial crisis. A crisis came in February 1667 when the Navy Board reported that the cupboard was bare. It owed £930,000 in back pay to its sailors and needed £500,000 from Parliament immediately to refit for the coming year. However, Parliament was not to be hurried. Before committing more money the Commons wanted to know what had happened to the £5 million or so previously allocated to the King. Pepys was the best-placed naval official to know. His calculations, jotted down in his diary, and meant for no one else's eyes, showed that £2,300,000 was unaccounted for. Where this vast sum went was never discovered. But such was the furore over vanishing funds that the House passed an unprecedented measure requiring the royal books to be opened. Horrified ministers circumvented that by offering a royal commission to examine war spending.

A delay of almost three weeks was caused while Parliament argued. Charles could have filled any funding gap by the usual method of raising a loan in the City but instead took the risk of saving money by mothballing the country's most powerful men-o'-war. Sails furled and crews discharged, the cream of the fleet, which the King had inherited from Oliver Cromwell, was crammed into Chatham Dockyard on the River Medway. Without consulting the Privy Council Charles had taken the decision not to put the battle fleet to sea in 1667. He would rely on other vessels and strengthened coastal defences to cope with any threat from the Dutch.

On Charles's side it would be argued that he had to retrench because Parliament was proving so slow in voting new monies for the war. Some had another explanation – that Charles planned to use the funds saved by mothballing to help govern without Parliament.

The Stuart predilection for absolutism was as strong in Charles II as it had been in his father. He aimed consistently to rule as his cousin Louis ruled.

Meanwhile, the international situation was in flux. The French were busily building a war fleet which, if added to that of the Dutch, would make a far more formidable force than Charles could muster, even including the mothballed ships at Chatham. English fears of such a threat were stilled when peace talks began in the Dutch city of Breda. Charles received repeated assurances from the Louvre that the Sun King would guarantee a peace deal. Charles's womenfolk in Paris, sister Minette and mother Henrietta Maria, were utterly confident that Louis could be relied on. In these circumstances nothing was done to reactivate the mothballed ships.

Throughout the negotiations, Buckingham had been the scourge of the government. He opposed everything ministers proposed and worked hard at pulling all strands of opposition together. In his *History of the Rebellion*, Clarendon recounted the Duke's methods of wooing MPs and fellow lords. He 'invited them to his table, pretended to have a great esteem for their parts, asked counsel of them, lamented the kings neglecting his business and committing it to other people who were not fit for it and ... reported all the licence and debauchery of the court in the most lively colours'.[4]

During the winter of 1666–7 Buckingham could no longer keep up the sage and sober image and began to overreach himself. After clashes in Parliament he threatened a duel with one member, and pulled off another's periwig. His antics had him twice consigned to the Tower, if only for a few days. Come the New Year he faced far worse. In January his enemies, alleging that he had cast the King's horoscope, levelled against the Duke the medieval charge of treason by 'imagining' or 'compassing' the King's death. Arlington was behind the move, perhaps in cahoots with the Lord Chancellor. Both men were butts of Buckingham's attacks and would have felt much more comfortable with him out of the way. In the event, he evaded the officers sent to detain him and, not for the first time, went

on the run. The most famous man in England was not seen again
until he gave himself up four months later.

The war, meanwhile, went disastrously wrong. In June a Dutch
fleet appeared at the mouth of the Thames, and after manoeuvring
for some days plunged up the river almost unchallenged. The Dutch
bombarded and then captured Sheerness, bombarded Gravesend, then
made up the River Medway to Chatham Dockyard and the pride of
the English fleet. There a chain had been slung from bank to bank
as a barrier to the dockyard. When the Dutch broke the chain, the
great warships inherited from Oliver Cromwell lay undefended. The
King's eighty-gun flagship, the *Royal Charles*, her stern proudly decorated with gold Stuart insignia, was boarded without a shot fired in
her defence. She was sailed back to Holland together with another
capital warship. The Dutch claimed to have sunk two dozen more
English craft. They spent days plundering the dockyard. Food stocks,
cannon, powder and ammunition were emptied from the warehouses and then the warehouses were set on fire. Dry docks were
destroyed. Even rowing boats were holed.

The King's trusted royal advisor John Evelyn was appalled and
afraid on learning of the attack. He knew that there was nothing to
stop the Dutch continuing up the Thames and firing every ship in
the river: 'all this through our unaccountable negligence in not setting out our fleet in due time', he noted in his diary. Fortunately the
Dutch were unaware just how defenceless the country was. On his
return to Holland, the Dutch admiral Michiel de Ruyter is said to
have remarked, 'Had I known landing would be so easy, I would
have brought an army.'[5]

Panic mixed with fury erupted in London on news of the debacle.
There were rumours that the Dutch were following up by landing a
French invasion force in Kent. 'Everybody was flying, none knew
why or whither,' recalled John Evelyn. It would seem that Londoners
still in the charred city were worried about an attack from the French
while the court worried about an attack from the mob. 'The truth is
I do fear so much that the whole kingdom is undone,' wrote Pepys.

'God help us and God knows what disorders we may fall into.' In the palace there was uproar with 'the Countess of Castlemaine bewailing, above all others, that she should be the first torn to pieces'. Pepys recorded that there were cries about betrayal and treachery in the streets, 'by Papists and others about the king'.[6] 'The common people and almost all other men are mad, some crying out we were sold, others that there were traitors,' wrote a correspondent in Kent.[7] The court, which was seen to be gobbling up money meant for war, was the main target of recrimination. In the first Sunday after Chatham, no less than the King's chaplain, Dr Creighton, inveighed 'against the sins of the court and particularly against adultery ... over and over instancing how for that single sin in David the whole nation was undone'.[8]

The King's activities on the night of the Medway attack became notorious. While his ships were burning and sinking twenty-five miles away, he and Barbara were reported to be supping at Lady Monmouth's house and making a game of hunting a moth. The story quickly spread around London, irresistibly conjuring the image of Nero 1500 years earlier. Here is one of the milder verses published anonymously in 1667:

> As Nero once, with harp and hand surveyed
> His flaming Rome, and, as that burned, he played,
> So our great prince, when the Dutch fleet arrived,
> Saw his ships burned and, as they burned, he Swived,
> So kind he was in our extremist need,
> He would those flames extinguish with his seed.*

Reaction would have been uglier still had Charles followed his first instinct after the attack. His personal courage had been proved on the battlefield, yet his first thought on hearing of Chatham is said to have been to get out of London and make for Windsor, presumably with his

---

* Attributed to John Denham, MP, courtier and poet.

womenfolk.[9] Defence against the invaders would have been entrusted to the drunken Cromwellian general who had given Charles the throne seven years earlier, George Monck, Duke of Albemarle. Happily for the King's reputation, he had second thoughts.

One of the prime targets for public fury over the next few days was Clarendon. He had opposed the war and had no part in its management, but forecast that if it went wrong he would be made the scapegoat for the war and much else too, and so it proved. The mob was at his door on the night of the attack: 'Some rude people have been ... at my Lord Chancellor's where they have cut down the trees before his house and broke his windows,' wrote Pepys. Nastier still, they had painted a gibbet on the gate with these words: 'Three signs to be seen; Dunkirke, Tangier and a barren Queen.' On recovering their courage the Chancellor's enemies at court followed this lead and called openly for his blood.

Clarendon was his own worst enemy. His arrogance and disdain for other views made many enemies, and though incorruptible by the standards of the day, and famously proud of his rectitude, the house of his that was attacked was palatial and cost a fortune, which invited suspicion. When he was an exile in the 1640s and 1650s, Clarendon had famously been on the breadline, swapping stories of penury with other refugee courtiers. Now he was sufficiently affluent to have spent a reputed £50,000 on his mansion. Almost before the ashes of the fire were cold he was using stonework from the shattered St Paul's to edify it. Rumours went around that bribes from the Dutch had provided the wherewithal for the building.

The penultimate scenes in the Chancellor's fall were played out by the King, by Barbara Castlemaine his bitterest antagonist, and by that other old enemy the Duke of Buckingham. The Duke had given himself up to the authorities in July, with typical display arriving at the Tower in a splendid coach filled with drunken friends. Barbara immediately intervened with the King on her cousin's behalf. She unleashed one of her infamous outbursts on her royal lover for jailing the Duke. For once Charles fought back, calling her a 'jade, that meddled with things she has nothing to do with'. His Majesty was a fool, she screamed back, 'for if he were not he would not suffer his business to be carried on by fools that did not understand them, and cause his best subjects and those best able to serve him to be imprisoned'.[10]

It is not clear exactly what happened next. Barbara, as so often, seems to have gone or been sent packing for a few days, but her intervention paid off. The Duke was brought before the Privy Council and quickly exonerated of the charge of treason. 'It is said', wrote Pepys, 'that when he was charged with making himself popular as indeed he is, he [answered] that whoever was committed to prison by my Lord Chancellor or my Lord Arlington could not want being popular.' Buckingham was released and readmitted to the Privy Council, where he now led the chorus telling Charles to disown the old, ailing and now allegedly incompetent Chancellor. James, the King's brother and son-in-law of the Chancellor, fought to save him but in vain: 'The friends of Lady Castlemaine openly told His Majesty "it would not consist with his majesty's honour to be hectored out of his determination to dismiss the chancellor by his brother, who was wrought upon by his wife's crying."'[11]

The King is said to have taken the final decision on Clarendon during a meeting with Buckingham set up by Barbara in her apartments. Some accounts insist that Charles's continued bitterness over Frances Stuart was a deciding factor: the King was thought to have accepted the allegation that Clarendon had promoted the young beauty's elopement with Richmond so as to prevent the King from divorcing his wife and marrying Frances. As a result his attitude to Clarendon hardened into 'a violent and irreconcilable aversion'.[12]

On 26 August 1667, at ten o'clock in the morning, Lord Clarendon waited on the King at Whitehall. The portly, limping minister was still deferential but querulous too, with the tall, sallow monarch possibly embarrassed at what he had finally been persuaded to do. The burden of what Clarendon said to the King was why? Why was he being dismissed? What fault had he committed?

Charles replied that no king ever had a better servant, but he couldn't change his decision. The sacking of the Chancellor took two hours of polite prevarication, the discussion ending abruptly when Clarendon brought up Lady Castlemaine's name and warned against her influence. In Clarendon's own loaded phrase, Charles, 'not being well pleased', jumped up and left without a word. The meeting was over.

By jettisoning Clarendon, Charles mirrored the actions of Prince Hal casting off Falstaff – except that in this case, Charles was not the newly serious prince but the eternal playboy and Clarendon, if not old, the serious-minded man of state. Clarendon's departure from the King took him through the Privy Garden past Lady Castlemaine's chambers. It was about midday and Barbara was still in bed. She ran out in her smock into her aviary looking into Whitehall to watch the old man go, her maid chasing behind with her nightgown. Pepys described how the twenty-six-year-old courtesan 'stood joying herself'. A crowd of 'gallants' also gathered to see the great man's fall, among them the Earl of Arlington and Baptist May. Clarendon's only words to Barbara as he passed were said to be, 'Oh Madam, is it you? Pray remember that if you live you will grow old.'[13]

The King justified Clarendon's dismissal to the Duke of Ormond, who had interceded on the Chancellor's behalf. Charles wrote: 'The truth is his behaviour and humour was grown so insupportable to myself and all the world else that I could no longer endure it and it was impossible for me to live with it and do those things with the Parliament that must be done or the Government will be lost.'[14]

A few days after that final interview between King and Chancellor, Secretary of State for the South William Morrice collected the great seal from the Chancellor's house. As Morrice handed the seal to the King later that day, Baptist May fell on his knees, kissed the King's hand and said, 'Now you will be king – what you have never been before.'[15]

Clarendon's enemies weren't yet satisfied. Led by Buckingham, a campaign began to have him impeached for treason. The grounds for this were generally feeble. Unable to stand up allegations of corruption, his opponents could only manage initially 'That he hath in a short time gain'd to himself a greater Estate than can be imagin'd to be gain'd lawfully in so short a time.'[16] At first, Clarendon was confident of carrying the day in any trial. But the King's continued animosity helped persuade him not to risk it and in October he fled the country into exile in France.

The Chancellor's eclipse was a triumph for the Villiers cousins, Barbara and Buckingham, but Barbara's own position in 1667 was increasingly precarious. The King had always seemed relaxed about her affairs, but his sticking point was her long-standing relationship with Harry Jermyn. According to the Comte de Gramont, the King 'did not think it consistent with his dignity' that his mistress should appear chained to the 'most ridiculous conqueror there ever was'.

Charles secured a promise from Barbara to give Jermyn up. Typically, she did no such thing and carried on the affair without much attempt to hide it. When rumour reached the King that Barbara was entertaining her old lover, Charles's remonstrances led to another furious row. The Gramont memoirs reported, 'The impetuosity of her temper broke forth like lightning. Reproaches against his promiscuous and low amours, floods of tears and the Medea-like threats of destroying her children and burning his palace followed.' According to the memoirs, peace was finally achieved after Charles promised to make Barbara a duchess in return for her giving Jermyn up and promising 'to rail no more' against his other women. Barbara would have to wait several years before Charles kept his side of the bargain.

12

ENTRANCES AND EXITS

Though Baptist May felt that Charles, now rid of Clarendon, could do as he wished, in reality the King's options were limited. The capital was in ruins with much of its population scattered into outlying towns and villages. Christopher Wren's vision of an orderly capital city spread along imperial boulevards could not be afforded. But plans were in train for St Paul's to be rebuilt and for houses to be built in stone, with wider roads and alleyways to separate them. In the meantime, thousands were homeless and often starving. For much of London's population in 1667, home was a shanty town.

Thanks to the crushing war with the Dutch, trade was in peril. The exchequer was depleted, taxation was down, and relations between the Crown and Parliament more fraught even than usual. Against such a desolate scene, almost the sole beacon of power and exuberance was the King's lust. The reason for the renewed burst of virility was that with Clarendon gone, Charles could, as Baptist May had purred at his feet, rule as he wished – or, more correctly, attempt to rule as he wished. Parliament was still tight with money and anxious about how state power was apportioned. More than ever, Charles wished to rule via his own cadre of supporters together with the Privy Council, though he had good reason to mistrust some of those who served in it.

The two most important people in government after the King were now Buckingham and Arlington, who despised one another. The King knew he needed them both on his side to keep the ship of state from running onto any more rocks. Due to his influence in both houses of Parliament, Buckingham was a necessary if uncomfortable ally. Despite his open hostility and resentment. In a poem entitled 'The Cabin Boy', Buckingham lampooned the King's abilities, disparaging his love of sailing and his seafaring skills, saying they were only as good as those of any cabin boy, while his knowledge of affairs of state was worse:

> But not one lesson of the ruling art
> Could this dull blockhead ever get by heart.

In a way, Buckingham's jest had weight. The King had never been schooled in the art of leadership. Any chance he might have had was left scattered in the courts of Europe while he was a penniless prince living on charity. A more studious and ambitious man might have used exile as an opportunity to refine his understanding of statecraft, as Machiavelli had done during his exile from Florence, but young Charles had chosen to dull the pain of exile in carnal pursuits. Though not lacking in intelligence, Charles was not a bookish man. His lack of education on matters of state, coupled with a mind that was not the most enquiring, put him at a disadvantage when dealing with more accomplished men.

The sinister looking but clever and agreeable Arlington, who had been appointed one of the two Secretaries of State a few years before, now carried more of the burden of government than ever. Buckingham, despite being appointed Captain of the King's Horse, had no substantive position in government. It was better, reasoned Charles, that Buckingham was inside the tent of state rather than outside making a nuisance of himself. It seemed Charles had, after all, learned some lessons of the ruling arts.

Apart from Arlington and Buckingham, three others made up what became known as the Cabal. They were Lord Ashley (later the Earl of Shaftesbury), a man of erudition and dangerously republican sentiments; Lord Clifford, who along with Ashley was one of the new Treasury commissioners; and the Earl of Lauderdale, the Scottish Secretary of State. By chance, the so-called Cabal spelled out the initial letters of its members' names: Clifford, Arlington, Buckingham, Ashley and Lauderdale.

This was no close-knit group of men pulling heartily together to drag the ship off the rocks. It was a group of self-promoting individuals each with his own views and strengths. Taken individually and together, the Cabal was not Clarendon. Together they allowed the King to rule without any one constraining influence. Individually there would be no one beady eye keeping watch over him. Charles could relax and try to recover the libido he had lost during war with the Dutch. When the Dutch navy triumphantly towed the *Royal Charles* down the Medway the King's libido went out with the tide. According to Pepys, he had not been able to keep an erection except by masturbation: 'The King's greatest pleasure hath been with his fingers, being able to do no more,' he scribbled salaciously.

In 1667, Charles and Barbara had an explosive row – perhaps their most serious to date – over Barbara's latest pregnancy. She already had five children by Charles, three boys and two girls.* Although she was not the most constant of companions, Barbara claimed this child was also the King's. Charles was not so sure. He had not, he said, slept with her in six months. Lord Halifax, who keenly observed the King's habits and character, noted that when it came to his lovers' infidelities, Charles generally 'had wit enough to suspect and he had wit enough not to care'. But with the matter of

---

* The children were: Lady Anne FitzRoy, 1661; Charles FitzRoy, 1662; Henry FitzRoy, 1663; Charlotte FitzRoy, 1664; George FitzRoy, 1665.

a child it was clear Charles *did* care. Barbara threatened that when the child was born she would bash its brains out in the palace and parade the King's other bastard children outside the palace gates. The row was so severe that Barbara moved out of Whitehall to stay with her friend Elizabeth, Lady Harvey, the flamboyant bisexual society hostess. There has been speculation that Barbara and Elizabeth became lovers. Though there is no evidence one way or the other, it is interesting that of all the friends she could have run to she chose Harvey. The row only ended when the King, as usual, backed down, went to Lady Harvey's and kneeled to ask forgiveness of his wayward lover.

Charles's behaviour here is quite peculiar. If he had truly cared for Barbara and suffered the pangs of jealousy when faced with evidence of infidelity, he might have found reason to end the relationship. Halifax wrote, 'It is a heresy, according to a true lover's creed, even to forgive an infidelity, or the appearance of it. Love of ease will not do it where the heart is much engaged.' In other words, a true lover would not have forgiven as easily as Charles. If Halifax is right, then Charles was not in love with Barbara but merely lusted for her.

As it happened, no child materialised from the pregnancy; either Barbara was mistaken and she was not pregnant or the baby did not survive into childhood – there is no record to tell us. Charles was not a man to dwell for long on domestic mishaps; he turned for distraction to one of his passions, the theatre.

Mercifully, the great fire had not destroyed the theatres, for they had been built to the west of the city so as to be convenient for the rich of St James's and Pall Mall. In the theatres was to be found amusement and escapism. The company Charles himself sponsored, the King's Company, had its home in a new state-of-the art theatre in Drury Lane (on the site of the present Theatre Royal), while the Duke's Men, sponsored by the Duke of York, were a stone's throw away at Lincoln's Inn Fields.

With the vogue for female actors, the theatre had become a hunting ground for the King, his brother James and their fellow rakes.

According to Elizabeth Knepp, a member of the King's Company, the King had first been smitten by Elizabeth Weaver, another member of his Company, shortly after the theatres reopened in 1661. When tired of the choices available among the latest batch of young women acting as attendants to the Queen, the Duchess of York or other ladies of the court, or when all those they wished to seduce had been seduced (or, like Frances Stuart, had resisted), the new corps of actresses, often little better than prostitutes with some singing or dancing ability, were there for variation. The more professional sort of female actor was often available for après-theatre fun, as the world they inhabited was one of bohemian tastes, where what would later be termed bourgeois habits were spurned and multiple partners accepted.

Thanks to a series of events designed to depress the royal spirits, those who habitually searched out new blood to distract the royal loins now turned to the belles of the stage. Among those who habitually procured such new delights were the Duke of Buckingham, Sir Charles Berkeley, Baptist May and the King's servant William Chiffinch.

Chiffinch was so omniscient, so omnipresent, that his role was known far and wide. Samuel Pepys knew him well and wrote about Chiffinch taking him into the King's private rooms to view a 'variety of brave pictures'. It was Chiffinch who had informed Barbara that Frances Stuart was entertaining a suitor in her rooms in Whitehall Palace while pretending she had a headache.

Looking around for possible young flesh for the jaded King, the pimps went into action. According to Pepys, Buckingham had become the leading light in the procuring exercise. He had a motive: he and his cousin Barbara had fallen out. She had not promoted his interests sufficiently with the King and Buckingham felt it would be better if her influence were terminated by the installation of a younger and more malleable model.

The pimps whittled a list of young actresses down to three. For a while, the King dallied with a dancer named Jane Roberts, though their acquaintance seems to have lasted very little time. That left two contenders. Buckingham favoured a young actress from the Duke's Men named Mary Davis. She was known as Moll, or according to some sources, Mall. Moll was reputed to be the illegitimate daughter of Thomas Howard, 3rd Earl of Berkshire, who was said to have helped pimp his own daughter to the King. According to another account, she was the daughter of a blacksmith employed by the earl on his estate.

Moll was aged about nineteen and, although billed as an actress, was what we might call a song and dance girl. She lodged with one of the company's two leaders, the venerable Poet Laureate Sir William Davenant, who according to John Aubrey was Shakespeare's unacknowledged son. This was quite possibly true, for Shakespeare was known to have had several illegitimate children. True or not, the rumour suited Davenant very well. It amused him to report that people thought he wrote with 'the very spirit of Shakespeare'. Davenant's personal taste in theatre stretched from Shakespearean tragedy to lewd contemporary comedy. He therefore recognised the importance of his young lodger to help fill the seats. Moll's chief attributes were her great figure, fantastic singing voice, a wonderful ability to dance provocatively and her easy morals. In 1667 she was the chief female draw for the Duke's Men.

Moll had a rival, for there was a faction among the King's pimps who favoured the female star in the King's Company – and anyhow, it was better His Majesty had a choice. This was Nell Gwyn, who was not as beautiful as Moll but made up for it in her character and her great ability not only to dance and sing but to make an audience laugh. The two actresses were rivals for the hearts of the London theatregoing crowd.

Those in the know made comparisons between the rivals. On 7 March, Samuel Pepys – who was addicted to the theatre – went to see the Duke's Men and reported on Moll's performance dressed in boy's clothing, that fashion of the day embraced even by the Queen: 'Little Miss Davis did dance a jig at the end of the play ... and the

truth is there is no comparison with Nell's dancing the other day at
the King's house in boy's clothes and this, this being infinitely beyond
the other.' In August, Pepys confided to his diary that he and his wife
were greatly pleased by Moll dancing dressed as a shepherd.

Her opponent in the competition to be the King's mistress was
younger, at just seventeen. There are many varying accounts of Nell
Gwyn's early life. Although she is one of the most famous characters
in English history, very little is known about her for certain. She is
variously reported as having been born in London, Oxford and
Hereford in 1650, although her descendant Charles Beauclerk has
ungallantly suggested she might have been born in 1642. It is possible
she was a teenage prostitute, following her father's death and the
family's descent into poverty. Her father may have been a soldier.
Some credibility is given to this by an entry in official papers according to which a Rose Gwyn, who was likely to have been Nell's sister,
petitioned one of the Duke of York's officials to help gain her release
from Newgate gaol where she had been thrown for theft. She wrote
that her father had 'lost everything in service to the late King'. This
evidently worked, for Rose was released and went on to a career as a
prostitute before marrying a highwayman.

Nell's mother was reduced to running a bawdy house, a brothel, in
Covent Garden, thereby making London Nell's most likely birthplace. In taunts from a fellow actress in 1667, Nell retorted that she
had been 'born in a bawdyhouse' and 'brought up in a playhouse'. In
another version of the tale she said she was 'brought up in a bawdy
house to fill strong waters for the guests'. Through an aunt who had
the franchise to sell fruit and refreshments in the King's Company
playhouse, young Nell left the brothel and secured a job selling fruit
to the patrons of the theatre, hence her abiding reputation as an
orange-seller.

The Restoration theatres where Nell found employment were
rumbustious places, entertainment venues where young actresses
could be bought for very little and where, occasionally, dramatic art
of the highest order might be experienced. All social classes went, as

did all types of man and woman, from the lewd and loose to the keen follower of the dramatic arts. In the pit, women wore their fashionable visors, or masks, and flirted wildly with the grandees in the boxes. The fruit-sellers not only plied their primary trade but also ran messages between the patrons and, as often as not, sold their own flesh as readily as a peach – the only difference being that the flesh of a peach was more likely to blush.

Charles had inherited his mother's love of theatre and had quickly restored the right to stage plays in London, rescinding the ban imposed under Cromwell's rule. Exhibiting very advanced taste, he allowed women on the stage for the first time. There was, as was often the way with Charles, an ulterior motive, for he loved to watch young women sing and dance. Among those to take advantage of the new dramatic freedom was Buckingham, keen to stretch his literary muscles. He rewrote an old John Fletcher play, *The Chances*. The work was put on by the King's Company at Drury Lane, where it was a great success, with Samuel Pepys' mistress Mrs Knepp in a lead role. Pepys recorded that she performed 'All Night I Weep' and 'sang it admirably'.

The theatre served a secondary function. The men who ran the newly opened theatres – Davenant at the Duke of York's and Killigrew at the King's Company – were chosen not merely because of their theatrical experience (though both had much), but because they were royalists through and through. Under them, the theatres became propaganda vehicles for the monarchy. Since the death of Charles I, royalist sympathisers had understood the power of a well-run public relations machine that could reinforce the idea of society being kept in order by having a divinely appointed king at its head. For all the Restoration theatre's fun and frolics, it had a more serious intent. Besides tales of cuckoldry and seduction, men like John Dryden wrote monarchist panegyrics in heroic couplets.

The Wits came to consider themselves not only as poets and playwrights, but as men entrusted with a tradition. As Vivian de Sola Pinto has put it:

The Wits were something a great deal more interesting than mere courtiers. They were the inheritors of the great tradition of the literary and Bohemian tavern clubs of the days of Shakespeare and Ben Jonson, which they handed on to their successors, the circle of Addison and Steele at the beginning and that of Johnson and Goldsmith in the middle of the eighteenth century.[1]

Perhaps this is right. But one must not get too carried away with the notion of the genius of such men. They were mostly nobly born amateurs, who turned their hand as readily to a game of cards or an evening of debauchery as to poetry or drama. Their collective merit should be judged in this light. A word of warning came from Charles Whibley:

> This union of poetry with the court had one evil result. It involved literature in an atmosphere of coxcombry. Social eminence appeared the very inspiration of Apollo. To deserve the bays nothing was necessary save to be a person of honour. All the resources of eloquent flattery were exhausted in the praise of noblemen who condescended to poetry. Criticism was thus poisoned at its source.[2]

Like their behaviour, the Wits' plays were mostly designed to shock. In the prologue to his play of bad behaviour, *The Man of Mode*, George Etherege implores the audience: 'Why should you, when we hold it, break the glass?'

As for the art itself, the writing of plays, the characters were often no more than versions of their creators, drawn as the writers imagined themselves to be. Etherege's *The Man of Mode* opens as two men of wit and fashion get ready to sally out to seduce new lovers, dump old ones, and have some fun by playing with the affections and hopes of other characters. The character Mr Doriment is often taken to stand for the Earl of Rochester, with that of Mr Medley being Charles Sedley, both notorious rakes.

For the times, what these unlikely *littérateurs* were doing was revolutionary stuff: they were writing about sex as an aspect of human activity that should be unconstrained by church or state, to be engaged in freely and, if necessary, outside marriage. Take away the baroque plot lines and what the rakes were expressing was in its essence the modern age. By his own leadership in transgression and immorality, Charles was unwittingly leading the charge into a moral enlightenment (or, if the reader chooses, a moral quagmire).

It was not all plain sailing; within a century, the work of the Restoration playwrights would receive a harsh critique from the stage of the Theatre Royal itself, spoken by the best actor of the following age:

> The wits of Charles found easier ways to fame,
> Nor wish'd for Jonson's art, or Shakespeare's flame;
> Themselves they studied; as they felt, they writ;
> Intrigue was plot, obscenity was wit.

These lines, written by Samuel Johnson and spoken by David Garrick at the opening of the Theatre Royal, Drury Lane in, 1747, pinpointed the self-obsessed heart of a sexual revolution. The Restoration comedies promulgated a moral code that was entirely self-serving and self-absorbed – or as the title of a play from a later century has it, 'It Pays to Advertise'.[3] Johnson, being nobody's fool, saw right through the enterprise. But what made these plays so revolutionary was not their amorality but the fact that they took sexuality, not love, to be central to human experience and worth writing about. Sexuality was now seen, albeit in elite circles, as a part of the human experience to be publicly celebrated.

In this sexually charged hothouse, young Nell Gwyn exhibited a rare personal quality – she had panache. This was the quality the contemporary wits and playwrights strove to exude in their own lives and struggled to impose upon the personalities of their fictional men-about-town. Nell's panache was not studied or learned, nor did it depend, as did that of the Wits, on a clever turn of phrase. Nell's panache existed *au naturel,* flowing from her irrepressible good nature and sense of fun, allied to a quick mind and the love of a good joke.

Her personality brought her to the attention of Thomas Killigrew, the King's Company's owner-manager. Killigrew decided to give Nell's exuberance a chance on the stage. The actors John Lacy and Charles Hart, the latter a great-nephew of Shakespeare, took on the task of schooling the ingénue in the performing arts. Soon Nell's full qualities were revealed and first Lacy and then Hart became her lovers. Nell was said to be illiterate and, though this seems unlikely for an actor, it is possible she learned her lines by repetition from colleagues. Unfortunately, straight acting was not among her talents. In Dryden's successful tragedy, *The Indian Emperor,* she played Montezuma's daughter, to unfavourable reviews. But unlike Moll Davis, she was something more than a song and dance act. In a comic role her personality and natural gaiety illuminated the stage. She became a great comic actress. Dryden thought so highly of her comedic talent that he wrote a series of parts for her.

Nell became a star and soon moved from her dingy lodgings in Coal Yard Alley to the south end of Drury Lane, just off the Strand and around the corner from some of the most fashionable houses in London. And there on May Day 1667, Samuel Pepys spied her when he came to see the celebrations at the May Pole, recently re-erected on the site after the Restoration, having like all the others in the country been pulled down by the Puritans. In a scene that gives us mid-seventeenth century London in all its spontaneous jollity and village-like community, the diarist sees another observer, young Nell, standing outside her front door in her 'smock sleeves and bodice', looking 'a mighty pretty thing'.

A portrait by Simon Verelst depicts Nell as having cute rather than classically good looks, her dress having slipped somehow completely below her breasts, which are concealed only by the folds of her shift, above which the blush of a nipple rises like a painted sun to greet the viewer.

But what would she have been like if, instead of paying for sex with girls, one of the rakes had paid for her education, as Buckingham had done with a farmhand's boy who showed promise?

The pimps weighed up Moll's looks against Nell's personality, and when it all came down to it, money was what mattered. The intermediary selected by Buckingham *et al* to secure Nell for the King was one of Charles's former lovers, Nell's friend and colleague, the celebrated singer Mrs Knight. Born Mary Anne Povey, Mrs Knight was the country's foremost female singer, having 'the greatest reach of any English woman'. In the strange logic of court intrigue, this talented former royal mistress was considered ideal to act as procuress for the next generation of mistresses.

Nell stipulated that if she was going to give up her career to become the King's mistress, she required £500 to ease the burden on her artistic soul. This was thought far too much and a sign that the girl was getting above herself. Moll in contrast nobly accepted the royal appointment for £200, though much more expensive presents soon followed, making Nell's requirement look cheap by comparison.

While the King was playing with Moll, Nell had been playing both on and off the stage with Hart. They became celebrated for their acting together. Playwrights wrote for them and their renown grew until in 1667 they reached the zenith of their fame with a play written by Dryden. It was called *Secret Love, or the Maiden Queen*, and in it the parts of the lovers, a courtier and a servant girl, were designed by Dryden to be played by Hart and Nell. When the play opened on 2 March, the real-life lovers sparred in scenes of banter reminiscent of *Much Ado About Nothing*, and became the sensation of London. On a night when the King went to see them play, Pepys, his fellow theatre addict, was also in the audience. 'There is a comical part done by Nell, which is Florimell, which I can never hope to see the like done again, by man or woman,' gushed the diarist. Nell had London at her feet – and she was only seventeen.

The catastrophe of the Dutch raid on the Medway in the summer of 1667 put a sudden stop to Nell's meteoric rise. In reaction to the military defeat, the theatres were closed. Nell was soon in financial trouble, as were her lover Hart and all those who depended upon the theatre for their livelihood. But Nell was not one to wilt under pressure. She looked for help to those redoubtable supporters of the theatre, the Wits. Through the Earl of Rochester, who had a town house in Lincoln's Inn Fields near the Duke's Playhouse, she was given a means of rescuing her financial position, if not her reputation. Rochester suggested that his friend and fellow theatre fancier Charles Sackville, Lord Buckhurst (later Earl of Dorset) should support Nell in turn for sexual favours. Sackville was a man of great estates and greater good humour, a patron of poets and a poet himself. His most notorious misdeed had occurred in 1663 when he, his brother and some others killed a man, claiming they had mistaken him for a robber. As was the way with the aristocracy, they were not brought to trial.

Although she and Charles Hart were living as man and wife, Nell took up Sackville's offer of £100 a year to live with him in a rented house in Epsom. Sackville invited along Sir Charles Sedley, another notable judge of young female talent.

Pepys became so overcome with curiosity that he and Mrs Pepys went to stay at the inn next door to the *ménage à trois*, ostensibly to take the waters. 'My Lord Buckhurst and Nelly is lodged at the house next door,' he reported. 'And Charles Sedley with them and keep a merry house. Poor girl, I pity her.'

Sedley was a friend of the Duke of Buckingham, a member of the Circle of Wits and a man without scruple. The least of his misdemeanours, it was said, was to have burned down Harefield House, the home of his relative Lady Chandos, by smoking in bed. He was a young man of title and learning and never had enough money. It was said that Sedley delighted the King because unlike all the other Wits at the court, despite his comparative lack of wealth, he never asked for anything.[4]

Among the Wits' favourite watering holes around Covent Garden and Holborn was the Cock Tavern in Bow Street, a thoroughfare of mixed and uncertain status. It had been the site of Sedley's most notorious public performance. One summer evening in 1663, accompanied by Sackville and Sir Thomas Ogle, Sedley had decided he should entertain the people in the street. Blind drunk, he and his companions went out on a balcony and mimed various positions of sexual intercourse. When this had attracted a crowd said to be one thousand strong, Sedley and Sackville briefly withdrew and reappeared stark naked. Uproar ensued while Sedley preached to the crowd, dipped his penis in his glass and then drank from it, before refilling the glass and drinking the King's health.[5] A riot ensued. Brought to court, Sedley was bound over to keep the peace on personal surety of five thousand pounds. Ogle and Sackville were let off with a caution. There was then no law covering lewd or indecent acts in a public place.

Sedley, a habitual philanderer, was married. His wife, Katherine, became mentally ill, developing the delusion that she was the Queen, or at least a queen, and demanding to be addressed as 'Your Majesty'. As her illness progressed, she agreed to live with an order of English Benedictine nuns at Ghent. Sedley was delighted and ensured his wife's acceptance by the nuns by agreeing to give the convent £400 a year to help them clear their debts. When poor Katherine entered the convent, she was tricked by a priest acting on her husband's orders into giving up her wonderful jewellery. The discovery of the loss of her jewels, emblems of her royal status, distressed Katherine even more. But her husband was now without the encumbrance of a mentally sick wife.[6] Later, Sedley's daughter, also called Katherine, became mistress to the Duke of York. Sedley was shocked by the affair; he knew only too well the manner in which men could abuse young women.[7]

While the wild triumvirate made merry in Epsom, hurried peace negotiations were under way. The diplomatist Henry Coventry and the parliamentarian Denzil, Lord Hollis, were dispatched to Breda to negotiate the best terms they could with the Dutch. When the treaty was signed on 31 July, both sides got some of what they wished, but not all. The weakness of the English position forced them to agree to lift restrictions in trade, including changes in navigation acts, to favour Dutch shipping. In return, England retained New York and New Jersey, which had been taken from the Dutch some years before. The English would much rather have swapped the American outposts for more lucrative properties in the East Indies but the Dutch declined the exchange. Following the treaty, England was a much-weakened power.

All was not well at court, either. The King's attempts to impregnate the Queen seemed to have faded. It was thought the waters of Tunbridge Wells might have somehow bestowed fecundity, but they did not. Although a relationship based on firm affection, the royal marriage remained unblessed by an heir. Charles was in need of new distractions to stop him from becoming withdrawn and out of sorts – something recognised by those who pimped for him.

As the summer turned to autumn, Barbara juggled her rope dancer, Jacob Hall, and the King. In Epsom, Nell Gwyn's famous charms could not prevent the taste of the spa's delights turning decidedly brackish. The lewd household split up and by the end of autumn Nell was back at the King's Company, looking for work. It was said that Charles had to bribe Sackville by repaying him the money he had spent on 'entertaining' Nell before he would allow her to resume her life in London. According to another version, Charles went so far as to elevate Sackville for his kind deed, making him Earl of Middlesex.

When Davenant gave Nell the lead in a play called *Flora's Vagaries*, she was glad to return to the stage, but found that audiences were not what they had been. The reason was a rival draw at the Duke's theatre in the comely shape of young Moll Davis, playing the lead part in *The Rivals*, a play adapted by Davenant from the original version, *The Two Noble Kinsmen*, by Fletcher. The King watched Moll dance a lively jig during the play and was impressed by his lover's famously beautiful legs. But he also was spending time at Drury Lane watching Moll's rival as star of the London stage, Nell Gwyn – a young woman with the personality and talent not only to win over an audience but to beguile a king.

13

THEATRICAL RIVALS

The year 1668 began with scandal and proceeded to rioting, with mobs on the streets of London protesting at the licentiousness of the court.

In January, gossip spread regarding one of the King's mistresses. It was reported that Moll Davis had quit the stage to become Charles's full-time concubine. The irrepressible Pepys learned the news from actress Elizabeth Knepp. She informed him that a house had been furnished for the actress, 'the king being in love with' Moll. Soon Moll was seen sporting a ring rumoured to have cost the enormous sum of £600. As for Nell Gwyn, Elizabeth revealed that it had been some time since the King had sent for her.

And so it looked as if Moll had well and truly won the battle of the actresses, although in January the King was reported by Samuel Pepys to have sent 'several times for Nelly'. It isn't known if these invitations were merely for the purpose of being entertained by Nell's singing and dancing, or for something more intimate, but it's thought that Nell was not yet the King's mistress.

In the New Year, the court had made another of its periodic visits to Tunbridge Wells, the spa town forty miles from London famous for its medicinal mineral waters and bracing social scene. The King and

Queen had a particular motive in going to 'the Wells' as the waters were said to have properties that encouraged conception.

While the Queen still hoped for pregnancy, there were entertainments to divert the royal party from their previous disappointments. The theatre companies had learned that it was good for business to put on shows at Tunbridge Wells during the summer season. Even during the winter, the stars would turn up to give solo performances or appear with much reduced companies of players. And so in the cold days of early 1668, Moll Davis went to the Wells. She had a song-and-dance routine entitled 'My Lodging is on the Cold Ground', which she performed in front of the King and Queen in such a brazenly come-hither manner that the Queen got up and left the room. The King also rose and took Moll to bed. John Downes, the theatre's prompt, in his memoirs remarked that the performance had been so effective it had 'raised the fair songstress from the cold ground to the bed royal'.

The King's love life was proceeding so urgently that Pepys found it hard to keep up. On 14 January, he recorded the gossip on the previous night's entertainment at a command performance in front of the King. According to the diarist's informants, various gentlemen and ladies of the court, including the Duke of Monmouth, performed a play called *The Indian Emperor*. Among those present were the King, 'my lady Castlmayne' and Moll, who flashed about the famous jewel-encrusted ring – now said to have cost £700 – while telling everyone it was a present from the King. Pepys relays the gossip that the King only had eyes for Moll – 'the most impertinent slut in all the world'.[1]

Throughout the play – a comedy – Barbara never laughed once and appeared melancholy and out of humour – as well she might, for she was being upstaged and humiliated by 'a homely jade' whose only talent was to dance 'beyond any thing in the world'.[2] Worse, at the age of twenty-seven, Barbara feared she was in danger of being supplanted in the royal bedroom by a strumpet who was not yet twenty. Even more intolerable for Barbara was the possibility that she was being supplanted not just by one young strumpet from Covent Garden, but by two. When Moll followed the King and Queen to Tunbridge Wells to take the waters, Nell Gwyn took the hint and went too.

On 16 January a much greater scandal broke out. It involved Anna, Lady Shrewsbury, her husband, and the King's great favourite, George Villiers, Duke of Buckingham. Proving to be among the wildest of all the women at court and already with a reputation as a *femme fatale*, Anna embarked on an affair with Buckingham. Despite the King having let it be known that duelling should stop, Lord Shrewsbury felt his reputation was so publicly on the line that he had little option but to challenge Buckingham.

Unlike the very public relationship between the wife and her lover, the duel was arranged well away from the eyes of society. It took place on the common at Barn Elms, across the Thames from the estates of the Bishop of London at Fulham Palace. Anna is said to have attended dressed as a page and holding her lover's horse, but this is a romantic invention. The fight was an intense and bloody matter. Shrewsbury and Buckingham were each attended by two seconds who joined in. On Buckingham's side, a second called Jenkins was killed, while one of Shrewsbury's seconds, Sir John Talbot, was badly injured. Buckingham caught Shrewsbury on the right breast with his sword, thrusting so hard his blade penetrated upwards through the shoulder, adding injury to insult. After her grievously wounded husband was carried from the field, Anna and Buckingham were said to have made love so hastily that Buckingham still wore the shirt splattered with the blood of his adversary. This, too, is merely a good yarn.

News of the duel caused uproar in London. 'This will make the world think the King hath good councillors about him, when the Duke of Buckingham, the greatest man about him, is a fellow of no more sobriety than to fight about a whore,' wrote Pepys. The great diarist expressed hope that the upshot would be that some better man would be brought into government to replace Buckingham.

He also poured disdain on the way government was conducted, remarking that when the King had been brought notice of the impending duel he had entrusted the Duke of Albemarle to ensure Buckingham was restrained, yet somehow the order had not been carried out. Commenting on this, Pepys wrote: 'And so between both, as everything else of the greatest moment do, do fall between two stools.'

The King made his choice; nothing would be done. As usual, he merely shrugged and pardoned all involved, citing the 'eminent services heretofore done by most of the persons who were engaged in the late duel'. Buckingham not only escaped the Tower, he continued to hold his position in government. Despite his *laissez-faire* attitude to the duel, Charles undoubtedly knew it had caused harm to the government, for he gave an assurance that 'on no pretense whatsoever any pardon shall hereafter be granted to any person whatsoever for killing of any man in any duel.'[3] Of course, Charles was in a bind; if he chose to make an issue of the actions of the richest and most influential person in the land, then he would force a crisis in the government. Arlington would thus become the natural choice to succeed as Prime Minister, something Charles did not wish for as Arlington was a Francophobe.

With his poise undiminished, Buckingham attended the state opening of Parliament on 10 February and presented a bill for religious tolerance towards non-conformists – a long-held interest – which, although the King used his traditional opening speech to counsel tolerance, met with stiff resistance. The implacable opposition of the politicians and the established church would within weeks have violent repercussions. The problem for Charles was that he simply did not have people in his government capable of persuading Parliament that religious toleration might be a wise course of action. Buckingham, in one of his many imaginative solutions, had once suggested bribing the entire upper and lower houses.

Buckingham became stronger again, thanks in great part to his brilliant political networking. Charles recognised his abilities to such an extent that he allowed him to assume the status of de facto Prime Minister. This so alarmed Charles's astute sister Henrietta that she wrote from Paris expressing her concern. Charles wrote back, 'I assure you that my Lord of Buckingham does not govern affairs here.'[4] He went on to say that he had little doubt that Clarendon – now in exile in France – would discredit the King, though it was Clarendon who was the author of the King's troubles.

On 18 March, five weeks after Buckingham's brazen appearance at the opening of Parliament, Shrewsbury died from the wound to his chest. With haste that shocked the most jaded courtier, Buckingham moved his adversary's widow into his country house. Buckingham's wife Anne (daughter of Parliamentary hero Sir Thomas Fairfax) objected, flatly stating that she couldn't share her home with her husband's strumpet. Buckingham instantly agreed, stating that that was why he had arranged for Anne's coach to be made ready to take her to her father's.

In an odd way, Buckingham's wild behaviour went some way to prove his jest that the King knew nothing about affairs of state. Charles's passive reaction to Buckingham killing a man and then installing his widow in his home could have been construed as giving Buckingham the right to say to his friends at court, 'See, the King does nothing!'

Meanwhile, Charles's extended family was thriving. His eldest son, the Duke of Monmouth, though only nineteen, was already such a firm favourite that his father made him captain of the Life Guards. Moll Davis became pregnant by Charles and he installed her in a fine house in Suffolk Street, off Pall Mall. Barbara was strong and clever and had survived many changes in the sexual micro-climate inside Whitehall Palace, but the King was undoubtedly tiring of his demanding, overbearing chief mistress. Teenage actresses were much more fun. Charles decided one was not enough. Why not have both Moll *and* Nell?

On Easter Monday, 23 March, the bawdy house riots broke out. These were a more or less annual event which had been taking place

for decades, in which the London apprentices used the annual holi-
day to let off steam by attacking brothels and sometimes tearing them
down. It might seem odd that brothels should be a particular object of
scorn or hatred for apprentices, but apart from any moral or religious
impetus, apprentices had no money to spend in such places and were
also forbidden to marry. Denied what came naturally, their frustration
turned to bile. Usually, these riots were seen as 'the ancient adminis-
tration of justice' and any punishment meted out by the courts was
lenient.[5] But in Easter Week 1668, something new took place; the riots
were much bigger in size and longer in duration and the authorities
chose to crack down hard on the ringleaders. Some force greater
than usual was propelling the riots and the official reaction.

On the first day of the riots, small crowds of apprentices gathered
in Poplar, a seafaring town on the Thames to the east of the City. In
the seventeenth century Poplar was famous as the birthplace of 'The
King's Pirate', Sir John Mucknell, a former East India Company
captain who became a royalist privateer during the civil wars.
Charles, then Prince of Wales, had knighted Mucknell for his services. The seaport was also known for the quantity of its brothels,
catering for the hordes of seamen who lodged in the port between
voyages.

The first brothel to be attacked was one owned by Damaris Page,
'the great bawd of the seamen'. At first this was seen as signifying
nothing more than the usual Easter reaction of apprentices to the
seamier side of life around the capital. But the next day the crowds
swelled to several hundred across other parishes inside the city,
attacking brothels in Shoreditch, Moorfields and Smithfield. It
became clear that the riots were taking on a political edge, with
many tradesmen joining the apprentices. The leaders carried green
banners, the symbolic colour of the Levellers, the proto-democratic
campaign group, while others were rumoured to be former
Cromwellian soldiers. The crowds were organised into companies
with commanders at their heads. Within days, it was reported, up to
forty thousand were involved. Judging from the details in the charges

brought against alleged ringleaders, these numbers were gross exaggerations, but many hundreds, and perhaps thousands, descended on several parishes over several days.[6]

In the parish of St Leonard's in Shoreditch, a crowd of four hundred gathered. Court records state that they were armed 'in a warlike manner with swords, halfe-pykes, halberts, long staves, clubs and other arms', gathered 'traitorously prepared, ordered [to] raise public war against the Lord now King'.[7] According to the indictment against the alleged ringleaders, pulling down the bawdy houses was a 'pretence' for something more serious and political. The King's Life Guard, under its commanding officer, Sir Philip Howard, was called out to quell the riot. When Howard arrived at St Leonard's, he was met with a hail of stones. Sir Philip looked so grand, some of the crowd asked if he was the Duke of York. When false word travelled round that he was, more missiles were thrown. The protestors had no fondness for the King's brother as there were rumours he was secretly a Catholic.

And here was the heart of the matter: the crowd had not only gathered to destroy bawdy houses but to voice their dissatisfaction with the lack of progress on 'liberty of conscience' for Protestant non-conformists, the very reform Buckingham had recently tried to get through Parliament, supported by the King, but which was denied by both houses of Parliament and the established church. According to legal reports, some rioters said that if liberty of conscience were not granted, then the following May Day would be 'bloody'. The rioters threatened they would go so far as to pull down Whitehall Palace itself, the biggest and grandest bawdy house of all, and under suspicion as the centre of widespread Catholicism.

Similar scenes were repeated across the city, followed by audacious raids on Finsbury gaol and New Prison to release incarcerated protestors. Along the way, more bawdy houses were pulled down or set on fire. Among them were those of two brothel keepers who paid fees to the Duke of York, who afterwards joked about his loss of revenue, as they paid him £15 a year in liquor licences. The riots had an undoubted edge of grievance against a King who had failed to bring in the freedom of religious expression he had promised prior to the Restoration.

The riots were put down severely and a group of ringleaders was accused of high treason, an offence punishable by the hideous torture of hanging, drawing and quartering. The chief author of the charge of treason was the Lord Chief Justice, Sir John Kelyng, a man who made George Jeffreys, 'The Hanging Judge', appear like Rumpole of the Bailey. Kelyng had a deserved reputation for harsh sentencing and for massaging the law to suit the desired result. In 1660, he had participated in a secret undertaking before the trials of the regicides in which the judges agreed to relax the rules on witness testimony, making it easier to convict. The following year he had imprisoned John Bunyan for preaching. Most infamously, in 1662 Kelyng had presided over the trial for treason, on trumped-up charges, of Sir Harry Vane. Only months before the bawdy house case, Kelyng had himself been tried by Parliament for the outrageous practice of fining and imprisoning juries, a charge that Parliament quietly allowed to drop after making some general recommendations on how trials should be conducted. Clearly, Kelyng was just the man for a sticky case, and when called to find a suitably crushing charge against the rioters he came up with 'constructive waging of war against the King'.[8]

The word 'constructive' indicates that this was an example of the practice whereby novel extensions to laws are created in order to stretch their remit beyond their original scope. As has been pointed out by Alfred Knight, the 'constructive' approach is 'one of the law's most useful frauds'.[9] Rising to the challenge, Kelyng construed the bawdy house rioting to be war against the king and hence treason. Fifteen men were put on trial; four were found guilty and hanged, drawn and quartered. The hard-pressed people of London would have been only too aware that while a duke might get away with murder, the poor were crushed for daring to make their dissatisfaction known. As the great social historian Fernand Braudel has pointed out, 'Long before the 17th century rulers had learned that they survived not because they doled out justice but because they ensured peace in the land.'[10]

Meanwhile, the satirists were busy taking aim at a favourite target. Several satirical broadsides appeared attacking the Countess of Castlemaine. A satire called 'The Poor-Whores Petition' appeared in the names of two of the brothel madams whose establishments had been destroyed, Mother Cresswell and Damaris Page, and was addressed to the countess. It was extremely vicious and wildly funny.

The cod petition from the 'Undone Company of Poor Distressed Whores, Bawds, Pimps and Panders' addressed itself to 'The most splendid, illustrious, serene and eminent Lady of Pleasure, The Countess of Castlemaine'. The petitioners claimed that through the actions of 'rude and ill-bred boys' they had lost the practice of their 'venerial pleasures – A trade in which your Ladyship hath great Experience'. The petitioners pleaded for speedy relief from the rioters 'that a stop may be put unto them before they come to your honour's palace, and bring contempt upon your worshipping of Venus, the great Goddess whom we all adore'. It went on to take a sideswipe at Barbara's Catholicism, before in conclusion promising in return for her help to the 'inferior whores' to promote Barbara's 'honour, safety and interest'.

The best evidence for the petition being a fake is that 'Mother Cresswell' wasn't just any brothel madam – she was the King's brothel madam, as if by royal appointment. The scandal sheet *London the wicked citie* reported that Cresswell had received the 'highest accolade'. According to the Chevalier Phineas de Charles, 'His Majesty personally honoured her with his presence and deigned to inspect her house ... he saw that she had established a sound organisation which had administered network of emissaries and spies in England ... as well as in France.' So the good Mother Cresswell used her establishment as a centre for gossip and intelligence that might be useful to the King. She must have had a very particular and select clientele. The report was as good as placing a royal warrant over the door.

This portrait by court painter Sir Peter Lely captures a great deal of the King's character: quizzical, humorous, restless; anxious to be up and away from the painter's gaze, off to sail his latest yacht, ride to the races at Newmarket or seduce a new lady-in-waiting.

© Private collection/Bridgeman Images

Jane Lane with Charles II disguised as her servant during his escape from the Roundheads after defeat at the Battle of Worcester. Charles credited Jane with saving his life and never forgot the risks she ran for him. Their adventures became the stuff of royalist legend.

Isaac Fuller © National Portrait Gallery, London

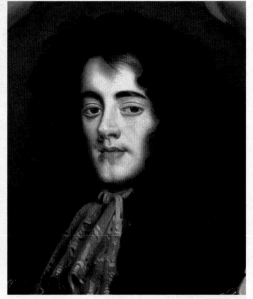

Lucy Walter, the 'brown, beautiful, bold but insipid creature' who gave birth to the first of Charles's illegitimate sons, James, later Duke of Monmouth. She was the King's first and possibly only real love but was vilified by his friends and forced to give up her son.

© This painting is part of the Pembrokeshire County Art Collection, held at Scolton Manor and is on public display in the Manor House

James Scott, 1st Duke of Monmouth, was the first of Charles II's many illegitimate children. His mother was Lucy Walter. He was the King's favourite son but caused chaos when he claimed the right to succession over his uncle James.

Peter Lely © Private collection/Photo © Philip Mould Ltd, London/Bridgeman Images

Barbara Villiers, Countess Castlemaine, Duchess of Cleveland, was Charles II's most flamboyant mistress. It was the fashion for ladies to be portrayed as the penitent sinner, Mary Magdalene. Scandalously, Barbara is portrayed holding her illegitimate child by the King, dressed not as the Magdalene but the Virgin Mary. *Peter Lely © Private collection/Photo © Philip Mould Ltd, London/Bridgeman Images*

Catherine, a Portuguese princess, arrived in England to marry Charles II in 1662, to discover that her honeymoon was to be spent under the same roof as the King's pregnant mistress. This set the tone for the unfortunate queen's marriage. *Dirk Stoop © National Portrait Gallery, London*

Upon her betrothal to Charles II, Catherine was given a grand send-off by her father, King John IV. She took part in a great procession around the Ribeira Palace on Lisbon's waterfront while the English fleet waited to carry her away to a new and unpredictable life.

© De Agostini Picture Library/G. Dagli Orti/ Bridgeman Images

James, Duke of York, the King's younger brother and heir to the throne. He was as eager a philanderer as his brother. His conversion to Catholicism destabilised the monarchy and threatened to lead to civil war. *Peter Lely © Royal Collection Trust © Her Majesty Queen Elizabeth II, 2014/ Bridgeman Images*

The statesman Edward Hyde, Earl of Clarendon, was Charles's most able adviser. But increasingly the King found Hyde's criticisms at odds with his own frivolous and playful temperament. When Hyde dared to criticise Charles's favourite mistress he had to go. *After Adriaen Hanneman © National Portrait Gallery, London*

Louis XIV of France, the Sun King. His secret payments to Charles II enabled Charles to rule largely without parliament and to live a life of pleasure as an absolute monarch. *Houasse, Rene Antoine (1645–1710) © Chateau de Versailles, France/Giraudon/Bridgeman Images*

Nell Gwyn rose from early life in a brothel to become the mistress of a king. Here she is portrayed as Venus, with her son by Charles II, Charles Beauclerk, playing the part of Cupid. The King had a painting of Nell, nude, hidden behind a secret sliding panel in his bedroom.

Theatrical star Mary 'Moll' Davis
vied with Nell Gwyn for the favours
of the King. Though she remained a
long-term royal mistress, she lacked
the wit and charm which made Nell
a royal favourite to the end.

*Jean Baptiste Monnoyer © The Trustees of the
Weston Park Foundation, UK/Bridgeman Images*

Frances Stuart posing as Britannia. It was
said of her that 'it was hardly possible
for a woman to have less wit and more
beauty'. But she had the will to keep the
lecherous king at bay for three years.

*Jacob Huysmans © Brooklyn Museum of Art, New York,
USA/Gift of Mrs. George C. Goodwin/Bridgeman Images*

Italian heiress Hortense Manchini was an
early candidate for the hand of Charles when
he was Prince of Wales. The match was
never made, but having grown into a strong-
willed beauty she left her husband and came
to London to seek out the man she had not
married many years before. *Jacob Ferdinand Voet ©
Private collection/Photo © Christie's Images/Bridgeman Images*

Louise de Kérouaille, the baby-faced Breton aristocrat who supplanted Barbara Castlemaine as Charles's chief mistress and acted as spy for the French King. Created Duchess of Portsmouth, her greed and her influence over Charles made her the most hated of all his mistresses. *Simon Peeterz Verelst © Royal Collection Trust © Her Majesty Queen Elizabeth II, 2014/Bridgeman Images*

Pepys recorded that he did not find the 'poor whores' satire amusing – a rare failure of humour no doubt connected to his lustful esteem for the woman he always referred to as 'My Lady Castelmaine'. Barbara cannot have been much pleased either. The satires surely contributed to the harsh treatment meted out by the law to the chief rioters.

It cannot have helped Barbara's mood that while she had to endure the satire of the brothel keepers' petition, the King's interest was increasingly elsewhere. With his brother, he continued to tour the theatres on the lookout for the latest young star to seduce. Among the willing were Elizabeth Farley and Beck Marshall, the latter said to be the daughter of a well-known divine. As these young women came and went, Charles remained particularly interested in Moll; she would continue to live in her St James's house for many years, and was to have a daughter by the King. The impure animal magnetism that drew Charles to this rather coarse young woman was not entirely slaked by her. By the early summer, his attentions had swerved more positively towards Nell Gwyn.

Nell was not above helping her cause along with the occasional piece of foul play. Gaining the King's favour solely by befriending him was not going to get her what she desired: a position as Charles's mistress above that of all the other actresses he had bedded, including Moll Davis. One day Nell learned that Moll was to spend the evening with the King and decided to stage a surprise. She invited Moll to tea that afternoon. In the morning she was said to have visited her friend Aphra Behn, the bisexual spy and author. Behn was a fascinating character; her poetry exhibited a disdain for traditional sexual restraint, with laudatory descriptions of heterosexual couplings and homosexual and lesbian relationships.[11] Politically, she was not so radical and was an active royalist, spying for the King in Holland. In 1666 she had gone to Antwerp where she rekindled an old affair with an exiled Cromwellian officer in order to gain inside knowledge of plans to launch an invasion intended to bring down the monarchy once again.

As the King did not bother to pay Behn for her services, she was put in debtor's prison. By the date when she was supposed to have helped Nell Gwyn's plan to sabotage her rival, she was perhaps yet to have been set free. But this would not have prevented Nell from visiting her. According to the story, Behn provided Gwyn with some jalap, a herb which acted as a powerful emetic. The jalap was baked into cakes, which were then offered to Moll. In the evening, after supper, Moll and the King retired to bed. At some stage during the evening Moll suffered the sudden and uncontrollable eruption her rival had planned. After that, relations between monarch and dancer cooled more than a degree or two.

The affair of the cakes provided wonderful copy for the writers of the many satires that circulated in the chapbooks,* always hungry for the latest stories of the King and his many mistresses. The fact that the King tolerated these scurrilous barbs exhibited his essential tolerance but also revealed a lack of concern about his position as the focal point of the nation's public life. If the monarchy could be reduced to gossip about the King's bed being fouled by an incontinent actress, where had the majesty gone?

From his time in exile, Charles seems to have learned much about the relationship between power and sex, but little about the link between power and majesty. He now spent so much time around the playhouses that theatre folk regarded him as one of their own, a fellow bohemian on whom they could play a prank. On the greater stage of the nation's affairs, Charles continued to play one of his other roles: that of the imperturbable monarch in the midst of a chaotic age. The fact that his own style of government was responsible for the chaos never seemed to cross his mind. However, he played the role of the unflappable and kindly king to such tremendous effect that many of the people, though far from all, were convinced by it.

---

* Chapbooks were cheap pamphlets, usually of only four pages, containing poems, ballads and stories, illustrated with woodcuts.

On 7 May, the Queen miscarried once more. She had carried the child for ten weeks. No satisfactory diagnosis of Catherine's inability to carry a child through to full term was possible then and none can be ascertained with any certainty now. Perhaps she had a genetic defect that allowed her to carry a child close to full term, only for it to miscarry. Another theory is that she took large doses of quinine, prescribed for pain or cramp. This would have been prescribed by the King's 'feverologist' Robert Talbor, who was known to have access to supplies of the bark of the cinchona tree, from which quinine is derived. In his published handbook *Pyretologia* (1672), Talbor's prescribing of quinine during pregnancy is described. Quinine in large quantities is known to have serious side effects and can lead to miscarriage. It is possible that the fate of the House of Stuart, and of the nation, hung on the notions of a dangerous quack doctor.

Whatever the cause of this latest miscarriage, the event was a cause of great sadness for both parents. Charles continued, after his fashion, to support his childless queen. No contemporary source tells us anything of the degree of pain felt by Catherine, nor how well she dealt with this recurring sorrow, but we know that as a matter of course she took comfort in religion and in the small coterie of friends her good judgement and a sense of fun had brought her, so we may speculate that she found some ease in these. We know better how Charles dealt with this renewed blow to his authority as a king and as a husband, as he buried his despair in the arms of his bohemian lovers.

The episode provided continuing ammunition for Buckingham, who moved on from schemes whereby the King would divorce or kidnap the Queen to wild notions of the King becoming polygamous. While he always rejected such schemes, Charles drifted ever further away in sentiment from his Queen. His thoughts strayed again to Frances Stuart, the beautiful girl who had rebuffed his advances and married the Duke of Richmond and Lennox. Charles had now forgiven Frances and when she contracted smallpox, he feared it would harm her looks.

He was so concerned about this that within hours of his wife mis-carrying, he wrote to his sister in Paris: 'I was at the Duchess of Richmond's, who you know I have not seen this twelve months ... She is not much marked with the smale pox ... and I hope she will not be much changed ...' Only after detailing his hopes and fears for Frances did Charles turn to his own domestic troubles: 'for my wife misscaried this morning and though I am troubled at it, yet I am glad that 'tis evident she was with childe, which I will not deny to you; till now, I did feare she was not capable of.'[12]

Charles seems to be suggesting here that during previous preg-nancies, Catherine had aborted very early but that this pregnancy had developed to a late stage. In his letter, he stated that the physi-cians intended to give Catherine a course of 'physique' which they said would make her 'holde faster next time'. This astonishingly frank letter displays Charles's odd ability to pour out his most private desires in great and immediate detail, while revealing that matters which should have caused him more immediate concern came like an afterthought added before his nib ran out of ink.

While the Queen was not always at the forefront of the King's thoughts, there were many others who were. Among them were the female players at the theatre in Drury Lane. And the King was almost always in their thoughts too, either as benefactor and patron – after all, he had made it possible for women to become actors – or as a figure to place in a play. After starring in a string of plays both good and bad – *The Virgin Martyr, The Mulberry Garden, Love Lies a-Bleeding* – Nell Gwyn took the lead in *An Evening's Love*, written by Dryden, with a part tailor-made for her. Nell's character, Jacinta, directs criticism at Wildblood, a womanising English gentleman: 'You dispatch your mistresses as fast as if you meant to o'errun all woman-kind,' she reproves, in a line surely directed at Charles. Replicating the King's infatuation with Nell, Wildblood likes to look 'downward' to his social inferiors for lovers. It seems remarkable that Dryden, who had just been appointed Poet Laureate in succession to Davenant, could deliberately poke such public fun at his benefactor.

As with the laxative incident, Dryden's lampoon reveals how Charles had become not so much a monarch as master of the revels, 'one of the lads', Good-time Charlie. Since Dryden was one of his favourites, and a doughty royal panegyrist, Charles took no offence. With his patron's approbation, Dryden had another hit on his hands. John Evelyn was on hand to lend a dissenting voice, finding the play very lewd and 'polluted by the licentious times'.

The licentiousness that so alarmed the endlessly mortified Evelyn spilled over from the stage into the pit and the boxes. On one memorable afternoon during a performance of Ben Jonson's *Catiline's Conspiracy*, one of the actresses performed her part while mimicking Elizabeth Harvey, the famous society hostess. Elizabeth lived the sort of life which naturally led to many interesting episodes. When she found her complicated bisexual love life constrained by the presence of her husband, the King kindly responded by sending him as ambassador to Constantinople. On that particular afternoon, Barbara was in the audience, having paid the actress to make fun of her friend, with whom she had fallen out. Why they were no longer friends is not known, though perhaps their newfound enmity might point to a cooling of ardour or to unrequited advances. Whatever the cause, more was to follow: when a character in the play asked what should be done with the character whose voice bore an uncanny similarity to that of Elizabeth Harvey, Barbara jumped up and, unrestrained by the presence of the King, shouted, 'Send her to Constantinople!'

In revenge, Elizabeth Harvey used her connections to have the offending actress thrown in prison. Barbara used her superior connection with the King to have the actress freed, and the impersonations of Lady Harvey continued. While attending a command performance, the King was shocked to see the offending actress pelted with oranges by thugs hired by the object of her derision.

Most likely Nell and Charles became lovers some time during 1668, though Nell did not become the King's paid-for mistress until

later. The event that may have led the King finally to make the move
is retold in several versions, relayed and exaggerated in the chapbooks sold by street vendors. The story goes that one afternoon when
Charles and his brother attended the King's Theatre, Nell was in the
adjoining box. This was unlikely to have been a coincidence, for as
a star member of the company she would have been able to ensure
she was seated where she wished. A flirtatious conversation sprang
up, leading to Nell and the King heading either straight back to
Whitehall in his coach or, in another version, to a tavern to dine.

The latter version allows room for a fine piece of embroidery on
the tale. After dining, Charles and James, like respectable blue
bloods through the ages, discovered that they carried no money. Nell
was left to settle the bill. 'Od's fish!' she exclaimed, mimicking the
King and employing one of his favourite expressions, 'I'm sure this is
the poorest company I was ever in.' This amused Charles so much
that he was immediately smitten and called for his coach to take
them away to the palace. Nell would soon crack the joke that Charles
II was her Charles the Third, for she had already been lover to
Charles Hart and Charles Sackville.

So began Nell Gwyn's extraordinary journey into both the King's
bed and the hearts of the English people. She continued to act
throughout that year and the next, making her final appearance at
Drury Lane only in 1670. As her appearances began to tail off, it sig-
nalled her reliance on a new source of money. Charles found in Nell
an attribute not present in any of the other women who caught his
attention – a rude and boisterous wit allied to an evident joy of living.
For sure, others had great animal attraction, from Lucy Walter
through to Moll Davis. Some had great beauty, as with Frances
Stuart or Barbara Palmer. But Nell Gwyn had wit and an unabashed
ability to say what she thought, even in front of a king. This beguiling unaffectedness was a sure antidote to some of the other women
with whom Charles whiled away his evenings. She was also cheap to
maintain, with none of the naked avarice of a woman like Barbara,
who measured her status in coaches, estates, houses and titles. Nell

wanted comparatively little and seems to have genuinely liked the King. With her, he could relax.

According to Nell's descendant Charles Beauclerk, writing in the twenty-first century, Charles was lonely.[13] By this analysis, the King's frenetic social life was the sign of a man anxious to keep moments of solitude and reflection to the minimum. But his constant need for activity, for diversion and amusement indicates something more profound: a restless emptiness caused by his childhood, the execution of his father, exile and the loss of a role.

Nell had the ability to amuse and to help him feel wanted for himself, and not simply for the gifts he could bestow. She did receive gifts, but they were commensurate with her station in life. Not for Nell the estates in Ireland, or the title to go with it that Barbara received. To begin with, the actress was given a house that Charles rented for her in Lincoln's Inn Fields and a coach was put at her disposal.

News of an old love interest surfaced from France, relayed to Charles in a letter from Minette. Hortense Mancini, the vivacious girl whose hand he had been unable to grasp in marriage in 1659, had left her husband and been thrown into a convent, as has been the fate of many put-upon women over the centuries. After making the nuns' lives hell she had found refuge in the Parisian palace of her uncle, Cardinal Mazarin. From there she had fled further from her vengeful husband by returning to Italy, taking her jewellery with her. All this amused Charles, who noted that Hortense had robbed her dull husband before leaving him. Charles wished the wayward spouse a 'good journey', not knowing that within a few years Hortense would re-enter his life.

Charles's complicated sex life did not prevent him continuing with his favourite pastimes, including tennis, sailing and attending the races. His ultimate form of escape was sailing. With a passion for the relatively new Dutch sport of yacht racing, he had amassed a collection of boats of all sizes. The star of the collection was the former coal boat the *Surprise*, the ship that had carried him away from England in 1651. With the ship renamed the *Royal Escape*, Charles

loved to show it off to visitors, helping to cement the mythology surrounding his providential escape from his enemies. He never tired of
telling visitors about it.

When not sailing, Charles loved to be at Newmarket for the races.
He had a modest town house repaired and fitted out as a retreat; otherwise he stayed with friends such as Lord Cornwallis, whose estate
was close by. Finally he tired of these arrangements and during the
year he bought Audley End House, a fine mansion near Saffron
Walden built by the Earl of Suffolk during the reign of James I.
Charles paid £50,000 for the house, which was so grand in scale
that most of the court could accompany him for the races. Although
his new house was seventeen miles south-west of the racecourse,
Charles was a fine horseman and had been known to ride a round
trip of sixty miles in a day. The gallop up to Newmarket was a joy to
the sporty King. After a while, his love of racing and his active nature
coalesced and he was no longer content with being a spectator but
began riding in the races. He gained the nickname Old Rowley after
a favourite horse of that name, even delighting in the fact that the
ordinary people called him by it. One story goes that when he overheard a maid enquiring where Old Rowley was, he put his head
round the door and said, 'Old Rowley's right here.'

When not engaged in sports, his need for female company was
always to the fore. This insatiable desire led to all sorts of stories,
many of them fabrications recorded by the often gullible Pepys. Here
he is on the gossip from Newmarket on 18 July:

> Creed told me this day how when the King was at Newmarket . . .
> that my Lord Cornwallis did endeavour to get the King a whore,
> and that must be a pretty girl the daughter of the parson of the
> place, but that she did get away, and leaped off of some place and
> killed herself, which if true is very sad.

As 1668 drew towards its close, Charles was still infatuated with the
two actresses, Moll and Nell. Although Nell had become the crowd's

favourite as the 'Protestant whore' and London's leading comedi-
enne, Moll continued to hold the King in rapture for her pure
animal sexuality. At the theatre on the afternoon of 21 December, the
ever-watchful Pepys caught the nature of the relationship and the
hostility it caused: 'It vexed me to see Moll Davis in her box over the
King's and my Lady Castlemaine's head, look down upon the King,
and he up to her; and so did my Lady Castlemaine once, to see who
it was; but when she saw her she looked like fire, which troubled me.'
Though the King's desire for his *maîtresse en titre* was on the wane,
Pepys's admiration evidently was not.

There is one important piece of evidence that Nell was increasingly occupying the King's erotic fantasies: a portrait by his court
painter Peter Lely. The painting, executed some time during 1668,
shows Nell naked, reclining against a chair, gazing out at the viewer
with Lely's trademark come-to-bed eyes. A *putto* lifts the wisp of
fabric covering her modesty, playfully attempting to see what the
viewer's eyes cannot. The pose in the painting is as awkward as anything Lely ever did. Compared to the reclining nudes of a master
such as Titian executed a hundred years before, it is a clumsy thing.
Contrasting it with the *Venus and Cupid with an Organist* that had
been in his father's collection, the naked Nell is very ungainly. When
compared to the superlative *Venus of Urbino*, in which the central
nude figure similarly gazes at us with resolute eyes, with only a languid hand covering her groin, we see just how wanting Charles's
senior painter was. But, then, all that was beside the point; the painting was intended as mere titillation, and Lely provided nothing
more.

By late 1669, Nell's theatrical career was fizzling out. She was
devoting more time to being a royal mistress, albeit second fiddle to
Barbara's first. But Nell had taken over as the King's premier erotic
dream. In his bedchamber, he kept the portrait of the naked Nell
hidden behind a secret panel on which was painted a staid Dutch
landscape. By sliding back the panel, Charles could reveal Nell in all
her glory. Charles enjoyed showing off the painting to his closest

circle. One cannot imagine Barbara, or any of the other society ladies of the court, agreeing to have their likeness depicted in such a brazen manner. But Nell was a girl from the backstreets and show was her profession. Another nude portrait depicted her as a female Cupid. This portrait was so popular that prints were made of it. Samuel Pepys had a framed copy above the mantelpiece in his Admiralty office – something with which to brighten up a dull winter's day at work.

Nell eventually became pregnant by the King and had to postpone appearing in a production of a Dryden play, *The Conquest of Granada*. On 14 or 15 May 1670, she gave birth to a son, christened Charles after his father. The christening was a grand event, and it said something for Nell's rising social status that the child's godparents were Buckingham and Buckhurst, though the choice said little for her adherence to Christian virtue. Nell eventually acted in *The Conquest of Granada*; it was her last theatrical appearance.

In recognition of her fulltime role as mistress to the King, in 1671 Charles moved Nell into a grand house on the north side of Pall Mall, followed shortly after by a move to 79 Pall Mall, situated on the other side of the street at the most fashionable, eastern end by the palace, backing onto St James's Park. It was an address fit for a royal mistress but it was not an outright gift, being on a lease from the Crown. It was a tsarist gift, one that could if necessary be taken away. It was at this house that John Evelyn spotted Nell and the King having a 'very familiar' conversation while Nell leaned over her garden wall and the King looked up from the walk below. Evelyn was displeased by what he saw, although it did not take much to cause the fastidious scholar and public servant to be irked by the simpler pleasures of less pious people, from former orange-sellers up to the King himself. Doubtless, Charles would never have invited his trusted servant to his privy chamber and then slid back the panel on which the Dutch landscape was painted to reveal Nell portrayed in all her naked glory.

The relationship between the actress and the monarch became so close and enduring that the King's initial caution in the matter of gifts was superseded by greater generosity. As time went by the bond between the girl from the slums of Coal Yard Alley and the King endured, she was awarded an income (called a 'pension') of £4000 a year – later increased to £5000 – and given several properties including a house at Windsor, named Burford House, and an estate in Nottinghamshire. In the amoral way of the Restoration court, she was handed the annual income from duties paid on logwood – income that should have correctly gone into the public exchequer.

This piece of good fortune illustrated one of the problems the King faced in mid seventeenth-century England: the system that enabled the monarch to give public money to his current favourite mistress also ensured that the exchequer did not have a dependable stream of income. Public finance was run through a system of private operators. Officials in charge of gathering money and taxes did not see themselves as directly beholden to the state as they had purchased their positions, often at great expense. Nell's popularity was such that, should the public have been informed of the diversion of the tax money, it was unlikely there would have been much objection.

Although given gifts of money and property, what Nell really wanted was a title for her son. This was not initially forthcoming. On Christmas Day 1671, she gave birth to a second son. The boy was christened James, after the Duke of York. Nell continued to hope her sons might have titles, like the other royal progeny. But the King was loath to give way to her request.

For the vast majority of the British people Nell was to maintain one great advantage over her more aristocratic rivals – she was a Protestant. In a country increasingly jittery over religion and the question of the succession, this mattered. The story is told by several sources (though without any well-defined initial source or date) of Nell travelling through Oxford in her coach when an angry crowd assailed it, mistakenly thinking it was that of a Catholic mistress. As the scene turned ugly, Nell poked her head out the window and said, 'Good people, be civil; I am the Protestant whore!'

Nell understood the mood of the English people a great deal better than her royal lover; or perhaps Charles knew it too, but did not care what the people thought of him and his apparently Catholic court. Either way, his indifference would help to lend credence to rumours and accusations that would ripple through the nation for years to come. Unbeknown even to the gossiping court, there was substance to the speculation thanks to the influence of a foreign king – Louis XIV of France.

14

A SECRET PACT

No one was more interested in the backstairs gossip from Whitehall than Louis XIV of France, the Sun King. One of Louis's instructions to his ambassador in London, Charles Colbert de Croissy, was to rake through the palace dirt and report. 'I think it would please the king if you were to send . . . gossiping letters about everything that happens in the private life of the king of England,' Croissy was told by his brother, Louis's chief Minister Jean-Baptiste Colbert.[1] Thereafter the ambassador gathered every detail he could of Barbara's and Charles's multiple affairs and the tantrums and deceptions attending them. The thirty-year-old French king wanted chapter and verse on all the other major players in Charles's court, too.

Louis delighted in sex no less than his philandering cousin in England. Both exhibited the same rampant libido as their grand-father Henri IV and both presided over courts swimming in licentiousness. But although the French king may have gained some vicarious thrill from digging through the Whitehall dirt, Louis's prime interest in wanting the details was less prurient. His strategic aim was the conquest of Flanders. That required the com-pliance of England and had him greedy for information on all things English. For hours on end he buried himself in bulky reports from across the Channel, studying the minutiae of Stuart rule and gobbling up material on England's Parliament, its navy, its currency, religion, pastimes, wars, even literature. The Sun King played hard like Charles, but he worked hard too on getting to know the opposition.

A first step in the seduction of England had come back in 1668 when the French initiated talks on a possible commercial treaty. The ambassador was instructed to use the talks 'to soften the animosity of the English and give a sop to their traders' while establishing ties with 'political men'. He was told to use 'all pretexts' to prolong the commercial talks till these contacts were established.[2]

Initially, the focus was on the two rival heavyweights in the ruling Cabal, the Secretary of State, Lord Arlington and George Villiers, Duke of Buckingham. The French king wrote: 'If each has a strong motive for helping me, they will both, however they may detest each other, plot for a common object.' He added: 'The affair is so important that I am willing to make any sacrifice of money.'[3] In that respect Louis would prove a man of his word. He would douse England's warring politicians, their mistresses and their king in bribes throughout the following decade.

Colbert de Croissy was authorised to buy the allegiance of the stridently pro-Spanish and anti-French Arlington, a former ambassador in Madrid, with a massive bribe – silver plate worth 100,000 crowns plus a yearly pension of 10,000 crowns, although in the event the bribe was not proffered. At his first meeting with Arlington, Colbert de Croissy found him so hostile to the idea of an alliance with France that he referred back to Louis before talking money. Louis instructed him to withhold the offer for the moment. As for Buckingham, he was pro-French anyway and for the moment Colbert held back from approaching him directly.

The ambassador's next target was Barbara Castlemaine. She had been as ardently Francophobe as Arlington. Back in 1665, when Louis dispatched a special mission to London in his vain attempt to prevent the second Anglo-Dutch war, the Frenchmen had put their failure down to an anti-French alliance struck up by Lady Castlemaine and the Spanish ambassador, Count Molina. Since then the Spanish had stirred Barbara's ire by attempting to interest Charles in a new mistress. A petulant Barbara was ready to switch camps.

At the age of twenty-eight Barbara was still a heart-stopper to look at, but her ties with the King had loosened. She had lost her apartment in the palace when Charles moved her out to Berkshire House, the mansion that he bought for her just beyond the palace complex. According to some, he no longer slept with her. His appetites were satisfied by such as Moll, Nell and the odd mopsy arranged by Chiffinch or Baptist May. Moreover, the spectre of Frances Stuart loomed again to darken Barbara's skies. After only about a year in exile, Frances had been allowed to return to court thanks to Queen Catherine, who made her a lady-in-waiting at Somerset House.

The news prompted Barbara to take to her bed for two weeks, reportedly incandescent that her rival was being allowed back. Frances was no longer the fresh, unspoiled beauty who had so frustrated the King. The attack of smallpox which had so concerned Charles earlier that year had left her with some disfigurement and also damaged one eye. But the King still found her attractive. Perhaps her misfortune softened his attitude, for after staying aloof from Frances for a year he started visiting her at Somerset House, often at night. It was quickly assumed that she finally did succumb to the royal lust. Charles was reported to have let this drop as fact – indeed boasted of it, according to one source – during a drunken session with Frances's husband, the Duke of Richmond.[4] The latter was later given a diplomatic post, as ambassador to Denmark that kept him mostly out of England. He died abroad just four years later. Frances did not remarry.

At various moments during the 1660s the King appeared to be on the point of disowning Barbara but her survival instincts always won through. At the end of the decade, in January 1669, Pepys recorded, 'My Lady Castlemaine is now in higher command over the King than ever – not as a mistress, for she scorns him but as a tyrant to command him.' Two months later he heard a courtier from the Duke of York's household say that Lady Castlemaine was 'never more great with the King than she is now'.[5]

Barbara's supreme self-confidence had left her seemingly unabashed by the bawdy house riots and the stream of written attacks on her. She as good as challenged the mob by parading through the streets in an eight-horse carriage. Far from abusing her, Londoners filled 'the streets, balconies and windows . . . to admire her'.[6]

The French ambassador's first meeting with Barbara was encouraging. The Lady signified her readiness to accept overtures from France. As an instance of her willingness to change horses, Barbara divulged details of a talk that she had held with the King about the possibilities of a French alliance. Charles had told her that the Secretary of State, Arlington, 'would not hear' of such a move. That was less than earth-shattering news, but even so Louis thought it well worth the ambassador's time to pursue Barbara and had his foreign minister Lionne instruct Colbert to go ahead.

'The King,' Lionne told the ambassador, 'thinks well of your efforts to obtain the help of the Countess of Castlemaine, and read with interest of her frank way of telling you how King Charles had confided to her that Lord Arlington would not hear of an alliance with France.' Louis called this 'a good beginning' and authorised a 'handsome present' for the lady. 'You can give it as if from yourself,' Colbert was told. 'Ladies are fond of such keepsakes, whatever may be their breeding or disposition; and a nice little present can in any case do no harm.'[7]

Colbert was displeased at the prospect of having to dip into his own pocket. He told his masters that he was running out of money. 'I have given away all that I brought from France, not excepting the skirts and smocks made up for my wife,' he complained, 'and I have not money enough to go on at this rate. Nor do I see the use of going to much expense, in satisfying the greed of the women here for rich keepsakes.'

He put forward another objection too. 'If handsome gifts are lavished on Madame Castlemaine, his majesty may think that, in spite of his assertions to the contrary, we fancy that she rules him, and take it in bad part. I should therefore advise giving her only such trifling tokens as a pair of French gloves, ribands, a Parisian undress gown, or some little object of finery.'[8]

Louis ignored the warning. In May 1669, Ralph Montagu, the English ambassador in Paris (and Edward Montagu's son), informed Arlington that a very expensive gift was on its way to Barbara. He wrote:

> I went to Mariall's to look for gloves and I saw a present which I am sure must cost a thousand pounds packing up. I found since that it is for my Lady Castlemaine which you will quickly know there. I asked him who it was for, but he would not or could not tell me. I asked him who paid him; he told me, the King of France.[9]

Charles was indeed sensitive to the suggestion that he was manipulated by anyone. The considerable ego of the man bridled at the idea of letting himself be used. Back in 1667 he had walked out of that final meeting with Clarendon when the old Chancellor blamed Lady Castlemaine for his dismissal. The King's touchiness was reflected in letters to his sister. In one letter he wrote: 'One thing I desire you to take as much as you can out of the French King's head that my ministers are anything but I would have them be.' In other words, that he controlled his ministers, not vice versa. In another letter he told the Duchess, 'Whatsoever opinions my ministers have been of I would and do always follow my own judgment.'[10]

What only a tiny handful of people knew was that the two kings were already negotiating a military and political pact, and there were no ministers or advisors, let alone lovers present while the basics were hammered out. The matchmaker was Minette, Charles's adored sister. She had been encouraged by Louis to push her brother towards an alliance with France and had become the inter-mediary while Charles and Louis circled round each other, trying for a pact and giving even their closest advisors no inkling of what was afoot.

Minette, the youngest of Charles's siblings, was fourteen years his junior. She was pretty, petite, promiscuous, witty and a ruthless schemer in the Stuart cause. When, in 1663, assassins in Switzerland murdered one of the men who had signed her father's death warrant, Minette was suspected of being behind the killing. Plots to murder other republican refugees are thought to have been funded by her as well. Minette was married to King Louis XIV's only brother, Philippe. Like Buckingham, sent home in disgrace after making an open play for the bride's affections while officially escorting her from London to Paris, the then unmarried Louis had flirted with her out-rageously, and had been reprimanded for it by his formidable mother, Anne of Austria. The marriage between Minette and the ill-tempered Duke of Orléans, whose courtesy title was 'Monsieur', was a disaster. Monsieur turned out to be a transvestite bisexual. He and Minette are said to have enjoyed a deliriously happy honeymoon last-ing two weeks, followed by years of backbiting, jealousy and then hatred. Much of the ill will centred around Monsieur's ostentatiously gay lover, the Chevalier de Lorraine, but it was also stirred by Minette's infidelities. She had a string of lovers who were said to have included even the Duke of Monmouth, her teenage nephew. The hot blood of Henri IV ran strong in her veins too, as, of course, it also did in young Monmouth's.

Of all Charles's women, Minette was probably the only one he came close to trusting. 'She has much more power over the king her brother than any other person in the world,' Colbert de Croissy told King Louis, 'not only by the eagerness the other ministers have shown to implore her favour and support with the King and by the favours he has accorded simply at her request . . . but also by the King's own confession and the tears he shed on bidding her farewell.'[11]

The pact for which Minette acted as nursemaid was the notorious secret Treaty of Dover between England and France. This was a breathtaking military and political deal. Under its terms Louis was to pay Charles huge subsidies to join France in attacking and dismembering the Netherlands, while, in return for still more money, Charles was to declare himself a Catholic. Louis was also committed to sending his brother monarch troops and further dollops of cash 'in case the said King's subjects should not acquiesce in the said declaration and rebel against his said Britannic Majesty'.

It is difficult to believe that the wily Charles seriously intended to risk his throne by declaring for Rome and banking on a French invasion should things go wrong. His father had lost his head for far less. He recognised that some thought him 'mad', but in a long interview with Colbert, Charles dismissed the objections. He argued that anti-Catholicism had been overplayed and that he was much better placed to suppress opposition than Charles I had been. If his father had had so many troops as Charles now had, 'he would have stifled at birth the troubles that caused his ruin.'[12]

From the start in 1668, negotiations between the two monarchs were clothed in secrecy. Contact between Charles and his sister was through letters in cipher while her contact with Louis was head to head, duchess to king. In December 1668, Charles, writing to his sister, assured her that his plan – or 'grand design' as he called it – was known only to himself and to 'one person more'.[13] On the French side only Minette and Louis were in the picture.

Charles obsessed about Buckingham finding out. Perhaps the only streak of consistency in the Duke's entire body was his hatred of Catholicism, and Charles knew that his boyhood friend would explode were he to hear of his grand design. Minette and Buckingham were old friends if not more than that, and the King pleaded with Minette to be prudent. 'Write but seldom to him,' he urged of her correspondence with Buckingham, 'for fear something may slip from your pen, which may make him jealous that there is something more than he knows of.' In another letter referring to the

Duke, Charles warned: 'The great secret, that which concerns Religion ... he must not be trusted with.'

There were leaks. In April 1669 there was talk in the Duke of York's household about a military deal with France. Pepys was told by a York courtier 'that for a sum of money we shall enter a league with France' and that Charles would use the money to dispense with Parliament. According to Pepys's contact, Lady Castlemaine was 'instrumental in this matter'.[14]

While the two kings haggled over a deal, domestic tragedy struck once more in the Palace of Whitehall. Queen Catherine miscarried a third time. The miscarriage was caused, it was thought, by a farcical incident in which one of the King's many pets – a tame fox – jumped on her bed and ran across her face. The effect on the Queen can be imagined. No more pregnancies were reported after this date. It confirmed what many in the court had predicted – that the marriage would remain childless.

On the diplomatic front, another year of haggling and hesitation were to go by before the two kings could agree the main strands of the secret treaty. When concluded, it gave Louis what he most wanted – effectively a free hand for territorial expansion northward. And it seemed to promise Charles the money he needed to rule without Parliament. Lords Arlington and Clifford were later brought in to finesse the details. Along with the King's brother James and the Catholic courtier Lord Arundel they alone of the English were allowed to know of the grand design.

Minette arrived at Dover in May 1670 supposedly on a visit to her beloved brother, but in fact to speak for her cousin the Sun King in the final haggling over the pact. It had to be done in Dover because of difficulties put up by Monsieur, the Princess's husband. His relationship with Minette had become venomous after she persuaded Louis to imprison the Chevalier de Lorraine, her husband's gay lover, for boasting that he could wreck her marriage. The Chevalier was sent to the Château d'If, the grim island prison immortalised by Alexandre Dumas in *The Count of Monte Cristo*. When approached by Louis to agree the trip, the vengeful Philippe replied, 'To England? I won't even let her go to Flanders.' He eventually agreed, but stipulated that his wife go no more than ten miles inland.[15]

Dover Castle rang with revelry during Minette's visit. Charles's riotous court decamped en masse to Dover and Minette brought a sizeable entourage from France to the party. Including servants they numbered more than 230. The guests were treated to ten days of balls, parties, theatrical displays and receptions. They ignored the ten-mile limit and partied as far afield as Canterbury. While the merrymaking went on, unknown to all but a tiny handful the final touches were being put to a document laying out one of the most shameful deals a British monarch has ever concluded.

Minette left Dover on 1 June. Before she embarked, precious stones were presented to the principals. Barbara, in the unaccustomed role of giver rather than taker, bestowed a jewel reportedly worth £2500 on Minette. In turn, Minette ushered forward one of her young ladies-in-waiting, Louise de Kérouaille, holding an open casket of jewels. Minette invited Charles to take his pick. Mlle de Kérouaille would make a far better present, he replied.[16] According to reports, he prolonged the final treaty agreement solely in order not to lose sight of the girl. He even pressed Minette to leave Louise behind. His sister refused. She had promised Louise's mother to protect her and would keep her word. Louise sailed back with her.

After Minette's departure, Buckingham, perhaps influenced by her, put forward a proposal that must have had the King choking on his own good luck. The Duke proposed a military alliance with France against the Dutch. Charles, of course, said yes, Buckingham was charged with negotiating it in St Germain and a second treaty was born. With French connivance it ended up with exactly the same provisions as the secret document, except that there were no references to any return to Catholicism. Buckingham confessed his surprise that the talks had gone so smoothly. He was never to know that the deal was already done.

Minette had been back in France for under a month and was relaxing at St Cloud when she suddenly collapsed. She complained of an unbearable pain in her side and, in agony, gasped that she had been poisoned. This was on the evening of 29 June 1670. At 3 a.m. next morning, at the age of twenty-six, the Duchess died. When the news reached England it was accompanied by rumours that Monsieur her husband or his lover the Chevalier had poisoned her. Twenty-one years earlier, when Charles learned of his father's execution, he had fled the room in tears and closeted himself in his chambers for two days. Now, on hearing about Minette, he was in tears again and shouted, 'Monsieur is a villain,' before retreating into his inner sanctum. He was unreachable for five days.

An autopsy suggested that the Duchess had died of peritonitis but suspicion flared in England. It was put about that the spiteful Chevalier had arranged for her to be given poison in a cup of chicory water. Louis was blamed for letting it happen. A vengeful mob gathered outside ambassador Colbert's residence in London looking for Frenchmen to string up. Troopers had to be called in to disperse them. Buckingham, who had once been so smitten by Minette, was no less bitter. Colbert gained the impression that little short of war would appease the Duke. King Louis feared that the secret alliance was dead.

It wasn't dead. Charles emerged from his seclusion shouting for the arrest of the Chevalier de Lorraine, but his diplomatic wits were soon restored and he sent a suitably gracious reply to King Louis's messages of condolence. Amity was quickly restored and the second treaty was ready for signature by Buckingham in Paris. The ever volatile Duke had been won back to the side of France by days of lavish receptions laid on for him by the Sun King. This wooing was helped no doubt by a bribe of 10,000 livres a year from Louis that with typically French subtlety went as a pension granted to his mistress, the now notorious Countess of Shrewsbury.

Buckingham's last days on this French trip were concerned with another woman, Minette's lady-in-waiting, Louise de Kérouaille. Recalling the King's avid interest in her at Dover, the Duke decided that she might be the one to topple Barbara as *maîtresse en titre*. A new era was about to dawn. It would last for fourteen years.

15

THE FRENCH RIVAL

The plot to topple Barbara Castlemaine and replace her with the young French beauty, Louise de Kérouaille, took shape in Paris in the late summer of 1670. The main progenitor was George Villiers, the Duke of Buckingham, who was in France supposedly finalising the Anglo-French alliance and patching up relations in the aftermath of Minette's death. Buckingham and Barbara had clashed bitterly over the question of the King's divorce, and now he was bent on destroying Barbara's influence with Charles. He canvassed the Palais Royal with the idea of getting the delightful Mlle de Kérouaille to set her cap at Charles and found Louis XIV enthusiastic. It is not clear what discussions went on, either with the Sun King or with the girl and her family, but all evidently agreed. As for Charles, it was suggested that he might honour his dead sister by bringing her entrancing lady-in-waiting to England as a lady of the Queen's bedchamber. Charles leapt at the suggestion.

Accompanied by Buckingham, Mlle de Kérouaille set off on the journey from Paris to London in September 1670. The aim of their mission of seduction was no secret in diplomatic circles. The Marquis de Saint-Maurice, Savoy's ambassador in Paris, reported, 'The Duke of Buckingham has taken with him Mlle. de

Kérouaille ... He would like to dethrone Lady Castlemaine, who is his enemy, and His Most Christian Majesty [Louis XIV] will not be sorry to see the position filled by one of his subjects, for it is said the ladies have great influence over the mind of the said King of England.'[1]

Dethroning Lady Castlemaine would not be easy. She had been the King's principal mistress for a decade, hated by some but with strong supporters at court as well. John Evelyn called her 'the curse of the nation' but she was evidently also great, raucous company, with a heart that sometimes seemed as big as her terrifying temper. Her hold over Charles fluctuated, but at this point it had never looked stronger.

Thanks to Buckingham, the mission got off to a bad start. He personally escorted Louise onto the road to the coast. There he left her in the luxury of his ducal coach to follow on behind while he hurried ahead to arrange passage to England. On reaching Dieppe he took passage himself, intending to send back a royal yacht to pick the girl up. It didn't happen. The Duke totally forgot about the existence of his passenger. Louise spent ten frustrating days in Dieppe before raising help from England's ambassador, who duly obtained a yacht.[2]

It is said that Louise never forgave the Duke, but even if she was boiling with fury on finally landing in Dover it probably was not evident. While Barbara Castlemaine allowed every emotion to show and loudly voiced her anger or her joy, Louise contained her emotions. With her peaches and cream skin, huge dark almond eyes and mane of dark brown hair with golden tints, the softly spoken Breton was the epitome of aristocratic cool.[3] The first impression that she presented was of confident innocence, a refined and ravishing blue blood with an undoubted pedigree. 'Languorous' was a word repeatedly applied to her and 'childish beauty' the phrase continually used to describe her looks. It all added up to a ravishing but undemanding beauty who would do as bidden. It would take several years before the true worth of this manipulative young lady fully emerged and she became the most loathed of all the Stuart mistresses.

She hailed from an impecunious family of aristocrats in Brittany. Contrary to what might have been expected, though quite a beauty, she hadn't married in her teens thanks to the family's lack of fortune – put simply, she had no dowry. So her mother had obtained a place for her at Minette's court, where she might snare Louis XIV into becoming her pretty daughter's lover. Unlike in England there was no opprobrium attached to the mistresses of the monarch.

Buckingham's forgetfulness cost him Louise's favour, and his rival in the Cabal, the Earl of Arlington, took over as her protector, while Arlington's Dutch-born wife acted as the girl's mentor. At the French embassy Colbert was in constant touch with her and debated with Paris her every move. She arrived in Whitehall when the prospect of Charles divorcing his wife had become a real possibility again.

Divorce had become a live issue because of a Private Member's Bill in Parliament designed to enable Lord Loos, heir to the Earl of Rutland, to remarry. Loos had divorced his wife for adultery and followed up by having her children bastardised by law; he needed a further Act of Parliament to enable him to marry again and the Bill he tabled offered a possible precedent for a royal divorce. Charles's behaviour encouraged the belief that he was interested in the possibilities the Bill might offer. As a rule, the King avoided Parliament, but to the amazement of MPs he was there every day that the Loos Bill was being debated. He laughed off the resulting suspicions. Why was he there? 'It's better than going to a play,' he retorted. However, Westminster rang with rumours about a new queen. Poet and MP Andrew Marvell outlined them in a letter to a friend. 'There is some talk of a French Queen to be invented for our King,' he wrote. 'Some say a sister of the King of Denmark; others a good virtuous Protestant, here at home. The King disavows it; yet he has said in public he knew not why a woman may not be divorced for barrenness as a man for impotency.'[4]

The Bill finally went through in March 1670, and in no time a royal Bill of divorce was drawn up. Baptist May, ever the King's man for delicate jobs, was charged with tabling it in Parliament. The circumstances suggest that he had secured a seat in the House of Commons just for this purpose. The Queen was reportedly in tears at the prospect and Barbara was no doubt cursing too. Any new Queen was a threat to her and she stood alongside the York faction in working on Charles to stop the legislation. At the last minute her side won. Three days before the motion was to be made, the King called for Baptist May and told him the matter 'must be let alone'.[5]

If Bishop Burnet's account of the marriage debates is correct, much worse than divorce was then suggested by the ever-active Buckingham. The Queen had just literally got lost in London playing a masquerading game that was the rage of the court. It involved disguising oneself and going singly by sedan chair to gate-crash the parties of perfect strangers. Playing this game too heartily, the Queen suddenly found herself utterly alone in the city, with her chairmen vanished and no one from the court in sight. Her disappearance and later her description of her desperate efforts to get back to Whitehall gave Villiers an idea. He proposed kidnapping Queen Catherine and whisking her off to a plantation in America. Each year that was the fate of hundreds of unfortunates who were tricked or forced onto America-bound ships and sold there as indentured servants. Many were effectively slaves.[6] Burnet reported that Villiers' idea was to 'steal her away and send her to a plantation, where she should be well and carefully looked to, but never heard of any more. So it should be given out that she had deserted.' According to Burnet's source, the Duke argued that Catherine's desertion could be construed by the Church of England as grounds for him to divorce her, 'grounded upon the pretence of a wilful desertion'.

Buckingham had even nastier suggestions, as related much later in Smollett's *History of England*: 'Buckingham had proposed infamous means for ruining her reputation in such manner that she might have been charged with breach of conjugal faith.' Happily for Catherine, the King rejected his ideas 'with horror'.[7]

The hapless Queen now came in for a share of the lampoons

directed at the women of the palace. The hostess at many a lavish court ball, her love of dancing gave a contemporary poet a target for the following cruel piece:

> Reform, great queen, the errors of thy youth
> And hear a thing you've never heard called truth
> Poor private balls content the fairy queen
> You must dance (and dance damnably) to be seen
> Ill-natured little goblin and designed
> For nothing but to dance and vex mankind.
> What wiser thing could our great monarch do,
> Than root ambition out, by saying you?
> You can the most aspiring thoughts pull down
> For who would have his wife to have his crown?*

The poet ended this ill-natured diatribe against the Queen with the following words:

> What will be next unless you please to go
> And dance among your fellow fiends below?
> There as upon the Stygian lake you float,
> You may o'erset and sink the laden boat;
> While we the funeral rites devoutly pay
> And dance for joy that you are danced away.

Unsurprisingly, the poet's satire was not published in his day. The more merited target, Barbara, was still milking Charles for titles, jewels, land and money. In August 1670 she was granted a royal pension and a clutch of new titles – Countess of Southampton, Duchess of Cleveland and Baroness Nonsuch. The honours were proclaimed to be in recognition of the 'eminent services' performed by her father, Viscount Grandison, who had died seventeen years before, and for

---

* This poem has been attributed to Marvell, though this is now doubted.

her own 'personal virtues'. The King also accepted paternity for her first and third sons, Charles and George Palmer, by according them 'the precedence of children of a duke'.[8]

Charles's largesse to Barbara year in, year out remains astonishing to contemplate. There were more five-figure dollops of cash, more plate from the jewel house and more grants from the excise, as well as 'rents' from office holders. Marvell says that Lord Berkeley paid no less than £10,000 to 'his landlady Cleveland'. Even this was seldom enough. Lady Castlemaine's outgoings were enormous. She wagered thousands at the gaming tables, lost in tens of thousands and wallowed in finery. At one point in 1670 she was seen at the theatre one afternoon wearing jewellery reckoned to be worth some £40,000. Attending a court ballet in February 1671, she is described as 'very fine in a rich petticoat and halfe skirt, and a short man's coat very richly laced, a periwig cravat, and a hat . . . her hat and mask was very rich'.[9] Such was her expenditure, Barbara found it difficult to keep up Cleveland House, her mansion in St James's, and had to sell part of its grounds.

Barbara is said to have 'added a new paramour every year'. They came from across the social scale and included actors, showmen and courtiers. From the theatre there was the leading tragic actor of the day, Charles Hart, Nell Gwyn's mentor and possibly her first lover. Barbara reportedly took him unprotesting into her bed to get even with Charles for taking Moll and Nell into his.

Another figure from the theatre was the young poet and playwright William Wycherley. She picked him up after shouting her congratulations to him from her departing carriage having just viewed his first comedy in Drury Lane. They got together the very next night, and judging from the dedications to her in his works he was bewitched: 'I can do your Grace no honour, nor make you more admirers than you have already; yet I can do myself the honour to let the world know I am the greatest you have.'

Wycherley was strikingly handsome. Similarly, that other young catch, the ensign John Churchill. She was generous to both these stripling lovers, backing Wycherley's theatrical productions financially and famously once handing over a huge lump sum to Churchill, reputedly £5000. The future national hero appears to have been less generous to his mistress than she was to him. The story ran that a long time later they were both at the gaming table, where he was banker, when she ran out of money and he refused to lend her half a crown to carry on. The bank never lends, he told her coldly.

It was put about that the £5000 gift to Churchill was from a sum of £20,000 that Barbara had conned out of a randy old rake, Sir Edward Hungerford, as her price for going to bed with him. When Barbara was first approached by Hungerford, she reportedly asked £10,000 for one night, a sum to which the ardent Sir Edward agreed. The money was handed over but she failed to show up. The bewitching Barbara then persuaded the old man that she certainly would turn up the next night for another £10,000. She got the money; Sir Edward got nothing. The transactions inspired Alexander Pope to write one of the more polite couplets about Barbara:

> Who of ten thousand gulled her Knight,
> Then asked ten thousand for another night;
> The gallant too, to whom she paid it down,
> Lived to refuse the mistress half-a-crown.[10]

Barbara could be generous to other lovers besides Churchill. She paid a pension to her muscular rope dancer, Jacob Hall. It was through Barbara that Hall secured a royal warrant, in which he was described as 'master of the King's rope dancers' and authorising him to 'use rope dancing, tumbling, vaulting and other feats of activity throughout the kingdom'. He used it to stage displays just outside the palace.

Although one of Charles's attractive characteristics was his lack of jealousy, what else but fear of discovery by a jealous King prompted Barbara to disguise herself for assignations with young Wycherley?

According to the antiquarian William Oldys, 'the Duchess of Cleveland used to visit Wycherley at his chambers in the Temple, dressed like a country maid in a straw hat, with pattens on, a basket or box in her hand.'[11]

The King found out about Wycherley anyway. Barbara had arranged to spend the night with the playwright in Pall Mall at the lodgings of the famous singer Mrs Knight. Charles was tipped off about it by a maid. Always an early riser, he arrived in Pall Mall at dawn to find Wycherley at the stair head muffled in his cloak, struggling to disguise himself. The King strode past the petrified writer into the bedchamber to discover the Duchess. She was either on the bed or in it. What was she doing? Charles demanded. Sardonically, Barbara replied that it was Lent and she was here 'to perform her devotions'. The King, equally sardonic, replied: 'Very likely, and that was your confessor I met on the stairs.' We don't know if either kept a straight face.

During a similar episode, the Duke of Buckingham, now Barbara's deadliest enemy, decided to play the same trick on her that she had perpetrated on Frances Stuart three years earlier, in 1667. He manoeuvred the unsuspecting King into making a surprise visit to Barbara when he knew that he would find her in bed with Churchill. When the sovereign appeared at her apartment, Churchill is reported to have jumped out of the window, but not before Charles recognised him. He called after the fleeing ensign, 'I forgive you, for you do it for your bread.'

It's questionable whether Charles did forgive his much younger rival. The future victor of Blenheim and Ramillies would so distinguish himself with an act of individual bravery during the next Dutch war that the Duke of York decided to reward him. He selected Churchill as a gentleman of his bedchamber. The promotion was stopped, vetoed apparently by the King.

Charles's own finances were always under scrutiny when Parliament was in session, which was one reason why he yearned to rule without Parliament. That ambition would have been bolstered when an MP had the temerity to refer in the House to his sex life, and almost got himself murdered for doing so. It happened in December 1670 when Sir John Coventry proposed a tax on theatres: 'That ... every one that resorts to any of the playhouses who sits in the boxes, shall pay 1s; every one who sits in the pit shall pay 6d; and every other person 3d.'

Oh, no, a loyalist MP retorted, that couldn't be done because the players were the King's servants and part of his pleasures. To which Coventry replied by asking 'if the King's pleasure lay among the men or women players'.

Charles was furious. This was the first time that his personal behaviour had been criticised openly in Parliament. The official record in the parliamentary archive states that Sir John's remark was 'reported at court and highly resented'. Resented indeed. Some time later the Duke of York told Bishop Burnet that 'the court', in other words the King, had resolved 'to set a mark' on Coventry to deter other would-be critics. This meant branding or disfiguring him. Some forty years earlier Charles's father had ordered one of his critics, a Dr Prynne, to lose part of an ear in retribution for a supposed slight on Queen Henrietta Maria, and more of both ears when he persisted in publishing anti-episcopal works. In Coventry's case the target was his nose. The order was passed through the King's son the Duke of Monmouth, commander of the Life Guards, and an ambush was set. Upwards of fifteen to twenty Life Guards lay in wait for the MP and jumped him on his way home from the Cock tavern, where he usually had supper. He grabbed a flambeau from a servant and fought back, sword in one hand, torch in the other. Eventually, after wounding three of his assailants, he was pulled to the ground and 'his nose was slit to the bone ... to teach him what respect he owed to the King's character'. Fortunately for him the Life Guards were disturbed before they could finish the job and they made off. The retribution meted out to Coventry was possibly chosen to be particularly degrading because nose slitting was often a punishment for prostitutes.

Parliament exploded in righteous indignation at this 'assassination' attempt on one of their number. Warrants were issued for men known to have participated in the ambush, and an angry sounding Act of Parliament was rushed through. It ruled that 'if any person shall ... by lying in wait, unlawfully cut out or disable the tongue, put out an eye, slit the nose, cut off a nose or lip, or cut off or disable any limb or member of any other person, with intent to maim or disfigure him; such person, his counselors, aiders, and abettors, shall be guilty of a capital felony'.[12]

The Coventry Act, as it came to be called, included a clause asserting that there must be no pardon for Coventry's assailants. But this was little more than the mere sound of thunder. Two of the attackers fled abroad and were ritually banished. Nobody else suffered. The King's involvement, which was confirmed much later to Bishop Burnet by the Duke of York, ensured that no one would be severely punished. Charles had the constitutional right to pardon and he exercised it.[13]

A satirical broadside published in 1671, 'The Haymarket Hectors', warned:

> Beware, all ye Parliamenteer
> How each of his voice disposes,
> Bab May in the Commons,
> C. Rex in the Peers,
> Sit telling your fates on your noses,
> And decree, at the mention of every slut,
> Whose nose shall continue, and whose shall be cut.

A few weeks later, before the Coventry affair had had time to settle, the Duke of Monmouth was directly involved in another scandal and cover-up: the beadle murder. He was the leader of the gang of young aristocrats who made a late-night foray into an area of London full of brothels and killed a member of the watch. A satirical poem about the affair written by Dryden suggests that the young blades were pursuing revenge on a prostitute. They blamed her for infecting Monmouth and another of the party with the pox:

> T'was an injury beyond repair
> To clap a king's son and a great duke's heir.[14]

It seems they tried to storm the brothel and became involved in an altercation with the watch. This led to the young bloods drawing their swords, and seeing off all but one of the watchmen. He was left on his knees in front of Monmouth and his friends, praying to them for his life. One of them ran him through. Another is thought to have thrust at him also.

His killers included two, maybe three dukes – Monmouth himself, the young Duke of Albemarle, who had just inherited the title, and possibly the Duke of Somerset – and a gaggle of other young aristocrats. There was no question of them facing justice. Charles issued a proclamation calling the watchman's death 'a sad accident', and followed it quietly by the issue of 'a gracious pardon unto our dear sonne, James Duke of Monmouth, of all Murders, Homicides, and Felonyes whatsoever at any time before ye 28th day of Feb. last past, committed either by himself alone or together with any other person or persons'. To wrap the matter up and reassure the public that young aristos wouldn't be allowed to run riot, the King announced that the guards 'have orders upon all occasions to assist the watch in any part of town against all persons, whatsoever quality they be'.[15]

Meanwhile, the backers of the enchanting baby-faced twenty-year-old from Brittany, Louise de Kérouaille, were worried as 1670 turned into 1671 that she would never snare the King. When she arrived in London, she had been allotted rooms in the palace, and initially all had gone as planned. Her looks and manner made an immediate impact. She was being called 'that famous beauty' inside a month of being introduced at court, and the King's interest grew by the day. 'The king is always finding opportunities to talk with this beauty in the queen's room,' reported the French ambassador, Colbert de Croissy.[16]

Louise's chief mentors in England, Henry Bennet, Earl of Arlington, and his astute Dutch wife, Elisabeth van Nassau-Beverweer, joined the ambassador in deluging the young Breton with advice on how she should handle the King. Like Elisabeth, the widely travelled Arlington spoke good French. The two basic rules they offered were 'not to speak to him of affairs [meaning the business of court], and not to show any aversion to those who are near him'. In short, said Colbert, let the King 'find only pleasure and joy' in her company.

Seven years earlier, Barbara had greeted her new rival Frances Stuart with a show of feigned friendship. Louise was advised to pretend friendship to Barbara as well. But Louise had more than Barbara to face. Nell used all her caustic wit to deflate the new rival. Louise began to use tears to get her way with the King, Nell called her 'the weeping willow'.

At first, all went as Colbert and the Arlingtons hoped. The ambassador reported gleefully that Barbara was losing ground to La Bonne Bretonne, as Louise's admirers were calling her. 'The influence of the Duchess visibly wanes', he wrote: 'The trouble and expense which the Condé Molina* has been to get her round to the Spanish side, have been thrown away.'[17]

The French evidently expected a quick bedding of Louise by the King. The ideal climate for an affair to blossom was provided by the masquerade ball, which, with its fans and disguises recently popularised in England, had become the rage at court through the winter of 1670–1. To the court's surprise, nothing happened; Louise seems to have behaved towards her royal admirer like Frances Stuart before her. She flirted and encouraged the ardent King but swerved away at the crucial moment.

As with Frances, coquettishness seemed to work. Her rooms in the

---

* The Spanish ambassador.

palace replaced Barbara's house as the magnet for the King. 'His Majesty goes to her rooms at nine o'clock every morning, never stays there for less than an hour, and often remains until eleven o'clock,' wrote Colbert. 'He returns after dinner, and shares at her card-table in all her stakes and losses, never letting her want for anything. All the ministers, therefore, seek her friendship.'[18]

But from the French king to the Earl of Arlington, there was now growing alarm at her failure to tie Charles down by becoming his mistress. Louis XIV asked testily when this young woman would fulfil her mission. His ambassador Colbert de Croissy offered the view that France had better continue pretending to be Barbara's friend: 'I think it safe, while undermining that lady, to keep her on our side by appearing to be with her,' he counselled Louis. Arlington's ill-tempered comment to Colbert was that the girl should succumb immediately to the King or lock herself away in a French nunnery.

It became accepted later that Louise had been playing the long game. Beneath the languorous exterior was a calculating schemer who decided to yield only when she was absolutely sure of her hold on the King's affections and had learned how to manipulate him.

It took over a year before she was ready.

16

A SPY IN THE BED

Thirteen months after her arrival at court, Louise de Kérouaille finally deigned to allow the King to bed her. So began the reign of the greediest, most politically powerful and most hated of Charles's mistresses.

The circumstances were very different from those of eleven years before, when Charles had first slept with the then Barbara Palmer. That affair had begun so clandestinely that historians still don't know in which country it was first consummated. There was no such secrecy about the coupling of Charles and Louise in 1671. It was as much a drum-beating public ceremonial as a sensual coming together.

Louise's mentors, the Earl and Countess of Arlington, provided the venue, the magnificent Euston Hall, set in the Suffolk country-side. Euston was a showcase of Caroline extravagance, a flamboyant Baroque chateau in the French style, with frescoed ceilings, domed pavilions and galleries lined with the works of Italian masters. John Evelyn's first sight of the hall left him starry-eyed, full of superla-tives – 'a very noble pile ... magnificent ... commodious ... splendidly furnished ... elegant ... handsome ... beautiful'.[1] It was said to be reminiscent of the Luxembourg Palace in Paris.

In October, the Arlingtons threw a huge party at Euston Hall that lasted fifteen days. Some two hundred courtiers and blue bloods attended. Louise was among them, conveyed to Euston in the royal coach. The young Breton was the centre of attention, feted and indulged during her stay. The unstated object of the party was Louise's surrender to the King. Her subsequent actions seem to confirm that she had always planned to give herself to him, but until the Euston Hall party none of her backers could be sure of her.

The party was timed to coincide with the autumn race meeting, twenty miles away at Newmarket. From Restoration year onwards the King's custom had been to carouse at Newmarket in the royal lodge, a mini pleasure palace built by his grandfather James I, whose unquenchable thirst for young men equalled his own appetite for young women. The dissipation here was always even more unbridled than in Whitehall and October 1671 was no different. Evelyn described that year's gathering as 'more resembling a luxurious and abandoned rout than a Christian Court'.[2]

After Louise's arrival at Euston, Charles and the gallants and ladies from Newmarket descended. They included the Duke of Buckingham and his notorious mistress, 'that impudent woman' the Countess of Shrewsbury. Buckingham also brought his own orchestra, a team of 'French fiddlers'.[3]

As Charles entered the Euston estate, he must have been in an ebullient mood. The forty-one-year-old monarch had just ridden one of his own horses to victory in Newmarket's premier race (and today the world's oldest horse race), the Town Plate. Stuart menfolk were enthusiastically competitive, especially with each other, and Charles had just beaten among others his dashing eldest son, the Duke of Monmouth. And now he had Louise to look forward to. On reaching Euston he was all over her and her response was equally uninhibited. John Evelyn, who recorded her spending almost the whole day in her 'undress', described Charles 'toying' with the 'young wanton'. The high point of the festivities was a mock marriage between Charles and Louise, who was ceremonially disrobed en route to the marriage bed with 'the stocking flung, after the manner of a married bride'.[4]

When Barbara Castlemaine set up a mock marriage between Charles and Frances Stuart with the two of them in bed, she had known that the lady would ultimately say no. Colbert and the Arlingtons arranged this one expecting the lady to say yes. And at last she did. Not only that – nine months later almost to the day she gave birth to a boy.

On receipt of the news from Suffolk, Louis XIV had his ambassador present his congratulations to Mlle de Kérouaille. 'I have made that young lady joyful,' replied Colbert de Croissy, 'in assuring her of the pleasure with which his majesty learned of her brilliant conquest. There is every prospect that she will hold long what she has conquered.'[5] Elisabeth Arlington was sent a beautiful diamond necklace for 'services rendered'.

The King's behaviour was to fulfil Colbert's prediction. He allotted his new favourite a vast suite of chambers in Whitehall, overlooking the Thames, showered jewels and other precious gifts on her and, crucially, let her raid the public and privy purses on an even bigger scale than Barbara managed – and for even longer than Barbara. Such was the scale of her gold digging that she was credited with an income of more than £130,000 in one year.

At first, Arlington oozed enthusiasm for Louise. He told the French ambassador how much better it was to deal with a lady like Mlle de Kérouaille than with 'lewd and bouncing orange-girls and actresses, of whom no man of quality could take the measure'. Mlle de Kérouaille was no termagant or scold either, he added, in a dig at Barbara Castlemaine. 'When the King was with her, persons of breeding could, without loss of dignity, go to her rooms, and pay him and her their court.'

Louise's hold on the King was further strengthened in July 1672 when she gave birth to the baby son conceived at Euston. He was christened Charles Lennox, bringing the total of sons at the palace called Charles to four, which occasionally caused confusion. Louise

pressed the King to acknowledge her little Charles and even legitimise him by marrying her.[6] She saw no reason, she said, why the
King, who was 'Defender of the Faith' and head of the church,
could not give himself a dispensation 'to have two or three wives at
once'.

Louise even imagined herself replacing Catherine as queen.
Ambassador Colbert de Croissy noted her excitement when
Catherine was taken ill in December 1672. 'She has got the
notion ... that it is possible she may yet be Queen of England,' he
wrote. 'She talks from morning till night of the Queen's ailments as
if they were mortal.'[7] In fact, the Queen's condition looked all too
mortal. The King's principal physician Sir Alexander Fraizer diag-
nosed her as suffering from consumption (pulmonary tuberculosis).
He gave her between two months and a year at most. Luckily for
Catherine, this turned out to be nonsense and by Easter 1673 she had
recovered to live another thirty-two years.

Barbara and Louise were total contrasts. To get her way with the
King, Barbara employed verbal brute force, haranguing and deriding
the King, sometimes with a ferocity that visibly shook him. The softly
spoken Louise employed tears, embraces, sulks and gentle pleading
with him and in extremis she feigned illness. She had a further
advantage in her refined tastes for music and Italian art, which
appealed to him. The rivals were alike in one respect only. They
were both addicted to the gaming table and both lost so heavily they
could have ended in debtor's prison. But both knew the King would
always bail them out.

In the same month that the fourth Charles was born, Barbara
gave birth to a daughter. Baptised Barbara FitzRoy, she was the first
of the known offspring of the Duchess of Cleveland who was certainly not the King's – being universally credited to Churchill. The
King took the appearance of little Barbara with equanimity. A fort-
night later he attended the formal marriage of the Duchess's second
son Henry FitzRoy to Isabella Bennet, the only daughter of Barbara's
old lover, the Earl of Arlington.

The court continued to throw up scandal, as the King indulged himself and his wild companions. Sir John Reresby described a drunken night during a visit to England by the King's nephew, William of Orange. The latter was in London with a view to arranging his marriage to Mary, the eldest daughter of the Duke of York. 'One night', reported Reresby, 'at a supper, given by the Duke of Buckingham, the King made him drink very hard' till he was 'more frolic and gay than the rest of the company' and tried to break into the palace apartments of the maids of honour.[8] William would have succeeded except for rescuers arriving in time to stop him. Sir John reflected that the Princess Mary probably 'did not like him the worse for such a notable indication of his vigour', although, since William's future bride was no more than nine years old at the time, one wonders. One wonders, too, whether William was driven that night by drunken lust for women or a desire to please his sex-mad uncle. He was after all latently gay.

None of the women around Charles seems to have had any time for Louise. The Queen was immediately averse to her but tolerated her, it is suggested, because the baby-faced girl never attempted to outshine her. Of the King's principal mistresses, even the sweet-tempered Duchess of Richmond, the former Frances Stuart, couldn't stand her. Not surprisingly, neither could Barbara Castlemaine or Nell Gwyn.

Barbara bitched and mocked and tried to upstage the newcomer. Three days after the fake marriage at Euston Hall, Louise went to the races in the grandeur of the King's coach and six, with two other coaches in attendance. Barbara responded by driving through the streets in a coach and eight and talked of laying on a coach and twelve. At the New Year's Eve ball, Barbara made sure she outshone Louise – and no doubt everyone else – in the most glittering ensemble of the season, reportedly sporting £40,000 worth of jewellery.

Nell spread the rumour that Louise wore dirty underclothes and she lampooned her whenever she could. The cocky actress's put-downs were quick and often savage. One of the most quoted arose from a chance meeting with Louise when Nell was dressed in 'an exceeding rich suit of clothes'.

'Why, Nellie,' said Louise, 'you are grown rich, I believe, by your dress. Why, woman, you are fine enough to be a queen!'

'You are entirely right, Madam,' Nell replied, 'and I am whore enough to be a duchess.'[9]

In 1674, Nell commissioned a silversmith to construct the ultimate in bedroom furniture, a silver bedstead. As a symbol of her triumph over Barbara she ordered as one of the bed's decorations a miniature figure of Barbara's lover, Jacob Hall, 'dancing upon a rope of wire work'. Barbara's reaction is not recorded.

Louise was the one truly political animal among the rival courtesans, and was an amazingly rewarding agent for France. According to her French biographer, Henri Forneron:

> To her, more than to any statesman, France is indebted for French Flanders, the Franche Comte [and] Alsace ... During fifteen years she was holding Great Britain in her delicate little hand, and manipulated its king and statesmen as dexterously as she might have done her fan ... She made that country a tool of Louis XIV's policy.[10]

She worked not as a loud advocate of any particular policy but by pushing or undermining the advocates of certain policies, be they continuation of the Dutch war, religious toleration or Charles giving Louis XIV a free hand in Europe. Political careers turned, flourished or ended thanks to quiet words from Louise de Kérouaille.

Her rewards were enormous. There were gifts and pensions from both kings, plus all manner of pay-offs and bribes for favours done and favours promised. And there were honours in both France and England. The two kings each elevated her to the top of the aristocratic tree in their respective countries. Charles made her an English duchess and Louis made her the French equivalent. If the people of England hated her as a Frenchwoman and a Catholic –

and they certainly did – the aristocracy in both countries hated her still more for lording it over them. In one spat over precedence in Tunbridge Wells, a relatively lowly English marchioness told Louise that she had no intention of giving way to a woman who lived from prostitution. Louise, who considered herself far above other ladies at court, was so mortified that Charles had to console her by dispatching a platoon of horse guards to escort her home in the style of a queen.

Louise's first taste of serious politicking came with her involvement in the selection of a second wife for James, Duke of York, heir presumptive to the English throne. This issue would become a major factor in the growth of the anti-Catholic fury that was beginning to build in England and would eventually kill off the Stuart dynasty. It surfaced after James's first wife Anne died of cancer in March 1671, revealing on her deathbed that she was a Catholic. Three months later her only surviving son with the Duke, the seven-year-old Duke of Cambridge, followed her to the grave. This put pressure on James to remarry quickly and sire a new male to come after him in a dangerously threadbare line of succession. Anglican England clamoured loudly for a Protestant bride while on the far side of the Channel, the King of France manoeuvred secretly for a Catholic one. James, as obsessed with sex as his brother, let it be known that whoever was chosen had to be beautiful. Ruinously, he also wanted a Catholic bride. A search lasting nearly two years began.

Louis XIV's preferred choice was the widowed Duchess de Guise, a loyal cousin of his. He looked to his ambassador in London, Colbert de Croissy, to try to set up the match, and Colbert turned to Louise and a Catholic priest in the Queen's entourage to use their influence. 'I shall neglect no means to ensure success in this affair,' Colbert assured the King. 'I hope to triumph over every difficulty through the Queen's confessor and the new mistress.'[11]

The new mistress wouldn't play ball. She had a candidate of her own and rubbished Madame de Guise, who was described as 'of low stature' and 'ill formed', certainly not the beauty whom James had specified. Louise had come to know the Duke well in her year at the palace and claimed that any attempt to foist Madame de Guise on him would send him flying into the arms of some German princess. Louise's candidate was thirteen-year-old Marie-Eléonore, eldest daughter of a family friend, the Duchess of Elboeuf. Lobbying hard, Louise obtained portraits of Marie-Eléonore and her twelve-year-old sister and presented them to James. Colbert complained that Louise's campaign had been so effective that 'nobody will now listen to the praises of Madame de Guise'.

The Sun King was not amused. He instructed Colbert to sabotage any Elboeuf match. 'I have reasons', he said, 'which would make such a marriage disagreeable to me and I therefore hope you will adroitly apply yourself to cause hitches so that it will never take place.'[12] It didn't.

King Louis, the master manipulator, if not always the wisest, prevailed. A shortlist of eleven royal women – all of them Catholic – was drawn up. Marie-Eléonore and her younger sister were excluded on grounds of age and a princess from a French client state, the Duchy of Medina, was eventually chosen. She was fourteen-year-old Mary Beatrice d'Este, daughter of the Duke of Medina. A deeply religious Catholic, Mary was more inclined to become a nun than a queen and she had to be persuaded. It took an interview with Pope Clement X to do it. For the price of another Catholic chapel being allowed in the Whitehall Palace complex, the pontiff agreed to persuade the girl that her duty lay in helping with the conversion of England.

A striking part of the Elboeuf episode was Louise's audacity. While she was risking the Sun King's displeasure by wrecking the chances of his cousin the Duchess de Guise, she simultaneously pressed Charles to ask a huge favour of the French king on her behalf. In July 1673, Charles spoke to Colbert of 'his desire' that Mlle de Kérouaille should be granted the French crown property of Aubigny in Berry and the ducal title that went with it. The title would entitle her to a tabouret, the elaborately upholstered stool whose owner had the right to sit rather than stand before the Queen of France. It was the ultimate honour for a woman in the slavishly hierarchical palace of the Louvre. Granting it to Louise would have elevated her above almost the entire aristocracy of her native country. At this stage Louis wouldn't go that far for her. Louise was granted Aubigny but not the full ducal title. That would come the following year.

After her display of independence, Colbert changed his view about Louise, and so did Lord Arlington. The ambassador rubbished her to his minister at St Germain and reported that Arlington shared his view. 'Arlington', wrote Colbert, 'neither likes nor esteems Mlle de Kérouaille and reproaches her with having as soon forgotten the obligations he conferred on her, as any of the good dinners she has eaten.'

Despite the ambassador's distaste for the Breton adventuress, there was no question of France discarding her, nor indeed of Arlington daring to do so. The years 1672 and 1673 were those in which the two kings, Charles and Louis, attempted to implement the secret undertakings agreed in Dover back in 1670, and King Louis was counting on Louise to help keep the slippery Charles to his commitments. (Not that the Sun King was any more trustworthy than his English cousin.) Charles, meanwhile, remained besotted with his twenty-two-year-old mistress. The partying went on.

At the beginning of January 1672, one of the consequences of Charles's largesse to his favourites had emerged when he abruptly reneged on his debts to the banks. 'The Great Stop', as it was called, ruined numbers of bankers in Lombard Street. The government ceased repaying them capital and paid interest only. The money this saved for the exchequer – well over £1 million – was supposed to be used to complete construction of the fleet for the coming war with the Dutch. This short-term fix persuaded bankers the King was a bad investment; it would be more difficult for him to borrow in the future.

Three months after the Great Stop, the touch paper to war was lit. King Louis launched his long-planned invasion of the Netherlands with a force of 130,000 men, and Charles too declared war. He also took what seemed to be a big step towards Rome by issuing the Declaration of Indulgence, suspending the religious laws which had penalised Catholics and Dissenters since his grandfather's time.

None of it went to plan. On land, the Dutch stopped the French armies and then turned them back. At sea the brilliant Dutch admiral Michiel de Ruyter bested the Anglo-French navies in successive battles. And at home the Declaration of Indulgence fuelled an anti-Catholic paranoia that would become the dominant force in English politics for decades. In abrogating laws enacted by Parliament, the declaration also raised fears that Charles aimed at absolutist rule on the pattern of his cousin at the Louvre.

The paranoia focused first on the Duke of York. His choice of another Catholic to be his wife fed suspicions that he, like his first wife, was a secret Papist. Anglicans shivered at the thought that England was only one life away from Papist rule. Apprentices demonstrated against the match, effigies of the pope were burned, furious broadsides circulated. A report to the incoming Secretary of State, Sir Joseph Williamson, judged the public mood 'to be as bad against the Duke as ever it was against his father in the height of his troubles'.[13]

Such was the clamour that with the New Year of 1673 the King reversed his position on Catholics. In February he rescinded the Declaration of Indulgence and in May signed the savagely anti-Catholic Test Act. Subtitled 'An act for preventing dangers which may happen from Popish recusants', the Test Act required every servant of the crown to take the oath of supremacy, recognising the King as head of the church, swear allegiance and disavow the Catholic doctrine of transubstantiation. For good measure, they were also ordered to attend an Anglican service to take a Protestant sacrament.

The King's U-turn secured him £1.2 million from Parliament for the war – more than he expected – but failed to stem the anti-Catholic tide. Parliament demanded a stop to the York marriage. When informed that a proxy ceremony had already taken place in Italy, MPs attempted to prevent the marriage being consummated.

Their efforts were futile. The new Duchess, now aged fifteen, landed in England in November 1673 to be greeted by her forty-four-year-old husband. A long wait now began for her to deliver a son.

After the Test Act was passed into law, the Duke resigned as Lord High Admiral, so confirming suspicions about his religion. A second prominent Catholic casualty was a member of the so-called Cabal, Sir Thomas Clifford, the Lord Treasurer. He resigned his post and a few days later he was found dead. He is believed to have hanged himself.

The next casualty, and the most surprising, was the Duke of Buckingham. An eager promoter of the French alliance, Buckingham realised that he could be cast as scapegoat for the war. In a disastrously incoherent speech of self-justification from the bar of the House of Commons, he targeted his bitterest rival Arlington as author of the worst decisions. Together with his supporters, Buckingham sprayed around allegations of treason and corruption on a colossal scale, accusing unnamed individuals of creaming off hundreds of thousands of pounds. MPs were unimpressed by his performance. The Commons voted to ask the King 'to remove the said Duke of Buckingham from all his employments that are held during His Majesty's pleasure and from the Councils for ever'. Charles was forced to dismiss his oldest friend.

Buckingham was also humiliated in his private life. Relatives of the Earl of Shrewsbury, killed by Buckingham in a duel, brought an action against him and the dead man's widow for their 'wicked and scandalous life' and 'the insolent and shameless manner' of their existence. Neither fought the action, but instead they submitted to a committee of bishops, which drew up a deed, binding the guilty pair to a lifetime separation under forfeit of £10,000 each to the King. They complied, with the Countess retiring to a nunnery in France. Buckingham went back to his wife, who amazingly cried with joy.

Back in the political world, Arlington was desperate to inherit the Treasury from Sir Thomas Clifford. Both Louise and Barbara lobbied Charles on his behalf. Charles, who had so often accepted his courtesans' nominations when made by one or the other on their own, said no to the two of them acting together. Not regarding Arlington very highly, Charles was astute enough on this occasion not to listen to his mistresses and demoted Arlington to the less important position of Lord Chancellor.

The Treasury went to a tall, lean Yorkshireman who was assumed wrongly to be in Buckingham's pocket. This was Sir Thomas Osborne, later Earl of Danby. Louise quickly made him a friend and, according to rumour, made him her lover too. Her practice was always to be close to the men of power. Osborne was one of the most capable administrators of the age and did much to put the affairs of state on an even keel. Years later, after his fall, Louise would make allies of his rivals and successors, the Earls of Sunderland and Shaftesbury. The one significant player she never made up to was the Duke of Buckingham. She always remembered how he had left her stranded in France.

While Buckingham plotted and James pursued a wife, the King had begun to pay for the decades of debauchery. In 1674 he is said to have suffered at least three of what were described as apoplectic fits. The first 'took him in the Duchess of Portsmouth's presence', a careful phrase pregnant with innuendo. Courtiers urged him to take it easy and Louise apparently begged him not to come to her at nights. We have no knowledge of when or where the second fit took place but the third occurred in the Privy Garden. The fits may have been the first signs of the health problems that would recur in future years.

Ill health marked the coming winter too. The Queen once more took to her bed in February 1674, this time with a serious bronchial infection. Her illness plunged her into her own paranoia. The Venetian minister in London, Girolamo Alberti, reported in dispatches that Catherine had talked of being poisoned and expected to die. She was said to have complained to one of her ladies of the king's amours and claimed that 'he had killed her'. But by March she had recovered and in September the king was briefly cohabiting with her, a practice he had abandoned for years. Needless to say this didn't last, and the following year she was so 'tormented with jealousy' at the 'flaunting of his mistresses' that she couldn't disguise it.[14]

The King and Louise were also laid low, but with another kind of infection, described as the 'pox'. It was probably syphilis. Details of their infection were relayed with relish in diplomatic dispatches to France. In May 1674, Ruvigny, one of the special envoys King Louis sometimes dispatched to England, wrote to the French Foreign Minister de Pomponne:

> I have a thing to tell you monsieur, for the King's information, which should remain secret as long as it pleases his majesty to keep it so, because if it gets out it might be a source of unseemly raillery. Whilst the King was winning provinces, the King of England was catching a malady which he has been at the trouble of communicating to the Duchess of Portsmouth. That prince is nearly cured; but to all appearance the lady will not so soon be rid of the virus.[15]

The envoy went on to say: 'She has been, however, in a degree consoled for such a troublesome present by one more suitable to her charms – a pearl necklace, worth four thousand Jacobus, and a diamond worth six thousand, which have so rejoiced her that I should not wonder if, for the price, she were not willing to risk another attack of the disease.'

The King recovered quite quickly but Louise suffered miserably for nearly eight months, and the infection may well have been the cause of her later persistent ill health. She travelled to Bath and Tunbridge Wells and possibly Epsom for the waters. She tried one fearful remedy after another. She didn't let the King forget the episode. More than two years later another French ambassador, Honoré Courtin, was to inform French Foreign Minister Louvois that he had witnessed a confrontation between King and courtesan over the former's behaviour: 'I tell you privately', Courtin wrote, 'how three days ago the Duchess of Portsmouth in my presence attacked the king about his infidelities. She did not hide from me what she had suffered from his misconduct with trulls; and he himself then described to me how his head doctor had prescribed for her.'[16]

The head doctor alluded to was most likely Richard Wiseman, the King's chief surgeon, who was an expert on treating the pox. Following the best knowledge and practice of the time, Wiseman knew the patient must be purged and bled. Both these actions were essential if the body's controlling 'humours' were to be restored to equilibrium. Bleeding involved opening a small vein with a knife and drawing off a small amount of blood. Purging involved administering various potions designed to make the patient vomit and excrete until both stomach and bowels were empty. Even then the purging was not complete. The patient was sweated – wrapped up in sheets and blankets and placed in a bed surrounded by hot bricks in a sealed room. How Louise must have loathed the discomfort, let alone the indignity, as her usually cool countenance was reduced to that of a beetroot sticking out of a blanket.

Along with this savage regime, Wiseman administered opium and various herbal mixtures laced with gold and mercury. The opium would certainly make the patient feel better but the mercury was the sole part of the treatment that actually worked on the infection. For reasons not then understood, the skin ulcers that were an early symptom of syphilis could be cleared up by the application of mercury. Only the wealthy could afford this treatment. The less well-off would suffer the horrors of London's many dedicated sweating houses, then, when the ulcers vanished of their own accord in a matter of days or weeks, believe themselves cured and pay their fees, only to suffer in years to come from more terrible symptoms such as dementia as the syphilis entered its final stages. Thanks to Wiseman's mercury, Charles and Louise were given a chance of a cure, though it was little wonder Louise complained to the ambassador.*

---

* For a fuller details of the horrors of treatment for syphilis, see the Appendix: Some Aspects of Sex in the Seventeenth Century.

Given Charles's wild sex life and the proliferation of sexually transmitted disease in seventeenth-century London, it can be assumed that Louise was by no means the only lady of the court to be infected by him and by other gallants. Understandably few, if any, seem to have made a fuss.

Both Barbara and Louise had another kind of threat to worry about too. As Catholic members of the Queen's household, both were directly threatened by the Test Act. However, there was a way out for them. A concession allowed Queen Catherine to retain a small number of Catholic ladies of the bedchamber. One can only guess at the lobbying of the Queen that went on as she decided whom to pick. In the end she chose Louise but omitted Barbara. The woman who had so humiliated the Queen ten years earlier was thus cast out of the official palace hierarchy which she had fought so ruthlessly to join. Revenge over Barbara must have been sweet for the sad little Portuguese.

For Barbara, it was a galling moment of defeat. But she was not finished. Sidelined and in debt, she pestered Charles for more money. He gave her Nonsuch Palace – after all, she already had the title. Nonsuch was a Renaissance palace ten miles south of London built for Henry VIII by the finest Italian craftsmen, including men who had worked on Fontainebleau for the King of France. The palace was so lavish in its construction that it cost one and a half times as much as Hampton Court to build yet was only a third of its size. It became a favourite haunt of Elizabeth I and after going through several owners, including at least three of the men who had sentenced Charles I to death, it came into the ownership of the politician and courtier Sir Robert Long, via a 99-year lease from the dowager Queen. When Long died in 1673, the palace was bequeathed to his son. But Charles overrode the will and gave it to Barbara. This was to spell the end for the palace. Barbara eventually sold it for scrap. It was torn down and its bricks, timbers, fine metal-work, carved masonry and gilded tiles sold off to pay her gambling debts. The palace's parkland was turned over to farmland.

Astonishingly, Barbara would remain a powerful presence around the court for a further two years.

The war ended in 1674, when Charles was forced to make terms with the Dutch because of an empty treasury. Like the previous disastrous struggle with the Dutch, the war was far costlier than at first envisaged. It nevertheless saw his high-maintenance women finding new avenues to cash. One avenue involved the King issuing them with warrants for prize money and goods from captured Dutch ships supposed to bolster the Treasury. But before the women could profit from it, the Cabal collapsed. The new Lord Treasurer, Sir Thomas Osborne, too capable by half, stopped the payments. He ordered that 'neither Madam Kerwell's nor the Duchess of Cleveland's nor Nell Gwyn's warrants would be accepted.' The loss to Louise alone was reported to be some £30,000, but Louis XIV came to her aid with the offer of his share in the next East Indiaman captured from the Dutch.

How well the mistresses were still doing despite the war can be gauged from the luxuries surrounding Louise. Her apartments in the palace consisted of more than twenty rooms plus a gallery seventy feet long. They were a magnet for aristocratic and lesser gawpers. John Evelyn saw them one December morning when accompanying the King and a retinue of courtiers. They found the young woman in her dressing room newly out of bed, with maids combing her hair. Evelyn was impressed by the opulence. 'What engaged my curiosity,' he recalled, 'was the rich and splendid furniture of this woman's apartment, now twice or thrice pulled down and rebuilt to satisfy her.' Among the exquisitely worked tapestries, the Japanese cabinets and profusion of silver, he spotted 'some of Her Majesty's best paintings',[17] presumably wrested from the Queen to end up with the notoriously acquisitive young Breton.

Evelyn, sanctimonious as ever, wondered how Louise could live with herself: 'What contentment can there be in the riches and splendour of this world, purchased with vice and dishonour?' The next mistress in Charles's life would enjoy herself too much to bother about such considerations.

17

A SENSATIONAL ENCOUNTER
WITH THE PAST

At the beginning of 1675 Charles was in financial straits and relations with his government and Parliament were in turmoil. The latest war with the Dutch had not settled much and the habitual blame game over foreign policy and finances continued between Parliament and monarch. The cavalier Parliament was turning out to be as much a thorn in Charles's side as the Long Parliament had been in his father's. Matters were even worse now that James, Duke of York, had sired an heir, causing growing unease over the possibility of a line of Catholic kings. Charles and the head of the Treasury, Lord Danby, who was in effect the prime minister, disagreed on the question of religion, with Danby determined to secure a resolutely Protestant kingdom, while the King, following the secret treaties with France, was wary of shutting out all religious observance but Anglicanism.

As was his way, Charles sought distractions from his problems. Along with his mistresses and his racing he became immersed in plans for a new observatory at Greenwich. Its primary purpose was described as being 'to find out the so much desired longitude of places for the perfecting of the art of navigation'. The King took a strong interest in 'useful experiments concerning navigation, of which he has a marvellous understanding'.[1] A new Astronomer Royal, John Flamsteed, proved to be equal to his task. He took tens of thousands of observations and produced a catalogue of nearly three thousand stars.[2] By refining the tables giving navigators the true position of stars and other heavenly bodies, ships' captains could work out their position. All this fascinated Charles, although Bishop Burnet thought it unseemly for a king to be so well versed in nautical affairs.[3]

And then over the horizon sailed the mesmerising – and once upon a time stratospherically rich – Hortense Mancini, the star beauty to whom Charles had proposed when he was penniless and been turned down flat. In a marvellous twist of fate the temptress, now totally broke, arrived in London to re-enter Charles's life and become his last truly grand passion. Hortense was flamboyant, outrageous, fiercely intelligent and ostentatiously bisexual. After turning down Charles all those years ago in Paris, she'd escaped from a disastrous marriage to the fabulously rich but unhinged Duc de la Meilleraye.

Hortense's life contained a dichotomy: on the one hand it epitomised the hedonistic life of the French court, in which Louis XIV encouraged sexual excess, and on the other it demonstrated her intense reaction to the control that men exercised over women. For Hortense, there was nothing philosophical about her rebellion: it was purely personal. Her husband, who wanted to control his wife and her money with absolutely no regard for her wishes, made her life intolerable and she wasn't going to stand for it.

As the spoiled favourite niece of France's first minister, Cardinal Mazarin, Hortense's upbringing had been as sparkling and glamorous as it was possible to be. She lived within the innermost circle of the royal court. The French king was a childhood friend. In her memoirs, Hortense describes a world full of laughter and games, tempered by the knowledge that one day she and her sisters would be given to suitors chosen by their uncle for their political standing.

Hortense and her sisters had arrived from their native Italy because of politics. Their uncle, Cardinal Mazarin, felt his position was precarious following the civil war, the Fronde. To bolster his political connections, he hatched a plan to bring his nieces and nephews to Paris and arrange suitably advantageous marriages for them. For the young Hortense, life in Paris was full of entertainment and opportunity. The little girl from Rome was not only fun-loving but bright. She wrote about her childhood years in her memoirs:

> You will doubtless find it hard to believe that at that age when philosophical reasoning is usually the very last thing on a person's mind, I had such serious thought as I had about every aspect of life. And yet it is true that my greatest pleasure at that time was to shut myself up alone and write down everything that came into my head. Not long ago I came across some of these writings again ... They were filled with doubts and questions which I posed to myself about all the things I found hard to understand. I never resolved them to my satisfaction.[4]

Hortense suffered from the lack of a good education. There was, however, no lack of insight. When she came to look back over her life, she regretted not finding the answers to her early questions. Had she been better educated, Hortense might have been dismayed to discover a river of historical opinion stretching back beyond Aristotle by which women were seen as inferior to men.

She was to find this out soon enough via the practical lesson of marriage. The childhood idyll she shared with her sisters came to an end when their husbands were chosen for them. The future Charles II had already been rebuffed as being without prospects. A long affair between Hortense's sister Marie and Louis XIV resulted in disappointment when the King married a Spanish princess. Worse was to follow, for Louis further distanced himself from the Mazarins in 1659 following a scandalous episode when the Cardinal's nephew celebrated Easter Week by taking part in a black mass and orgy at the estate of the brother of Madame de Montespan.

With his health now waning, Mazarin desperately looked about for a suitor on whom to bestow the hand of his favourite, Hortense, and with it the Mazarin name and fortune. The choice he made could not have been worse. Armand-Charles de la Porte de la Meilleraye, a rich nobleman who was a commander of artillery, was related to Cardinal Richelieu (Mazarin's predecessor) and whose father had been a military hero. He seemed an amiable soul and was graciously willing, in return for the cardinal's gold, to set aside his own family title and change his name to Mazarin.

The marriage was a disaster. The new Duc de Mazarin was not the most alluring specimen. Hortense, who was merely sixteen when they were married, was high-spirited and flirted with all and sundry. The ardent letter-writer, Madame de Sevigné, excused the young woman's behaviour, writing cuttingly of the new Duc de Mazarin's looks that 'He bore on his face the justification of his wife's conduct.'[5] The upright Duke was tortured by his young wife's frolics. He began to exhibit signs of neurosis, retreating into medieval piety. Whether he was already unhinged or whether it was marriage that tore him from the hinges of sanity, we cannot say. He ordered his female servants' front teeth to be pulled out so as not to arouse passion in young men, and had to be dissuaded from doing the same to the two daughters Hortense bore him. The classical statuary in the Palais Mazarin mocked his piety and he took a hammer to their genital regions. Paintings were daubed with black to cover their taunting nudity. More amusingly, he forbade the milk-maids to milk the cows, seeing in this simple act some form of lewd Sapphic rite.

The Duke attempted to keep Hortense a prisoner and had her watched day and night. On the few occasions she was able to go out, spies shadowed her in the streets. When the Duke had to travel on official business, he insisted that Hortense accompany him, no matter how long the journey, nor even if she was pregnant and near to giving birth. He began to give away his wife's fortune in support of various religious purposes suggested by priests Hortense described as a 'cabal bigote'.[6] The Sun King gazed upon the combined wealth of the Mazarin/Meilleraye family and enquired how he might lighten its burden. The Duke dutifully handed the King large sums of money.

A virtual prisoner, her friends barred from seeing her, her servants regularly sent away, her pearls and jewellery confiscated, Hortense could stand it no more and one night she ran away. From that moment on, the woman who said she knew that a woman's place was not to cause gossip, did nothing but cause gossip. She was spurned at court and advised by the King to return to her husband. Such was the Duke's self-righteous and overbearing behaviour, Hortense decided she must leave him for good. As she made to leave the Palais Mazarin, her husband physically tried to stop her but Hortense forced her way past him in tears and fled to her brother's. A further attempt at reconciliation led to a suggestion from the King that she should enter a convent. She refused, went back to her husband, then fled into refuge at the royal abbey of Chelles near Paris, where the abbess was a cousin of the Duke's. Pacifying the Duke, Louis requested that Hortense move to another convent near the Bastille, which had a stricter regime. There she encountered another young woman about her own age, Sidonie de Lenoncourt, the Marquise de Courcelles. Together, they created mayhem with childish pranks at the nuns' expense. It was rumoured that they became lovers. The miscreants were relocated back to Chelles, from where Hortense's husband attempted to take her home by force.

Both sides resorted to law, Hortense suing for a legal separation and her husband hotly disputing the application. Hortense agreed to a settlement whereby she would have some degree of personal autonomy, living in an apartment separate from her husband. Inevitably, the arrangement did not work out. With the help of her brother, the Duc de Nevers, Hortense rode off to Italy disguised as a man, accompanied by the Chevalier de Rohan, who was probably her lover.* She had an affair with her equerry and her ensuing pregnancy became the talk of Milanese society.[7]

Soon Hortense ran out of ready cash and was forced back to France, destitute and in debt. By now she was the most scandalous woman in Europe. Louis XIV, always her amused admirer, accepted that the marriage was well and truly over. He gave her a small pension allowing her to travel about Italy and provincial France, until she eventually came under the protection of her old lover, Charles-Emmanuel, the Duke of Savoy. At his palace in Chambéry, surrounded by the foothills of the Alps, she found some sort of peace. Unfortunately for us, her memoir ends at this point.[8] But her story was far from over.

Hortense presided over a salon that was a Mecca for artists and intellectuals. Apart from the Duke, Hortense had at least one other affair while at Chambéry, with the historian Cesar Vichard. In 1675 this happy ménage was torn apart when the Duke died and his widow showed Hortense the door. She was rescued by Ralph Montagu, the ambitious and flamboyant British ambassador to Paris, and a would-be player in power struggles in London. Montagu was a famously successful womaniser, a favourite lover of the English court beauty Mrs Jane Myddleton. His success can only be put down to his personality and status, for in a portrait by John Closterman we see him in fine clothes, with a small mouth bracketed between a long, pointed nose and a large, rounded chin, peering out at the world like a contented hermit crab from beneath an enormous wig.[9]

Montagu brought Hortense to England with the express intent of having her displace the Duchess of Portsmouth in the King's favour

---

* The Chevalier would later feature in the rivalry between Nell Gwyn and the Duchess of Portsmouth, not for his amorous abilities but through his death. When Rohan was executed in 1674 for treason, Louise appeared at court in mourning, claiming a family connection. Gwyn then turned up in black, saying it was for the Crown Prince of Tartary. When asked within earshot of Louise what her connection was with the khan, she replied it was exactly the same relation as the Chevalier de Rohan was to the Duchess of Portsmouth.

and so increase Montagu's personal standing at court. Hortense's purpose was much less ambitious, being primarily one of finding a new home and benefactor. If that benefactor turned out to be the King, so much the better. It says a great deal for Hortense's beauty and style that although she was penniless and three years older than Louise, Montagu thought she was worthy of the task. Up to that point, Charles had always replaced his mistresses with younger women.

Hortense arrived on New Year's Eve 1675, dressed as a knight, accompanied by Vichard, and made an immediate impression. She had become something of a romantic heroine, her exploits written and gossiped about long before she appeared in England. 'She is one of those Roman beauties', wrote Charles de Saint-Evremond, 'who in no way resemble your dolls of France.'[10]

Saint-Evremond had fled from France after criticising Cardinal Mazarin. He was a bon viveur and essayist, who regaled his friends with his opinions on a wide range of subjects, including how they should run their own lives. He was specific about Hortense's attributes: 'There are none in the world so sweet ... Her smile would soften the hardest heart,' he gushed, describing her eyes, nose, voice and hair in luxuriant detail.[11] Saint-Evremond was clearly smitten – as the King would soon be.

Twenty-nine-year-old Hortense simply dazzled Charles. Although his other long-time mistresses, Nell Gwyn, Countess Castlemaine and the Duchess of Portsmouth, remained Whitehall fixtures, inside a year Hortense became the King's chief sexual obsession. In his usual emotionally disengaged manner, Charles held no rancour over the way in which his suit had been rebuffed in 1659 nor did Hortense for the manner in which hers had in turn been rejected in 1660. In an age of patronage and of marriage for economic or political gain, such quibbles were deemed affectations. Besides, there were similarities in Charles's and Hortense's stories. Both were sexual adventurers. Both preferred playful pursuits to more mature or responsible activity. And both had been cast adrift from their expected glittering futures to become impoverished mendicants in foreign lands, dependent upon the whim and generosity of others for their supper. With the Restoration, Charles's story had taken a turn for the better; now Hortense hoped that hers was about to enter a happy, or at least a comfortable, phase.

The Duke of York held a reception for Hortense and the King sent a senior courtier to pass on his respects. The French ambassador, the Marquis de Ruvigny, no doubt with a nod to his master's partiality, said she was 'more beautiful than anyone in England'.

Louise realised she faced a type of adversary altogether different from Nell Gwyn, the young upstart from the backstreets. Louise had underestimated Nell, but she would not make the mistake of under-estimating Hortense, possibly because she saw Hortense as a social equal who could exercise the sort of influence at court in which the sexy young actress had no interest. When Hortense arrived, Louise was pregnant with a child by Charles. So great was her anxiety that she miscarried.

For her part, Nell saw the new royal mistress as presenting a different challenge. If the King became fixated on Hortense and had children by her, Nell's chances of ever persuading him to bestow titles on her own children would recede. As part of her offensive, Nell badgered the King to ennoble their eldest son, Charles, just as he had his offspring by Barbara and Louise. During a visit from Charles, she is said to have called to her son, then aged six, 'Come here you little bastard and say hello to your father.' When Charles reproached her, Nell said that she had no other title with which to call him. Charles relented. In December 1676, the boy was given the surname Beauclerk and made Earl of Burford and Baron Heddington. The story is a good one and, given Nell's reputation for the rough wit of the streets, it has a ring of truth about it, if it were not for the competing story of Nell hanging her child out of a window until Charles cried out, 'Long live the Earl of Burford!'

A few weeks later, the younger boy, James, was made Lord Beauclerk. Nell was finally established and could hold her head up among the better-born women of the King's seraglio.

Apart from Nell and the Duchess of Portsmouth and their circles, one other important person was particularly dismayed at the arrival of Hortense in London. This was Louis XIV, who foresaw his influence over his cousin diminishing if his chief agent at the English court, Louise, was cast aside.

Louis's presentiments soon gave way to alarm. He received a letter from Charles saying that Hortense was short of money and asking him to press the Duc de Mazarin to increase his wife's pension. Louis chose not to get involved. But he recalled Ruvigny as ambassador and dispatched the more socially adept Honoré Courtin to look after his interests at the Court of St James. Louis evidently held Courtin in high regard, but the new envoy's mission did not begin well. He brought a demand from Meilleraye that his wife should return to France immediately and retire to a convent. This tempting offer was reluctantly turned down.

Louis XIV was faced with a potential new royal favourite in London who had good reason to feel that her old ally at Versailles was no longer her friend. When Hortense was ensconced in St James's Palace, any doubts the French king might have had as to the seriousness of the situation were dispelled. The new ambassador, Courtin, tried to persuade Meilleraye to create a favourable atmosphere at the Palais de Mazarin so that his errant wife might return home. This entreaty resulted merely in a long diatribe from Meilleraye setting out why his wife would be better off in a convent.[12] Courtin tried in vain to persuade Hortense's now neglected lover Vichard to intercede. Vichard saw his lover's gaze was elsewhere, found his circumstances hopeless, and left for France. Courtin's tenure at the Court of St James was going no better than that of his predecessor.

Meanwhile, Louise found her situation ever more unstable. She was increasingly isolated within the court, which now mirrored to a great extent the sentiment of the country against her. Not one to waste an opportunity, Nell Gwyn put on her darkest mourning clothes once more, this time in lamentation for her adversary's social death. By late summer of 1676, rumours circulated that the King no longer slept with Louise. He was now wooing Hortense and sleeping with Gwyn. Nevertheless, Charles continued to pay Louise all due courtesy. While the royal ardour might have cooled, the Duchess remained a key link with Charles's banker in Paris.

England and France were engaged in a dance of power and money. Ralph Montagu was dispatched once more to Paris to nego-tiate the sums France was willing to pay to keep England out of its war with the Netherlands.[13] In London, yet another new French ambassador, Jean-Paul de Barillon, had the task of keeping Louise's position secure and of helping to bribe any politicians necessary to further French interests.

In the midst of all this domestic and political turmoil, Barbara, Countess Castlemaine, Duchess of Cleveland, had thrown in the towel and decided to start a new life in France. She left on 13 March 1676. A vicious printed satire marked her departure. The lampoon named her various lovers, including the dramatist William Wycherley, and referred to the King's affair with Nell Gwyn for good measure:

> Why might she not fuck with a poet,
> When his Majesty fucks with a player?

Barbara moved to Paris, taking her two youngest daughters with her. According to the Gramont memoirs, she moved to be near her lover, Ralph Montagu.[14] As might be expected, she made a great show of leaving and of arriving, taking forty servants along and donat-ing £1000 to the convent where her daughters were to be educated. At their parting, the King showed his relief. His last words to her were, 'Madam, all that I ask of you . . . is to live so for the future as to make the least noise you can, and I care not who you love.' It appeared to be the final bowing out of one of life's great divas. But this grandest of all grand dames had not yet done with England, nor with its king, her lover.

With the Countess now in France, her eldest daughter Anne, Countess of Sussex, occupied her apartments. Anne and Hortense became firm friends, enabling the King, who recognised Anne as his daughter, to visit regularly. On occasion, Hortense stayed the night. The French ambassador wondered whether he might be able to arrange for Hortense to be replaced in the King's favour with the less threatening Mrs Jane Myddleton, the famous blonde-haired beauty who was the Italian's rival for the title of most beautiful woman in London. Jane Myddleton was not a woman to overburden her husband with irksome matrimonial duties. In time, she had sexual liaisons with many court characters. Apart from Ralph Montagu, she had affairs with Edmund Waller, the Duc de Gramont and others, but she never allowed herself to be co-opted as a royal mistress. By the standards of the day her reputation remained unsullied.

In March 1677, the French ambassador reported to Paris that Hortense had spent much of a day shut up with the King in a private Whitehall chamber to which only His Majesty and William Chiffinch had keys.[15] It had taken her less than three months to become one of the King's favourites. In no time, she was able to set herself up with a salon at which fashionable and well-connected London could gossip, discuss the theatre, play cards and make sexual liaisons. From Louise's point of view, the threat was serious because Hortense was not only well versed in courtly arts, she was able to hold her own in intellectual circles; indeed her entourage soon included many of the foremost figures of science and the arts. The reason for the swift turnaround in her fortunes was that Hortense had been put on the royal payroll.

Just as he remained open-handed with money, Charles continued to be careless with the favours of his mistresses. Soon after her arrival, Hortense made other conquests, one of the first being Prince Louis of Monaco. And just as John Evelyn was constantly at hand to disapprove of the antics of his contemporaries within the court (albeit secretly to his diary), Saint-Evremond was always at Hortense's disposal with the benefit of his wisdom. Unbidden, he wrote to her with a word of warning on the perils of getting tangled up with kings and princes, pointing out that rulers crave distraction via those favourites 'with whom they ease themselves of their burdens'. He went on to warn that disaster awaits a favourite who becomes too friendly with a king who seeks 'enjoyments they cannot find in their Grandeur':

> They look out, at last, for a bosom friend, to whom they may open a heart, which they keep shut to the rest of the world ... but how dangerous are such friendships to a favourite who is more solicitous of showing his love, than watchful on his conduct and behaviour! This confidant thinks to find a friend, where he meets with his master; and, by an unexpected turn, his familiarity is punished, as the indiscreet freedom of a servant who forgot himself.[16]

The essay fell on deaf ears. The young Hortense was having far too much fun. Of course, the worldly Saint-Evremond knew only too well that a letter containing unsolicited advice could not avert the social and amorous pitfalls he so cleverly dissected. So why did he write it? The reason was that he too was infatuated with Hortense. In another letter, he proclaimed, 'I love you', while elsewhere he wrote the pithy aphorism: 'With other Ladies our Love generally begins where our Reason ends; here our Love cannot end, unless we lose our Reason.'[17]

With even the fifty-three-year-old man of letters in thrall to the still youthful and beautiful Hortense, a large portion of London's male society seemed to be at her feet, in her bed or at her basset table.* For the unimpressed anonymous newssheets, she was 'The Italian Whore'. Those who saw in her a means of prising power away from

---

* The card game of basset originated in Italy, and was perhaps brought to England in 1677, two years after the arrival of Hortense Mancini. It was played exclusively in high society. The game was weighted strongly in favour of the banker and was designed to encourage continuous rounds of betting, which meant that players could generate huge losses, often losing entire family estates.

Louise, and hence influence from the French king, were pleased at her ability to hold Charles bewitched. Montagu was joined by Arlington in her circle of supporters. The plan seemed to be working; the King's new infatuation caused Louise great distress and she often wept at her situation. With a fresh lover to distract him, Charles strode the corridors of Whitehall at his ease, exhibiting little concern over the manner in which the enterprise of government was lurching from crisis to crisis.

Hortense's most scandal-provoking relationship was that with Anne Palmer, Countess of Sussex, Charles's daughter with Countess Castlemaine. In 1674, at the age of thirteen, Anne was married to thirty-year-old Thomas Lennard, Baron Dacre, who took the title of Earl of Sussex upon his wedding. Despite her youth, Anne quickly stole a leaf from her mother's love book, and scouted around for other partners. Within two years she gave gossips something radical to talk about by starting a relationship with Hortense. In a marvellously theatrical tableau, the two staged a public sword fight in St James's Park, dressed in nightgowns. It is impossible not to applaud this ironic and hedonistic display, staged in an age of male posturing and duelling.

The Earl of Sussex did not see the humour of it and sent his wayward wife to his country estate, where she lay in bed all day, kissing a portrait miniature of Hortense and declaring her everlasting love. Tiring of this petulant display, the Earl packed Anne off to Paris, to be looked after by – of all people – her mother, who had herself gone into exile because of her notoriety.

Even for Charles, the fact that his lover was having an affair with his own daughter was hard to ignore. Of course, some said Anne resembled the Earl of Chesterfield, but Charles had acknowledged her as his own and given her the surname FitzRoy. Now he had to face up to what he had created between the bed sheets. The relationship was the ultimate expression of the licentious court he had fostered. Since his accession in 1660, he had made love to dozens of women, several of whom had borne him children, one of whom was now having a relationship with his latest mistress. If an illustration were ever needed of the modern American saying, 'What goes around comes around', one might look no further. For the cynical court wits, always looking for some new sexual intrigue to amuse them, here was the very best of gossip.

On 4 November, celebrations were held for the marriage of James's fifteen-year-old daughter Mary to William of Orange, the Dutch head of state, at St James's Palace. It was William's twenty-seventh birthday. The King would have preferred Mary to marry the French dauphin, Louis, but the unstable domestic political situation made the match inadvisable. In Scotland, Charles's repression of the Presbyterians was continuing at a ferocious level, with scenes of escalating violence and barbarity. In England, the crackdown on religious dissenters was leading to increased numbers of non-conformists being thrown into jail and their families into poverty and starvation. In Ireland, disputes continued over land allocation between the Catholics who had been dispossessed by Cromwell and the Protestants who did not wish to relinquish the properties they had been given. Against these problems in all three kingdoms, James had to be dissuaded from marrying his daughter to a Catholic super-power next door.

Shortly after celebrating the wedding, Louise became ill. Her illness was reported, like all such gossip, by the French ambassador, Jean-Paul Barillon.[18] He was not alone in his interest in the Duchess's health. The celebrated Parisian writer Madeleine de Scudéry relayed gossip that Louise had clutched a crucifix while lying in her sickbed, pleading with Charles to take to a more righteous path and give up his other mistresses.[19] Nell Gwyn would have savoured the scene in which the delusional Louise acted the part of the virtuous and wronged woman in the relationship. The Queen never entered the feverish mind of *la Grande Horizontale*, for she was not just any mistress – she was the King's political ally and the key to his foreign finance.

As if in answer to Louise's prayers, Charles took action over

Hortense. As Barbara Villiers had discovered, there was a limit to the King's patience and understanding. Beautiful and exciting though Hortense was, Charles veered away from her embrace and back towards the less exhilarating but more predictable arms of Louise de Kérouaille – quiet, patient, calculating Louise.

In his late forties, was the boy-king, the eternal playboy, at last growing up? Or was he simply growing old? Neither seems to have been the motivating force. Women with strong personalities always captivated Charles, but with Hortense he had encountered a woman whose character was too close to his own. Both expected to live their lives as they wished, unencumbered by sexual or social constraints. Both expected everyone else to put up with their decisions and actions. With Hortense, Charles had met his match. Even Barbara's wildest infidelities could be seen as merely a mirror of his own. With Barbara, there had always been at least a chance that if Charles stopped sleeping around, so might she. But Hortense answered to no one, not even a king. She was a woman who would not only look a gift horse in the mouth, but kick it where it hurt.

Charles sought the resolution that would cause him least grief and annoyance. He avoided a showdown by allowing Hortense to remain on the courtesan payroll and stay on at court. The situation was not perfect, but thanks to his deeply developed pleasure principle, Charles habitually sought some sort of equilibrium. As for their relationship, they were now merely good friends.

18

PLOTS AND ALARMS

After the King's affair with Hortense Mancini cooled off, the Duchess of Portsmouth re-emerged as Charles II's *maîtresse en titre*, and she would remain so until the end of his life. Given the animosity that she inspired, Louise's mere survival in England bordered on the miraculous. Her nationality, her religion and her known dominance over the King, her lavish lifestyle at the country's expense and her rumoured promiscuity fused to make her a figure of hate. Outside the protective walls of Whitehall, she was known as the 'French whore', almost universally loathed, and even inside the palace she had few real friends.

Until the winter of 1678–9 Louise was able to live with the animosity and paraded proudly in public with her royal lover. In April 1678, she and the King, together with their six-year-old son Charles Lennox travelled in grand style by royal barge to Deptford for the launch of a new warship. Charles named it the *Lennox* after their son, who had been made Duke of Richmond and Lennox.

Louise was still the haughty young favourite, exuding confidence and power. In June, Jean-Paul Barillon, the new French ambassador, said of her, 'I cannot doubt that the King speaks to her of everything and that she is able to do much to insinuate what she wishes.' In

November, her confidence evaporated, when the King stood back, doing nothing as the alleged Catholic conspiracy against his life, the so-called Popish Plot, exploded round him, and its first innocent victims were dragged to the gallows. In the face of the anti-Catholic hysteria that now arose, a frightened Louise contemplated flight. In December, ambassador Barillon alerted King Louis to that possibility. 'Madam de Portsmouth', Barillon told his king, 'is not sure that she can stay in England. There are many persons who are minded to name her in Parliament as conspiring against the Protestant religion for the King of France. She thinks it would not be a great misfortune to be obliged to retire to France.'[1]

The Duchess was far from convinced that her lover would protect her if a worse crisis were to develop. Barillon wrote:

> She is afraid that her continued presence must embarrass King Charles, and she would prefer to get away while he preserves some kind of feeling for her than by staying longer to expose herself to the rage of a whole nation. Her position would be sad indeed if, after she lost the King's favour, she was assailed by Parliament and the people.

Louis had already been asked to provide protection if Louise was forced to flee and he had reassured her; but talk of her quitting England was the last thing that the French king wanted to hear. In 1678 he was planning to launch another stage in his step-by-step military conquest of the Spanish Netherlands and he needed to keep England, and especially her navy, from intervening. Louise's influence with King Charles in this period was seen – rightly – as crucial.

Financially, she benefited hugely. Charles continued to shower her with gifts and money and she was allowed to supplement the King's largesse by continuing to syphon off a fortune in pay-offs and bribes. An example was the traffic in royal pardons. Her agent Timothy Hall sold these to convicts, and those unable to pay were auctioned off on her behalf in the colonies as indentured servants, effectively slaves. Many thousands were sold in Virginia, Maryland and Barbados during Charles's reign at between £3 and £12 a head. The French records show that Louise's regular pension of £12,000 a year was swollen by supplements to reach an average of £40,000.[2] Even this was not enough. She found a way to dip her fingers directly into Treasury funds. In one year she extracted a colossal £136,668.

By comparison with Louise, Nell Gwyn was a poor relation. A surviving list of payments by a Treasury clerk to 'Madam Carwell', as the Duchess of Portsmouth was known, and to 'Nelly Gwynn' for the last six months of 1676 shows Louise receiving three times as much as Nell. The following year, Louise received five times as much.

This was a period of astonishing corruption. The King was as grasping for his cousin Louis's gold as his mistresses were for his own. In return for vast French subventions he continually prorogued Parliament to keep at bay the increasingly anti-French opposition, which howled and bellowed for war.

Charles became so completely beholden to his French cousin that, according to the French foreign affairs archive, he told the Sun King that he, Louis, could choose when the English Parliament would next be summoned. Without Parliament, England sat back while Louis XIV's military juggernaut was allowed to capture further chunks of Flanders whose names would one day be known in every English household – Ghent, Mons, Ypres, Valenciennes, St Omer, Cambrai. They proved far easier to take in 1678–9 than in 1914–18.

French gold found its way into the pockets of senior British statesmen to buy their support. At one time or another, France is believed to have purchased the loyalty of Lords Arlington, Buckingham, Danby, Sunderland, Bristol and Shaftesbury. Even the republican idealist Algernon Sidney, whose writings would inform the American Declaration of Independence, was on the Sun King's payroll. Ambassador Barillon wrote of him to King Louis: 'I gave him only what your Majesty permitted me. He would willingly have had more, and if a new gratification were given him, it would be easy to engage him entirely . . . I believe he is a man who would be very useful in the affairs of England should they be brought to extremities.'

Even the great Lord Clarendon, who liked to project an image of pure integrity, had not been immune to bribery. He had turned down a French bribe back in 1660, but the diary of the Cromwellian minister Bulstrode Whitelock shows him on the take that year nevertheless. It tells how in 1660 Whitelock paid his great friend Ned Hyde (Clarendon) 'a present' of £250 to be kept off the death list being compiled during Charles's hunt for the regicides. Hyde wasn't content with that. He charged his friend 'fees' on top totalling £37 18s. 8d.[3]

In Parliament, the dominant government figure in the later 1670s, the Treasurer (and Louise's lover) Lord Danby, relied on wholesale bribery to build a power base in the House of Commons, the so-called Court Party. It was calculated that he used secret service funds to pay sweeteners to more than 200 MPs. The scale of the King's sell-out to France was to be laid bare to Parliament in December 1678. It would come about in the slipstream of one of the many sexual entanglements of the woman Charles thought he was rid of, Barbara, Countess of Castlemaine. The former *maîtresse en titre* was living in effective exile in Paris, happily whiling away the time in various torrid affairs. In May 1678, Barbara returned from a trip to England to discover that the latest trophy of her regular lover, English ambassador Ralph Montagu, was her seventeen-year-old daughter Anne. News of Anne's new affair incensed Barbara. No doubt her first reaction was to rave and shout in one of those volcanic outbursts which she had so often employed to intimidate the King.

She dispatched a passionate letter to Charles demanding that their daughter be confined in a Parisian religious house and castigating her lover. The letter alleged that Montagu was leading a plot to displace Danby as Lord Treasurer and install himself instead. She claimed Montagu had boasted, 'For the King I will find a way to furnish him so easily with money for his pocket and his wenches . . . and lead the King by the nose.'[4]

Montagu made for London hoping to justify himself to Charles. He was not given the opportunity. The King cut off his explanations, relieved him of his ambassadorial and other posts and banished him from court.

The now former ambassador was far from finished. He blamed Danby for his fall and made common cause with the French ambassador, Barillon, in a plot to topple the minister. This had the enthusiastic support of the puppet master back in Versailles, Louis XIV. Since he blamed Danby for the marriage of the Duke of York's eldest daughter Mary to the principal obstacle to Louis's expansionism, the Protestant William of Orange, the Sun King happily countenanced the plot.

The intrigue got under way just as the country was plunging into the double crisis of the Popish Plot and the struggle over the succession. King Charles first heard of the plot one day in the summer of 1678. As he set out from Whitehall for his daily walk in St James's Park, he was approached by an acquaintance. Christopher Kirkby was a chemical experimenter who had assisted Charles in his scientific and alchemical investigations. On this occasion Kirkby had something much more immediate on his mind than the search for the philosopher's stone. He warned the King that there was a Catholic plot to assassinate him. By nature, Charles was disinclined to be alarmed by such tales. Previous plots had dissolved into the air like mercury vapour. But Kirkby insisted that this one should be taken seriously. He said he could produce proof in the form of a person who had personal knowledge of the plot, including documentary evidence. At Kirkby's insistence, Charles agreed he could bring what evidence he had to the palace, and strolled on towards the park.

Since Henry VIII had taken England away from the Church of Rome, there had been a variety of schemes to return the country to Catholicism. Elizabeth I was saved from plots to depose her and put Mary Queen of Scots in her place. The religious dispute rumbled on through the Gunpowder Plot against Charles's grandfather, James, right up until Charles's reign and his secret promises to his cousin Louis to reconvert the country. Charles had wisely stopped there, but there was no disguising the Catholic affiliations of so many of those closest to the throne – the Queen, the Duke of York and various mistresses past and present, including the Duchess of Portsmouth. The fear of 'Popery' ran deep and the Catholics around the King were objects of suspicion.

When Kirkby arrived for the arranged meeting at Whitehall Palace, he brought with him another man, an elderly clergyman called Israel Tonge. The cleric fostered an obsessional belief that Jesuits were plotting against Protestant England. He told Charles that the Jesuits were plotting to kill him and the Duke of Ormond, the Lord Lieutenant of Ireland, and cause rebellion in England, Ireland, Scotland and Wales, and with the help of the French, either to place James on the throne or, if he refused, to give the throne to the Duke of Monmouth. Charles listened impassively. When Tonge produced a document he said would reveal all, he asked Chiffinch to look after the affair and to arrange for Danby to investigate. Charles appears to have thought that the matter would end there. But the matter wasn't ended. Tonge's document would have a profound effect on Danby and the King's Council.

Kirkby and Tonge knew one another because they had once lodged in the same house in Vauxhall. Kirkby had boasted of his access to the King. This engaged Tonge's attention, for he was already involved in fomenting one of the oddest conspiracies in British history. Some years before, Tonge had come into contact with a failed clergyman named Titus Oates with whom he shared a hatred and fear of Catholicism. Oates had recently returned to England from living abroad.

By trade and inclination, Oates was a con artist. The one constant motif in his adventurous life was the gaining of money by misrepresentation and deception. Unfortunately for him, his skills at dissembling were usually undermined by his foul-mouthed conversation and disreputable habits. Even his father, a radical cleric, didn't like him. Despite this, a career in the church seemed a natural choice. Being by all accounts lazy and stupid, Oates failed to gain a BA from Cambridge, then lied about his degree in order to be ordained in the Church of England. He was soon sacked from his parish for incompetence, before conning his way into several jobs, including that of a ship's chaplain, all of which ended in scandal. With his options running out, Oates managed to find employment as a Protestant curate in the household of the Duke of Norfolk, a Catholic. While there, he was brought into close contact with the beliefs and values of the Church of Rome. In 1677, at the age of twenty-eight, he converted to Roman Catholicism.

Seeking to turn his spiritual awakening to his earthly advantage, Oates persuaded the Society of Jesus of his ardent desire to become a member of the order. He was enrolled in the school for English Jesuits at Valladolid in Spain. After a time, the Jesuits grew sick of his ignorance and peculiar personal mannerisms. They threw him out. Oates then managed to inveigle himself into the Jesuit school at St Omer in Flanders. The second chance turned out no better than the first.[5]

Back in England in 1678 and in dire poverty, Oates seemed doomed to spend his miserable life as a failed con man. Perhaps craving revenge on the Jesuits and certainly on the lookout for a new financial opportunity, for he was in desperate want of money even to buy bread, Oates found an unlikely route to both through Israel Tonge, the obsessive vicar who was now printing regular exhortations against the Catholic menace.

Tonge was not much above the breadline himself but he was the lifeline Oates had been searching for. Acting as a man who had been ill-treated by the Jesuits and had seen at first hand their plots against England, Oates persuaded the gullible Tonge of his wishes to reveal all. Together they would save the nation from a terrible spiritual threat. Tonge encouraged Oates to write down his experiences and his knowledge of the Jesuit plots. To what extent Tonge was complicit in fabricating the evidence rather than being merely a gullible fellow fanatic is unknown, though he was at first the main engine of the enterprise.[6] Oates's chief motives remain a matter for conjecture, as he maintained to the end that his invented evidence of a plot was true. According to Roger L'Estrange, the official censor turned satirist, 'the original design was to remove the Queen and to destroy the Duke of York.'[7]

Egged on by Tonge, Oates wrote forty-three papers on the Popish plots he had supposedly learned about during his time with the Jesuits. There had, he claimed, already been many attempts upon the life of the King; one had been foiled only because the weapons used by the assassins failed to fire their silver bullets. Such conspiracies seem to owe more to the often farcical nature of the plots against Cromwell in the mid-1650s and those by Puritan revolutionaries against Charles in the 1660s than to any reality. The first minister, Danby, nevertheless thought it better to treat the claims with respect than not. After reading the papers provided by Tonge, Danby realised that neither the ageing cleric nor the eccentric chemist Kirkby was the true force behind the comprehensive evidence of multiple plots and schemes. Tonge refused to be drawn on who else was involved. Disappointed that the King was dismissive of his claims, he arranged for Oates to come briefly out of the shadows to swear the truth of his evidence before a magistrate, Sir Edmund Berry Godfrey.

Among the most sensational of Oates's claims was that the Duchess of York's former secretary, Edward Coleman, was a conspirator. By making this claim, Oates scored an unwitting bull's eye. Coleman had converted to Catholicism in the early 1660s and was said to have played a part in many other conversions, including that of the Duke of York.

Although not a member of the aristocracy, Coleman's education and connections placed him within the royal establishment to the extent that in April 1661, Charles had appointed him one of his Gentleman Pensioners, a ceremonial troop of armed attendants or guards. Later, while working as secretary for the Duchess of York,

Coleman had carried on a form of private mission to forge links with and raise money via Catholic priests close to the crowns of France and Spain.

Thanks to his Catholic connections, Oates would have learned of Coleman's importance to the Catholic cause. What better name to pick as a member of his fictitious plot? And all the better since Coleman had engaged in private contact with Catholic priests who had the ear of Louis XIV in France, as well as that of the simple-minded Charles II of Spain. Were it not for the possible collusion of the Duke of York, such activities could have been seen as treasonable. By 1676, the Earl of Danby and the Bishop of London had found this activity so dangerous they had Coleman removed from his post in the Duchess's household.

Two weeks after Godfrey witnessed Oates's deposition, he vanished. His body was found five days later, on 17 October 1678, on Primrose Hill, with his own sword driven through it. Examination showed that Godfrey had been dead when impaled; the cause of death had been strangulation. The murder was the event Oates and Tonge required for their plot to be taken seriously. Suddenly, it was the talk of London.

A few days after Godfrey's death, and thanks to the Duke of York urging his brother to take matters seriously, Tonge and Oates were called before the Privy Council to be interrogated. Charles attended and personally quizzed Oates on his evidence, discovering many inconsistencies. Oates stuck to his story, which by now he had embellished with even more details. The entire inglorious confection was composed of names and events that Oates had squirrelled away during his time with the Jesuits, now to spew forth with the addition of a huge plot to overthrow Protestant England and Scotland. His list of plotters numbered more than five hundred Jesuits and many Catholic nobles and their associates. Charles ordered Oates to be arrested as being a false witness, nothing else.

Charles still thought Oates and Tonge had invented the entire plot. Unfortunately, he was almost alone in seeing through the conspirators' fictions. On 23 October he was visiting Louise at her apartments when Sir John Reresby dropped by. The King told him that he 'thought it some artifice, and did not believe one word of the plot'.[8] Parliament saw things differently, ordering that Oates be freed, and provided all assistance in tracking down the plotters. Oates was given an income of £1200 a year and an apartment inside Whitehall Palace itself, which must have irritated the King intensely.

The mania was to last for three years. At the height of his fame Oates was hailed by many as the saviour of the kingdom, a notion he held onto until the end of his days. He adored his fame and made much of his sudden elevation from poverty to well-fed celebrity:

> I had my guard of Beefeaters to protect me from being insulted or assassinated, my ten pounds a week duly paid without deductions, Venison Pasties and Westphalian Hams flew to my table without sending for, I was as much stared at, at the Amsterdam Coffee House and at Dick's as a Foreign Ambassador, when he makes his entry through Fleet Street.[9]

Of course, one reason why Oates was much stared at was not so much his notoriety but his looks. He was described by one contemporary as having his mouth in the centre of his face. This would put it about where a normal person's lower eyelid would be and so give him a very small forehead and an enormous chin. He was a man once seen never forgotten.

The plot hatched by the gullible Tonge and the exploitative Oates would ultimately lead to the execution of fifteen innocent men, among them the hapless Coleman. Shortly after Godfrey's death, one of the Queen's servants was arrested on suspicion of his murder, taking the plot right to Catherine herself.

The accused servant of the Queen, Miles Prance, a Catholic, was tortured in Newgate, admitted his guilt and named three others. He then recanted his confession and veered between admissions and denials of guilt until on his evidence the three luckless individuals he had named were executed. The flames fanned by the plot were to reach their zenith in the summer of 1679 with a series of trials and executions. All those found guilty declared their innocence. Charles himself believed them, but it was politically expedient for him to let the fifteen go to their deaths. As the accusations, the arrests, trials and executions continued, there was finally the beginning of a backlash, and a turning point was reached when the Queen's physician, Sir George Wakeman, was accused by Oates of plotting to poison the King with the assistance of the Duke of York. When this patently ridiculous charge went to court, Wakeman was acquitted.

Although the trial of the Queen's physician helped turn opinion against Oates, the hunt for plotters went on. The final victim of Oates' fabrications was the Archbishop of Armagh, Oliver Plunkett. He was hanged for complicity in the plot in July 1681. With this final travesty, the country had had enough of Popish plots. Oates was told to leave Whitehall Palace. In response, he made accusations against the King and the Duke of York. They were accusations too far. Oates was accused of sedition and taken to the Tower, where his rooms were somewhat less luxurious and the Beefeaters were there to guard him rather than for his protection.

As the grotesque nonsense of the Popish Plot played out, an interlinked but more important political struggle was taking place that posed much more danger to the house of Stuart. What was to become known as the Exclusion Crisis was a sustained series of attempts to bar Charles's Catholic brother James from the line of succession. Many feared the attempts would end with the country stumbling into a new civil war.

The seeds of the exclusion struggle had been planted midway through the decade, at a time when the Queen's continued inability to deliver a living heir and Charles's refusal to divorce her opened up the prospect that the Catholic James might one day sit on the throne. For Protestants in England, that conjured a nightmare vision of enforced conversion by a dictatorial regime that would be in thrall to Rome. They shivered to contemplate an England patterned on the absolutism of King Louis XIV. James's stolid, humourless personality, such a contrast to his brother's, was not reassuring.

In April 1675, a step had been attempted towards absolutism when the Earl of Danby, the Lord Treasurer, introduced another Test Bill in the Lords. The Bill stipulated that all public servants had to accept on oath that resistance to the King 'on any pretext whatsoever' was unlawful. It also sought to require all Members of Parliament and all office holders to forswear 'any alteration in the government in church or state'.[10]

The hugely contentious measure would have confined political power to Anglican royalists and it was fiercely contested. A highly charged debate in the House of Lords lasted seventeen days. Untypically the King curtailed his usual round of pleasures in order to watch. He saw the Bill finally squeeze through the Lords by a few votes, only to be killed off by a piece of procedural sabotage in the Commons. A furious Charles, whose charm usually masked any irritation he felt, prorogued the House and didn't recall it for eighteen months.

In the interim, talk in the salons and the political clubs had been dominated by speculation about James. How to contain the Papists if he succeeded his brother? Should he be allowed to succeed? Who might replace him?

Now, in October 1678, came the time for answers, when lack of money forced Charles to reconvene the Parliament he had prorogued eighteen months earlier. In his formal speech from the throne, the King revealed the Popish Plot, which he called 'a design against my person by the Jesuits'. He delivered the news almost as a throwaway line, giving no details of the plot at this time but speaking of 'foreigners contriving to introduce popery amongst us'.

Charles, as we have seen, didn't believe in the plot, and he didn't want it investigated by Parliament. If members of the Commons started probing they might turn up 'many things that were yet to be concealed'.[11] His prime concern was keeping a lid on the secret payments from Louis of France. So Lord Treasurer Danby had been instructed to bypass Parliament and leave the allegations for the judges to pursue. Danby, always a hardliner on Catholic issues, and the most devious of men, disobeyed his master, making details of the allegations available to the Commons. The King, though furious with Danby, had no option but to go along with him.

The effect was immediate. In the words of Sir John Reresby, the country 'took fire'. In his memoirs, Reresby recalled, 'It is not possible to describe the ferment which the artifices of some and the real fear and belief of others concerning his plot put the two Houses of Parliament and the greatest part of the nation in.' Over the coming weeks even the most level-headed were persuaded that the King was in imminent danger from Papist assassins and the very future of Protestantism was in the balance.

The furore developed into a threat to the throne itself, with the Earl of Shaftesbury, Anthony Ashley Cooper, playing a major part. Probably the ablest politician of the reign, Shaftesbury had helped restore Charles to the throne, but he had become increasingly alienated from the King because of his absolutism. He was the dominant figure among the loose grouping of constitutional monarchists, Presbyterians and radicals who would come to be known as the Whigs. Few historians think he ever believed in Oates's plot but he found it a useful weapon. He orchestrated an anti-Catholic campaign that had the crown trembling on Charles's head.

Shaftesbury showed his hand a week after Charles's speech. In the Commons, the Earl's ally Lord Russell tabled an address calling for the removal of the Duke of York 'from His Majesty's presence'. In the days that followed a similar address demanded the banishment from Whitehall of the Queen and all her retinue. Then came a Bill to ban Roman Catholics from sitting in either house. The Lords voted by the narrowest of margins to exempt York from the ban. But that was a limited reprieve in a darkening situation. Orders went out to arrest priests and Jesuits, while Catholics were barred from the court, the army and then from London. Search parties were sent to arrest those who had failed to leave and London's prison population bulged. Towards the turn of the year, some two thousand were held in Newgate, the Fleet, the Marshalsea and other gaols.

In the meantime Ralph Montagu was pursuing his vengeance against Danby. He had been promised 100,000 crowns from the French if he could ruin the minister inside six months. He relished the prospect and planned to do it through Parliament. On 18 December his moment came. During a series of tit-for-tat accusations in the Commons, Montagu produced a letter from Danby about the latest bribe Charles had asked of France. In return for staying neutral and not recalling Parliament, the King wanted a phenomenal six million livres a year for three years. The letter stressed the need for secrecy: 'all possible care must be taken to have this whole negotiation as private as possible,' Danby had written. 'I must again repeat it to you that ... you must not mention a syllable of the money.'[12]

Louise de Kérouaille undoubtedly played a key part in this most sensitive deal, just as she had in other transactions with Louis, and she was concerned at what Danby might now reveal. Though she and Danby had been lovers, in a letter evidently written before Parliament quizzed him, Danby made clear that they were lovers no longer. He wrote complaining of 'her ill usage of me' and indicated that he could do her damage. 'I dare not trust what I may do if I be hard pressed by the Parliament to speak things that may not please her Grace.'[13]

To her undoubted relief, nothing about her appeared publicly at this juncture. Danby had to shoulder the whole blame for the sellout to the French. In Francophobe England this inevitably meant his ruin. In April he was impeached and dragged through a baying crowd to be lodged in the Tower, where he passed five years without trial. One of the King's old boon companions, Silius Titus, sneered: 'By the trouble this great person has given us, we may plainly see how much easier a favourite undoes a Kingdom, than serves a Kingdom.'[14]

Having already lost Danby as a lover, the Duchess had now lost her greatest political ally. But her sexual antennae invariably homed in on the powerful, and she now established a similarly intimate relationship with Robert Spencer, Earl of Sunderland, who was made Secretary of State in April 1679. They were old friends. Eight years earlier, during those frolics in Euston Hall, the Earl's wife had happily played a part in the mock marriage ceremony that climaxed in the King's first bedding of Louise. Now, as her husband became enmeshed in the Frenchwoman's manoeuvres, and tongues wagged about their relationship, Lady Sunderland radiated the air of an embittered and wronged wife. In letters to Henry Sydney she called Louise 'a jade', 'that abominable jade', 'more of a jade than ever ... to everybody and in every particular'. She warned against relying on the Duchess's good offices to help the Prince of Orange, 'for she will certainly sell us, whenever she can, for £500.'[15]

Before Danby's fall, the King had dissolved Parliament and ordered a new election, hoping for a less fractious House. At the same time Danby had persuaded the King to exile his brother James before the new Parliament convened. According to a footnote in the *House of Commons Journal*, he convinced the King to 'send the Duke beyond the seas so there might be no colour for suspecting that the councels [*sic*] were influenced by him. He was sent away upon very short warning.'[16]

The crisis over the succession focused attention on the King's earliest love, the long dead, much vilified Lucy Walter. Her son with Charles had grown up to be the dashing if not too bright Duke of Monmouth, Charles's favourite child. As the Exclusion Crisis developed, Monmouth emerged as the popular favourite to displace James. His supporters dredged up the old stories of a secret marriage between his parents and of a 'black box' supposedly containing documents that confirmed it. The contents would legitimise Monmouth and give him a better title to be heir than York. Orchestrated by Shaftesbury, a bandwagon began to roll for the young man.

Charles rebutted the marriage claim in a move that must have been humiliating for a king. He provided James with a written declaration stating:

> I do here declare, in the presence of Almighty God, that I never was married nor gave contract to any woman whatsoever, but to my wife, Queen Catherine, to whom I am now married. In witness whereof I set my hand, at Whitehall, the sixth of January 1679.[17]

When York saw an announcement of Monmouth's latest appointment, as Captain General of the Army, describing him as the King's 'son', he asked his brother to reaffirm Monmouth's illegitimacy. Charles testily had the wording changed to 'natural son'. Following this, uncle and nephew, who had once hunted and raced happily together, were no longer companions.

In the Palace of Whitehall, Catholic Louise and Protestant Nell continued to contest for the King's bed, and Chiffinch continued to shoo gaggles of young women up the back stairs. While these girls remain anonymous, we know something of those who came in through the front door. One of them was Jenny Myddleton, the tall, voluptuous and auburn-haired daughter of Jane Myddleton, the court beauty of the 1660s. Jane, together with one of the most practised intriguers of the court, Elizabeth Lady Harvey, waved Jenny under the King's nose.

They chose their moment when Louise was off the scene in 1678 due to illness. Lady Harvey persuaded Nell to have Jenny accompany her on soirées with the King in Chiffinch's rooms. There is a suggestion that Hortense Mancini was also brought in on the plotting and took the girl along on visits to the King. Gossiping about it in a letter to Rochester, Halifax reported:

> My Lady Hervey who always loves one civil plot more, is working body and soul to bring Mrs Jenny Middleton into play. How dangerous a new one is to the old ones I need not tell you, but her

ladyship having little opportunity of seeing [the King] upon her own account, weedles poor Mrs Nelly into supping twice or thrice a week at W.C's [Chiffinch's] and carrying her with her; so that in good earnest this poor creature is betrayed by her ladyship to pimp against herself.

The ploy worked in so far as the girl was thereafter numbered among the long list of the King's minor mistresses, but any affair was fleeting. Louise returned to send the challenger and sponsor packing by ordering them to be barred from the royal chambers.

Despite Charles issuing two further rebuttals of the Lucy Walter marriage story, the Monmouth bandwagon rolled on. It was given added force in June when Charles charged Monmouth with putting down a Covenanter uprising in Scotland and the Duke returned in triumph. Bonfires burned in London, bells rang to mark his triumphant return and Monmouth was celebrated pointedly as 'the Protestant prince'.

Another, quieter bandwagon was rolling too – for the involvement of another Protestant hero in English affairs. A triumvirate of Whig earls – Essex, Halifax and Sunderland – favoured the candidacy of William of Orange, whose resistance to French aggression in Flanders had made him a darling of English Protestants. Publicly, the earls proposed a system of 'limitations' to restrict James's freedom of action were he to become king. Privately, they discussed replacing him altogether with his eldest daughter Mary or her husband William. In debating the role William might play if his wife succeeded, the word 'Protector' was used – which, one might have thought, would have sent shivers down royalist spines.

Between 1679 and 1681 Charles was to deploy the royal prerogative ten times to defeat exclusion bills and other Parliamentary threats by proroguing or dissolving Parliament. In one case he disguised his intention until the last minute, arriving at Parliament with robes and orb conveyed there secretly in a second coach. According to one unlikely story, he hid the crown in his codpiece.

He also tried to reduce the temperature by exiling Monmouth as well as James. With the main contenders for the succession abroad at least some of the time, others fought their corners for them. Halifax described London at this time as buzzing with so much politicking that 'a wasps nest is a quieter place to sleep in than this town is to live in'.[18]

All manner of options were canvassed. The most straightforward in theory would have been for James to announce his reconversion to the Anglican church. It was put to James. 'I will never be brought to do it,' he told an MP supporter. They would say it was only a trick, and 'that I had a dispensation and I was still a Catholic in my heart . . . and that was more reason to be afraid of popery than ever.'[19]

Inevitably, the divorce option was mooted again. This time it was raised by Shaftesbury, and once again the King turned it down. Charles was equally against legitimising Monmouth, though that might have solved everything.

The Duchess of Portsmouth, still an alluring young woman who delighted in flaunting her influence with the King, flitted between the different camps, trying to keep in with each but ultimately plumping heavily – and surprisingly, perhaps – for Monmouth and his backer the Earl of Shaftesbury. York had counted on her support against exclusion and was livid at her defection. He later grumbled that she had played 'a dog trick' on him.

Two factors probably determined Louise's support of exclusion. One was ambition for her son. According to Bishop Burnet, the Duchess was told that the exclusion of James might be followed by an Act of Parliament enabling the King to choose his successor. Why shouldn't he pick her son, the Duke of Richmond, rather than Monmouth? The possibility was said to have been planted in her mind by the ever-resourceful Shaftesbury to bring her into the exclusionist camp. If so, it succeeded.[20]

The other factor for her was fear. On the day in April 1679 that the Commons finished with Danby, Sir John Reresby noted that 'both houses began to reflect' on the Duchess of Portsmouth. In August, Barillon reported that Sunderland and Portsmouth 'are very worried about being attacked in the next session of Parliament'. The following January he warned that, if Parliament was recalled, 'Madame Portsmouth would certainly be attacked and perhaps chased out of England.'[21]

Defending herself privately, she coolly denied that she was a French dupe, letting it drop that pure self-interest dictated her loyalty. She told Henry Sydney that while she loved her country, when it came to France versus England 'she would show that she thought her stake here was much greater than there.'

Louise was not one to ignore personal attacks. She possessed a temperament as vindictive as Barbara's, if not as loud, and she was blamed when the suspected author of one attack on her was beaten up. This was the poet John Dryden, a friend and pensioner of Shaftesbury. He was set on by three men in Rose Alley in December 1679, after circulation of a verse labelling Louise a prostitute. The attack prompted this riposte:

> Though Portsmouth have strong ruffians she can trust
> As well to serve her malice as her lust
> Yet still she's slavish, prostate, false and foul
> Destroy our prince's honour, health and soul.[22]

Hard on the heels of the signs that Parliament would be gunning for her, a newsletter reported that twenty-two charges had been drawn up against the Duchess, possibly by the Duke of York. Louise's enemies circulated the charges in pamphlet form.[23] Some were ludicrous, others deadly accurate. They ranged from 'labouring to subvert the government of church and state' and fomenting that 'fatal' alliance between England and France, to trying to poison Charles and siphoning off 'prodigious sums' of money from the public purse.

For a proud and haughty woman, the most mortifying allegation in the list was that she was infected with the pox and thus a danger to the King. The accusation read:

> The said Duchess hath and still doth cohabit and keep company of the King, having a foul, nauseous and contagious distemper which once possessing her blood can never admit a perfect cure; to the manifest hazard and danger to the King's person in whose preservation is bound up the weal and happiness of the Protestant religion, our lives, liberties and properties and those of our prosperity for ever.

Of course, it was true. She had been infected – and by the King.

The treason charges, however, were never aired in court. Shaftesbury attempted to indict Louise as a common prostitute before a Middlesex jury packed with his fellow Whigs, but the King's loyal Chief Justice, Lord Scroggs, closed proceedings before the case could be made.

Behind the scenes, Louise continued her role as link between the two kings. This involved her trying to nursemaid the most breathtaking royal deal yet. It got off the ground in early July 1679, when Louise set up a discreet meeting between the French ambassador Barillon and Charles in her apartments. It was late at night, and judging from reports of their conversation, the atmosphere in those lavishly appointed rooms was charged with melodrama.[24] Charles told the ambassador that it was up to his master, Louis XIV, whether England continued as a monarchy or became a republic. In what was obviously going to lead to a bid for a great deal of money, Charles asked the ambassador to warn Louis that nothing could stop the English Parliament taking control of foreign affairs, the making of treaties and indeed war and peace if Louis didn't support him. It was the opening round in a series of negotiations that would end with Louis agreeing to pay to become, in effect, the secret ruler of England, while the notional ruler was left with his women.

During the haggling, Charles faced the humiliating experience of being asked if he could be trusted. The French ambassador recalled broken English promises from the past and quizzed Charles on why he was allowing so many innocent Catholics to be executed without intervening. Charles blamed his ministers, his brother and 'circumstances' – everyone but himself. The price for saving Charles was that Louis should sanction when England's Parliament would meet.[25] At a subsequent meeting in Louise's apartments, Charles told Barillon that 'he was prepared to bind himself not to summon a Parliament for several years, and only then if the King of France himself should consider that there was no danger in doing so.'[26]

Louise was directed by Charles to squeeze as much money as possible from the Sun King. However, this extraordinary deal did not go ahead. Before it could be sealed, Charles was taken seriously ill and it looked as if he were on his deathbed. In Westminster, there was panic, and in 'swift secrecy' James was summoned home from his exile in Brussels, preparatory to being proclaimed King. Opposition Whigs in the meantime discussed plans to raise an army against James under Monmouth's banner. Guards were posted at Temple Bar and ordnance ringed Whitehall. Charles's womenfolk wept at his bedside. All of it was premature. His doctors dosed him with quinine and he recovered remarkably quickly.[27]

Well again, Charles was persuaded to take the heat out of the crisis by exiling both the family rivals, his brother and his son: James to Scotland this time, and Monmouth to Utrecht. It didn't work. The people's temper continued to rise, stirred up by a blitz of broadsides, pamphlets and speeches from the Whigs and mass petitions demanding a recall of Parliament. One exclusionist petition pleaded for it to meet in London, the stronghold of the Whigs, and not in royalist Oxford. In the ancient city of spires, 'neither Lords nor Commons could be in safety but daily would be exposed to the swords of the Papists and their adherents of whom too many have crept into His Majesty's guards'.

It is a strange fact in the history of this crisis that there was very little violence, though the threat of it hung in the air throughout.

Within two months Monmouth was back in the country, without the King's permission. The thirty-year-old Duke arrived at the Palace of Westminster to find his entrance barred. His father refused to see him and he turned to his father's women for help. Louise refused him too. She declared that she would do nothing for him, 'so long as he was an enemy to the King and to her'. Nell Gwyn took pity on him and gave him shelter in her house. She reportedly hid him in a closet when the King called, but when the little actress did judge the moment right to plead his case and approached the King, he slapped her down. 'Be quiet!' he ordered after she brought up Monmouth's name.

Charles stripped the Duke of his remaining offices and again ordered him out of the country. Monmouth ignored the command and set off on what would prove to be the first of a number of semi-royal progresses through the western counties. Bells rang, bonfires burned and gentlemen brought out their tenantry to applaud the Protestant Duke as he passed. He even effected that magical curative power which reigning monarchs were supposed to possess: 'touching for the King's evil'. One of the barrage of propaganda stories put out by his supporters described the miracle cure of a girl with scrofula whose head he had stroked.

On several occasions, meanwhile, the King was reported to be on the point of succumbing to the Whigs and deserting his brother's cause. In March 1680, Whig leaders offered to abandon exclusion in return for concessions by the King, among them the dropping of Louise and Sunderland. At the mention of her name the King walked away. However, later that year the Duchess herself claimed to have worked on Charles so successfully that she reported him ready to surrender. His price was a supply of £600,000 from Parliament.[28]

Distrust killed the deal. There was so little faith in the King's word, and he was so chary of the opposition, that neither side was prepared to move first. A stand-off prevailed. The turning point in the crisis came in the spring of 1681 and was occasioned by another huge secret pay-off from Louis XIV. This disarmed Charles's Whig and Republican opponents, for it furnished sufficient money for him to defy them and rule without Parliament till the end of his life. The first instalment of the subsidy of five million livres was delivered to Charles's factotum William Chiffinch on 8 April 1681. The King had delivered his part of the deal by closing down Parliament just eleven days earlier.

In the years that followed, royalists were to focus on the injustice of setting aside not only James but his two children too, and a backlash against exclusion developed. James was welcomed back from exile, tens of thousands signed addresses 'abhorring' the campaign against him, and for a while the King appeared more securely on the throne than at any time since the 1660s. Admittedly Whig and Republican conspirators posed a threat to Charles, but for the most part the King was able to relax and continue to indulge himself and his women.

Indeed, 1682 was marked by a grand reappearance at court: Barbara, Duchess of Cleveland was back. There was a rapprochement between Barbara and Charles who, true to form, had found it impossible to deny her wish to return to England. The royal court had, after all, been the stage on which she had played out her life for sixteen rumbustious, exuberant, excessive years. Now she was back where she belonged.

Meanwhile, the following year, Louise's self-confidence almost brought her to grief. She had an affair with a French nobleman, Philippe de Vendôme, who bore the title Grand Prior of France. Vendôme was the nephew of Hortense Mancini. Handsome, charming and immoral, he arrived in England in June 1683 to visit his aunt. The chemistry that soon existed between Louise and the twenty-eight-year-old Vendôme was clear to everyone, and the story went round that Charles had caught the couple in bed.

The French ambassador, Barillon, told his master Louis XIV that 'prudence' necessitated Portsmouth telling her lover to go. 'But I do not yet observe any disposition on her part to do so. Those who would give her such counsel would be certain to displease her.'[29]

According to one view, Charles did not have it in him to confront his mistress: 'with increasing years, he had become so indolent and enervated, and so completely her slave, that he had no power of revolt left in him.' Charles sent Lord Sunderland to tell Vendôme to stop visiting the Duchess. The Frenchman complied for a few days but was soon back at Louise's door. This time Charles employed Barillon to intervene by 'gently' telling the suitor to go back to France. The young man, described by John Evelyn as 'a young wild spark', wouldn't listen.[30] He secured an audience with the English King and began to try to justify himself, only to find that Charles was in no mood to hear him. Vendôme emerged from the palace defiant and then stuck it out in London for months despite threats of being carted off to Dover by the royal guards and forcibly bundled onto a ship. Desperate to stay, he offered to keep out of London, insisting with extraordinary impudence that under Magna Carta the King had no right to deport him. The reply came that those rights extended to Englishmen alone. The troublesome lover finally condescended to go in November 1683. Louis XIV ensured that he never returned to England.

Far from the Vendôme episode cooling Charles's ardour for Louise, he seems to have grown warmer towards his errant mistress. Bishop Burnet recorded that Charles kissed and caressed Louise in public as he had never done before. Her hold on him was tighter than ever.

The widespread discontent over the shape and colour of the House of Stuart's rule that had surfaced during the Popish Plot and the Exclusion Crisis bubbled up once more in this period. Opposition groups ranging from downright revolutionaries to Whig grandees discussed ways of unseating Charles. Plans ranged from insurrection to assassination. Monmouth was again widely mentioned as a possible successor, not least by himself. In the midst of all the turmoil, one apparently viable plot emerged. The King and the

Duke of York would be murdered as they returned to London from the Newmarket races in the spring of 1683.

The plan was simple: to secrete a squad of assassins in the grounds of an old manor known as Rye House, situated beside the Newmarket Road, and when the royal entourage passed by to leap out and kill the King and his brother. The date was set for 1 April, when the spring races would have ended. But there had been a major fire in Newmarket and the races were cancelled. Charles and James returned to London early and the assassination never took place.[31]

In June, word of the plot leaked out. A large-scale round-up of suspected plotters saw the arrest of many revolutionaries and several important opposition figures including Lord Russell, Lord Gray, the Earl of Shaftesbury, the Earl of Essex, and Algernon Sidney. After the ensuing treason trials, eleven were executed, including Russell and Sidney. Many more were imprisoned and a large number fled into exile. One of the significant aspects of the plot was the eminence of many of those supposedly involved. Charles may have come within a whisker of being the second Stuart king to be killed by his own subjects, or he may have whipped up the whole thing as pretext for clamping down on the Whig and republican opposition. Historians differ on the matter.

Despite the upheavals, these were good times for Charles's mistresses, especially the Duchess of Portsmouth. The stories of her rapacity continued to mount. In return for persuading the King to bring his brother back from exile, she extracted a promise of £5000 from the Duke. She also benefited from the fallout from the Rye House conspiracy. One of the conspirators, Lord Gray, escaped to the Continent and was condemned to death in his absence, with all his estates confiscated. Charles was inclined to allow Gray's children to inherit their father's estates. Louise put a stop to that, ensuring the children were disinherited, and acquired a large chunk of the estates for herself.

As for Charles, he must have hoped that at last he could relax, secure in his position as ruler, the opposition crushed, no Parliament to deny him and a conduit to ready cash from France. Maybe now he could spend a comfortable middle age with his women, his horses and his yachts.

Fourteen months later, he was dead.

19

DEATH OF THE KING

On Monday, 1 February 1685, having spent the previous evening in the company of Louise, Barbara and Hortense, Charles rose from his bed at seven in the morning and collapsed, suffering a seizure. Fortuitously, two of the royal physicians were in the palace. One of them, fittingly named Dr King, decided Charles must instantly be bled, took a lance from his pocket, opened a vein in his arm and drew off sixteen ounces of royal blood.

Bleeding was thought to help restore equilibrium to the humours and hence to restore health. Dr King was taking a risk, for to bleed the monarch without the permission of his chief physician amounted to an assault and could be treasonable. Luckily for Dr King, when the King's chief physician, Sir Charles Scarborough, was called he agreed that the junior man's actions were justified.[1]

With the physicians fearing that the King could die at any moment, the Bishop of London was called. He informed the King that he must prepare for whatever might be about to befall him. Charles did not answer.[2] Over the next four days, Charles rallied and deteriorated in turn. He began to drift in and out of consciousness. A team of fourteen or more physicians came and tried all they knew. Several stayed beside Charles around the clock, together with senior churchmen. The Duke of York hardly left his brother's bedside. At night, several gentlemen of the bedchamber slept in the room with the man whom they had tended and grown to know so intimately over twenty-five years. The fire was kept blazing and his spaniels dozed by his bed. The atmosphere grew warm and fetid with the odour of lactating dogs and hardly-washed men.

The physicians bled the King several times, finally going so far as to open the veins in his neck. They gave him an enema and purging potions to drink. On Wednesday, Charles seemed briefly to rally, then his condition worsened once more. They shaved his head and applied to his scalp a blistering ointment made of poisonous cantharides to draw off bad humours. Between those and other remedies, the physicians expertly hastened his end. The King's doctors, of course, had no idea what was wrong. They tried more extreme remedies, including a potion made from a human skull, prepared in the King's own laboratory.[3] By Thursday morning he was close to death.

The Queen came to see him, as did his sons, all except for the disgraced Duke of Monmouth, his first son, whom he loved so much but who now lived in exile, dreaming he might succeed his father as king. Charles's health declined further throughout Thursday and the Bishop of London offered to administer absolution according to the Anglican Book of Common Prayer. Charles put him off, saying there was time enough for that. The King's refusal of the Anglican rites was noted with dismay by almost everyone present, most especially by the bishops who came and went. Soon the reason would become known. With his life ebbing away, Charles, a man who loved subterfuge and secrets as much as his father had before him, became the centre of one last conspiracy.

The doctors told the Duke of York that the King was unlikely to last another day.[4] The Duke recalled that at this moment 'all hope vanished.'[5] He acted swiftly, arranging for the French ambassador, Barillon, to be admitted to Whitehall. Once inside the palace, Barillon was summoned to the Duchess of Portsmouth's chambers.

When he arrived, the Duchess said she was going to tell him a great secret – the King wished to die in the folds of the Roman Catholic Church.[6] At the heart of this conspiracy were the King's brother James, Duke of York, and the Duchess herself, who was finally fulfilling the secret role given to her by Louis XIV fifteen years before. She would ensure Charles was faithful to the terms of the Treaty of Dover and converted to Catholicism. Even with the help of the King's brother, it was a dangerous and challenging undertaking. The ambassador was then summoned to an anteroom close by the King's bedchamber, where the Duke of York could speak to him in private. The Duke was anxious that when the time came, France would see him, the new king, as its friend and ally. It was important that Charles should receive the last rites of the Roman Catholic Church.[7]

Barillon went again to the apartment of the Duchess, who confided that she had not been able to locate a priest who could be brought secretly into the palace to carry out the ceremony. With time running out, Louise remembered – or was reminded of – Fr John Hudleston, a chaplain to the Queen, who had helped hide the King at Moseley Hall in Staffordshire after the Battle of Worcester. Hudleston was fetched from Somerset House, where he served the Queen at her private chapel. He came to the palace and made his way to the back stairs of the Queen's apartments, where he was asked to wait. Hudleston had been told to bring everything necessary to administer the last rites. In his haste, or by dint of being dim-witted or disorganised, he arrived without the sacrament.[8]

One of the Queen's Portuguese priests, Fr Benito De Leos, was called to bring it. Like his colleagues, Fr Benito could not have carried out the last rites for the King, for he spoke little or no English and could not have heard his confession. Meanwhile Hudleston was shown up to the King's apartments. At the King's request, Hudleston was admitted to his bedchamber. And so it was that Charles's last secret assignation was not with some actress brought surreptitiously up the river under cover of night but with a disorganised priest.

Hudleston knelt by the dying King's bed. When Charles told

him he wished to die in communion with the Roman Catholic Church, the priest replied that an act of penance was required before absolution could be given. At this, according to Hudleston, the King 'made an exact confession of his whole life'.[9] If this were so, it must have been quite something. For Charles II to have recounted even half of his many philanderings and adulteries would have taken not only some time but a quite Herculean effort for a dying man. One is forced to conclude that, whether out of kindness or due to an eye on posterity, Huddleston's testimony overstates the King's confession.

Whatever the actual form and duration of the confession, Hudleston was satisfied enough to utter the time-honoured words, *'Dominus noster Jesus Christus te absolvat.'* As he moved on to administer the oil of extreme unction, he was interrupted by a call to go to the door. There he found Fr De Leos with the forgotten sacrament. Hudleston administered Holy Communion. According to Bishop Burnet, the host stuck in the King's throat and a glass of water had to be called for. After this, the King asked for the act of contrition to be repeated.[10] For a man who had left so much to chance in life, Charles seemed unwilling to leave anything to chance in leaving it.

At midnight, the Queen came to visit for the last time. She was so moved by her husband's plight that she fainted and had to be carried to her rooms. When she recovered she sent word to Charles, imploring that if she offended she should be forgiven. 'Alas, poor woman,' said Charles. 'She begs my pardon! I beg hers with all my heart.' In this brief interchange lay all the previously unspoken regrets of more than twenty years of marriage, during which the Queen had failed to provide an heir and the King had taken up with many other women, leaving his wife to an unfulfilled and often lonely existence.

The King turned his mind to his other relationships. He asked his brother James to look after both the Duchess of Portsmouth and Nell Gwyn. The latter was perhaps the only one of his mistresses who loved Charles for himself. Charles instructed James not to let 'Poor Nelly' starve.[11] In the early hours, he was visited by many of his illegitimate children. The Dukes of Richmond, Grafton, Southampton, St Albans, and Northumberland all came. From what we can gather, none of Charles's daughters visited him, though this is not certain. Either they were not considered to be of such consequence as their brothers, or it was thought the deathbed was not the right place for young women.

At six o'clock on the morning of Friday, 6 February, Charles asked to be raised up in his bed and the curtains drawn back so he could see the sunrise. It was obvious to all that as the sun came up the King was sinking fast. His brother James was with him. The doctors could do nothing. Sir Charles Scarborough recorded their frustration and grief – 'Woe's me!' he wrote.[12] Shortly before noon, Charles died peacefully in his bed with his brother by his side. For the first time in British history, the throne was passed from monarch to monarch at a deathbed. That afternoon, between three and four, James was publicly announced as the new monarch. He would not have a coronation, as the Archbishop of Canterbury could not crown a Catholic.

Within hours, Charles's surgeons carried out an autopsy. The chief reason was to look for signs of poisoning, in case Charles had been murdered. Sir Charles Scarborough reported nothing suspicious. But according to Bishop Burnet, there were suspicious signs in the body which were covered up. Burnet wrote that 'Lower and Needham, two famous physicians, told me, they plainly discerned two or three blue spots on the outside of the stomach', but that when Needham called to have the stomach opened up it was taken away unopened. According to Burnet's hearsay evidence, another doctor called Short suspected foul play and spoke out about it. Shortly afterwards, Short was poisoned and believed himself the victim of a plot because of what he had said about the death of the King. Before he died, Short told two fellow physicians that he had been poisoned in the house of a Papist patient.[13] This might point to a Catholic plot, but it is doubtful whether any of it can be believed. A Protestant plot, designed to put Monmouth on the throne, seems equally unlikely, as

James was able to succeed unopposed and Monmouth's rebellion was yet some months away.

It was not until the twentieth century that renewed interest was taken in the autopsy. A theory was put forward that Charles died from mercury poisoning. The first person to propose this was not a pathologist but the romantic novelist, Dame Barbara Cartland, in 1959.[14] The first scientific paper suggesting the King had died from mercury poisoning came two years later, fittingly presented to the Royal Society, the learned body to which Charles had given his royal patronage.[15] Finally, using information from the contemporary accounts of the King's post-mortem, Professor Frederick Holmes deduced in 2003 that the mercury theory was correct.[16]

So how could mercury have entered the King's body? It would have been an uncertain way to murder someone, so foul play was an unlikely source. Charles was, however, fascinated by the alchemical mystery known as fixing mercury. During the many years of experimenting in his laboratory, he could have inhaled mercury vapour. For those working in laboratories, mercury poisoning was a well-known problem at the time. The alchemist Thomas Vaughan had died 'operating strong mercurie, some of which getting up into his nose killed him'.[17]

Perhaps the mercury had infiltrated the King's body via a different route. As we have seen, Charles contracted the pox in 1674 and it is worth noting that mercury was a treatment for syphilis.[18] There was even a saying: 'One night with Venus, a lifetime with Mercury.' Among the feared side effects of mercury treatment was neurological damage. The King suffered convulsions when his fatal illness took hold. But this was not the first time he had exhibited such symptoms. Ten years before, he had suffered convulsions during the celebrations for Louise de Kérouaille's elevation to the rank of duchess. In between those episodes, Charles was generally well and his behaviour was perfectly normal. The diagnosis of mercury poisoning must therefore be doubted.

This leads us to the question, was Charles suffering from tertiary syphilis when he died? The autopsy recorded none of the obvious manifestations of the disease, such as the lesions, chancres and rashes usually to be seen on severely infected patients, nor did Charles suffer any of the associated behavioural problems caused by the infection entering the brain. For some time before his fatal illness he had suffered from ulcerations on his leg. Such symptoms could be caused both by syphilis and mercury poisoning, but given the fact that the ulcers were localised we may assume they were leg ulcers of the simple type that older people are prone to, often due to a problem with the blood supply to the limb. We may discount syphilis as the cause of death.

We must mention one other theory, put forward in the early twentieth century by the eminent physician Sir Raymond Crawfurd, that Charles died of uraemia, or renal failure, which could possibly account for the reported 'convulsions'.[19] Crawfurd reached his diagnosis by reading the contemporary accounts of Charles's fatal illness and Sir Charles Scarborough's autopsy report.

With so many theories in the debate, we asked the eminent pathologist, Professor Sebastian Lucas of King's College Medical School, to examine the post-mortem notes along with the contemporary descriptions of the King's illness – in effect, to repeat what Crawfurd had done, but with the advantage of modern medical understanding. Professor Lucas reported that he could find no data on which to base any of the diagnoses discussed above. From the scant information available, Professor Lucas was of the opinion that the most likely cause of death was stroke. Charles suffered convulsions and loss of consciousness, followed by periods of lucidity, followed by more seizures. This, according to Professor Lucas, points to ischaemic stroke. He added that it is usually the case that the obvious cause of death turns out to be the correct diagnosis. Charles died because of thrombosis, a blockage of the arteries cutting the blood supply to his brain.

On 14 February, the funeral of Charles II took place in Westminster Abbey, where twenty-four years before he had been crowned king. For a king, it was a markedly low-key ceremony. In a break with tradition, no wooden effigy was placed on Charles's coffin, just a crown on a purple cushion. He was buried in a vault beneath the exquisite fan-vaulted ceiling of Henry VII's Lady Chapel, where his body now rests along with those of monarchs including Henry VI, Henry VII, Mary Queen of Scots and his grandfather James I. His father, Charles I, was not buried in the abbey but at Windsor Castle. A life-size wax effigy was erected to stand over the grave, and stood watch for over a century. Today, it is in the abbey's museum.

Following Charles's death, those who knew him did not take long to pass judgement on his reputation. In general, the report was not good.

'The ruin of his reign, and of all his affairs, was occasioned chiefly by his delivering himself up to a mad range of pleasure,' reported Bishop Burnet, although he was far from being a disinterested party; as a senior cleric in the Church of England he had considerable reason to be less than pleased with his monarch's lifestyle and ultimate choice of religion.[20] Burnet recorded that he thought Charles was not actually all that interested in religion, but at the end this seems not to have been entirely true. It was simply that Charles did not think religion should prevent a man having fun, and told the bishop as much. Lord Halifax cynically thought that Charles chose Catholicism because it fitted his licentious lifestyle better than Protestantism would.

Those who knew the King well and not only worked in government but spent evenings in play at the royal court were in a good position to know the marrow of the man. 'Men often raise their passions,' said Halifax with a wink, 'I am apt to think his stayed as much as any man's ever did in the lower region.'[21]

Of course, the women in Charles's life were allotted more than their fair portion of blame for Charles's wayward style. 'An excellent prince doubtless had he been less addicted to women,' summed up Evelyn. This addiction 'made him uneasy and always in want to supply their unmeasurable profusion'. He had, said Evelyn, many good qualities, but sadly for us he failed to spell them out.

Evelyn certainly thought that bad company ensured that Charles never fulfilled the nation's early expectations: 'Certainly never had King more glorious opportunities to have made himself, his people and all Europe happy ... had not his too easy nature resigned him to be managed by crafty men, and some abandoned and profane wretches, who corrupted his otherwise sufficient parts ... but those wicked creatures took him off from all application becoming so great a King.'

So what about the charge that Charles was corrupted by women? Such a view derives from the long-standing male fallacy that all men are somehow pure and all women impure. Charles was a man who knew what he wanted: female company and lots of it. Given the nature of society in the seventeenth century, and the lot of women, it seems unfair to be so hard on all Charles's women. Most were merely taking advantage of the few opportunities available. As for his mistresses, in a man's world they ventured more than most, having most to lose, including their reputations. On the other hand, they had a great deal to gain in terms of a life outside the ordinary. Without the literary talent of an Aphra Behn or a Duchess of Devonshire, women of the landed classes had few ways of striking out beyond the confines of an arranged marriage, which might lead, as it often did, to incarceration in a country house while their husband played in London. The women who attached themselves to Charles were beyond blushing but they were not necessarily to be condemned. Charles's licentious immaturity was merely their opportunity to live differently. Gifts of fine clothes, houses, lands and coaches certainly helped the social experiment along.

There are two mistresses whose behaviour and influence on Charles take them well beyond the role of mere adventurers or social climbers. Barbara Palmer, gold-digger though she was, sought influence and power. From her actions it is clear she considered herself to be an equal to the Queen – if not actually her superior, due to her success in bearing the King's children. She certainly persuaded Charles to give her trappings of rank that outshone those of the

Queen, having much grander apartments and a larger allowance. She interfered in affairs of state, holding an alternative court in which the most influential men of the day would congregate. She then used her influence to have statesmen intercede on her behalf with the King or to have her favourites promoted to positions that could benefit her. Charles allowed all this to happen.

Louise de Kérouaille also exercised influence over the King, and in a much more dangerous manner. She was an agent of France, an enemy power to which the royal family was closely attached through the Queen Mother and the King himself. Louise attached herself to Charles at the same time as he secretly attached himself to the French crown via the Treaty of Dover in 1670. The last decade or more of his reign, when he shook himself free of Parliament and ruled as an absolute monarch, he had a French agent in his bed and French money in his purse. Louise even helped ensure that her lover died a Catholic.

Whether or not Charles was manipulated by 'crafty men' is open to debate. He was certainly clever, and shrewd enough to see through the most shocking cases of perfidy – for example, he never believed for one moment that the Popish Plot was real. But he did allow innocent men to go to their deaths on the scaffold, most likely because it was politically expeditious to do so. And did it take manipulative advisors to convince him to mothball much of the fleet when war was brewing with the Dutch? His need for money drove that decision. Similarly, his desire to rule without Parliament – which led to many of the problems of his reign – was motivated by his own desire rather than that of cunning advisors.

Charles's childhood friend the Duke of Buckingham thought that, with or without the women, Charles was simply uninterested in statecraft. While this was undoubtedly so, he pulled off the considerable achievement of ruling for many years without the support of Parliament – a feat his father had been ultimately unable to manage. At his last, Charles left no great words on how to govern a kingdom wisely, for he had none to offer. It is the measure of the man that his last recorded statements are one of regret to his wife for not having treated her better, and another to his brother, imploring him to ensure that one of his mistresses should not starve. As an epitaph to a king and to a reign, it is not much, but as a memorial to the man it summed him up perhaps better than any epigram penned by Rochester or any of the other court wits or playwrights. 'Let not poor Nelly starve' could so easily stand in for, 'Don't forget that I was only a man.' To that could be added that he was a man who had never truly grown up.

Victorian historians such as Lord Macaulay thought that Charles's problems stemmed from the violent death of his father and his subsequent years of enforced exile. Some of his contemporaries agreed that his time in France corrupted him. In our own post-Freudian era, benefiting from modern psychiatry and psychology, it is tempting to use such tools to analyse Charles Stuart. We therefore sought the help of psychiatrist Dr Paul Harlow, formerly of the Maudsley psychiatric hospital in London, now retired. With Dr Harlow's guidance, we can venture to cast Charles as suffering from arrested emotional development, stuck irredeemably in adolescence, the symptoms being his hatred of any serious conversation, a strong desire to shirk responsibility, the avoidance of emotionally mature relationships and the need for endless female couplings. During his formative years, his lack of close contact with a mature male figure led him to exhibit what psychiatrists might see as Don Juan syndrome, a condition in which a man fails to take charge of his life in an adult, mature way. Such a pathology would certainly fit Charles II.

With his easy charm, under which lurked a violent temper when crossed, and a coldness or void at his core (as pointed out by Professor Ronald Hutton), it is also tempting to see Charles as a potential psychopath. The most commonly used test for psychopathy is the Hare Psychopathy Checklist. While conscious of the difficulties in applying any modern clinical test to the long deceased, and of the fact that we are not psychiatrists, we attempted to apply the checklist to

Charles II in the spirit of historical enquiry. We quickly discovered that many of the checklist's questions simply don't apply to kings. While Charles rated highly on many of the indicators for psychopathy such as superficial charm, promiscuity, impulsivity and proneness to boredom, others were much more problematical. The trouble is that when a man has absolute power and is not expected to explain his behaviour to anyone, it is all but impossible to apply the rules of normal social behaviour. How does one deal with a lack of guilt or a parasitic lifestyle in the case of a supreme ruler who believes in divine succession? Furthermore, for an all-powerful monarch, the question of failure to accept responsibility for one's own actions does not even come into play. Having decided that Charles scored highly on the list, but perhaps not highly enough to be classed as a psychopath, we set the checklist aside. However highly he scored, Charles simply enjoyed life too much, and engaged in it too well, to be a psychopath.

Whatever his problems and failings, Charles carried himself well enough throughout his life, usually with good humour and with a word for the most humble of his subjects (though he cared little about them). Occasionally, however, he could display a flash of irritability and a quick temper, which he usually attempted to hide. Although he displayed no deep feelings for his lovers, when his will was thwarted, he could display deep and lasting jealousy that gave rise to sudden rage. Generally speaking, as long as he got his way he was conviviality itself. He was not always quite the 'merry monarch'.

Abjuring the regal aloofness of his father, Charles's openly louche behaviour dispelled the divine enchantment that had previously attached to monarchy. None who came after would be considered an absolute ruler chosen by God – at least, not by their people. Having broken the spell, he brought the monarchy down to earth. Never again would an English royal court reverberate with such fun and vigour, so much youthful swagger and sexuality. Charles succeeded supremely in one thing: he facilitated an experiment in social change in which sexuality was no longer hidden away but put out in the public glare. For a quarter of a century, the royal court was presented to the world as being as much about pleasure as power. The King displayed his sexual potency to the nation and London's fashionable set raced to emulate him.

Charles's display of sexual power did not change the morals of the entire country, but it was extremely potent within the London elite where fashions were set and new modes of behaviour laid down. For centuries, Western civilisation regulated sexual behaviour, placing it within strict rules dictated by religious authority. What Charles helped to create was a revolution in which sexual behaviour was freed from this straitjacket; further, it could even be discussed and expressed publicly.[22]

Many, if not most, revolutions begin not with a bang but in fits and starts and so it was with the sexual revolution of the mid-1600s. Indeed, while there was sexual experimentation among the ruling classes, women were still very much at the mercy of their male counterparts. It would not properly take hold until the following century, while a sexual revolution embracing both sexes and all classes would have to wait until more recent times. In Charles's day, far from everyone was pleased with the revolution. There were still Puritans and non-conformists and those of a reformist or even royalist but serious turn of mind who felt Charles was letting down the country and his office. They ranged from the Puritan poet John Milton and his friend Andrew Marvell to the anti-monarchist political theorist Algernon Sidney and the disapproving royalist insider, John Evelyn himself. Although the enduring image of Charles came to be that of the 'merry monarch', in the years after his death his reputation and that of his court and government was not held in the highest regard. Twenty or so years after Charles's death, in an *Essay on Criticism* Alexander Pope ridiculed the topsy-turvy power structure of his circle – and its morals:

Jilts ruled the state, and farces statesmen writ;
Nay, wits had pensions, and young lords had wit:

The fair sat panting at a courtier's play:
And not a mask went unimproved away:
The modest fan was lifted up no more,
And virgins smiled at what they'd blushed before.*

With Charles's death, James II lost no time in making changes to Whitehall Palace his brother would never have dared commission. Wren was asked to take time away from St Paul's to design a new Romanist chapel. It was an exuberant space, with carvings by Grinling Gibbons and an Assumption painted by Antonio Verrio in a Baroque explosion across the ceiling. Charles would have loved it. Naturally, John Evelyn was on hand to be mortified. 'I could not have believed I should ever have seen such things in the King of England's Palace after it had pleased God to enlighten this nation,' he wrote.[23] A few years later, William III had the chapel dismantled and closed. The old palace was seen as unhealthy, being right on the riverbank. William and Mary moved to Hampton Court, which they had remodelled by the ever-obliging Wren.

England once again turned to age-old squabbling about whether too much freedom led to sexual immorality. The Act of Toleration of 1689 was initially of little help, reviving worries that religious toler-ance could lead to sexual licence of the (largely imagined) type that scared the devil out of Anglican worthies during the 1640s. In time, religious tolerance would grow and lead to a more broad-minded view of sexuality.[24] But immediately after the Glorious Revolution the answer was sturdy religion, strong law and chastity for all. Charles would have hated it.

During the reign of Charles II the walls of Whitehall were impreg-nated with every emotion from violent disagreements and sadness to joyous exuberance and lovemaking. Within a few years, all that was to be heard within its walls was the dull chatter of bureaucrats. William

---

* A jilt is a frivolous young woman; a mask is a woman of fashion who wears a mask to the theatre.

of Orange turned the palace into offices. It seemed only fitting that in 1698 the great palace he had made into such a rumbustious pleasure dome was consumed by fire, leaving behind only the stories and myths of a libidinous king, his unhappy queen and his beautiful lovers – 'When love was all an easie Monarch's care.'[25]

POSTSCRIPT:
THE KING'S DESCENDANTS
AND THEIR LEGACY

Charles's propensity to sire illegitimate children while failing to have any legitimate heirs has spawned a social phenomenon unique to England. It is difficult to travel around the country without meeting people who claim to be descended from the Merry Monarch. To all of those who are descended from the King, we must apologise if we do not mention their names here, as we can only include a few. Our intention is to show how Charles's legacy continues to shape the public face of Britain. Before moving on to his descendants we must, however, say something of his brother and his wife.

Because of Charles's lack of a legitimate male heir, his brother James inherited the throne, to be deposed after only three years because of his religion. A Dutch Protestant invader, William of Orange, ruled in his place, along with his wife Mary, the deposed King's own daughter. After failing to regain his throne at the Battle of the Boyne in 1690, James lived out his final years in exile at the palace of St-Germain-en-Laye, dying in 1701 from a brain haemorrhage, aged sixty-seven.

Following her husband's death, Queen Catherine lived on in England. Despite having been the most isolated and put-upon of queens, Catherine had begun to consider England as her home.

Both James and William were well disposed towards her and awarded her pensions suitable for her modest desires. Unfortunately, due to growing anti-Catholic sentiment, her position gradually deteriorated, and in 1699 she decided to depart for Portugal, which she had not seen for thirty-seven years. In Lisbon, she became a tutor to her nephew, the ten-year-old Prince John, heir to the throne. Catherine became established as a major figure in the country's political life and when her brother was unable to rule due to illness, she acted as regent. Fittingly, she lent her support to a trade treaty between England and Portugal in 1703.

Catherine commissioned a splendid home in Lisbon, the Bemposta Palace, and in 1705 she died there, bequeathing it to her nephew, Prince John. Today, her statue stands in front of the palace, a monument to one of history's most stoical women and, if the words are not too threadbare, to a thoroughly good person. Perhaps the best monument to Catherine is the fact that throughout everything, Charles grew to be fond of her and even learned to be kind to her, after his own fashion.

The story of Charles's first important lover does not end well. Born in the same year as Charles, Lucy Walter's misfortune – like that of Charles – was to have grown up in a time of war and political upheaval. Her tragedy was to have a relationship with a prince yet to establish himself in the world and who could not, or would not, care for her after she bore his child, James. The relationship between mother and father fractured early on, after Charles II set off for Scotland to seize his one great opportunity to win back the throne, the invasion which ended so badly at Worcester. Lucy's affair with Charles was therefore short-lived, lasting until 1651 or perhaps a little later. Two years after James's birth, Lucy's daughter Mary was at first claimed by Charles and later repudiated. The relationship continued in some form until 1656 or even later, if only for the sake of their son.

Given his later habit of keeping the mothers of his children well provided for, Charles's failure to look after Lucy was atypical. Perhaps during the critical years when he was struggling to establish himself as a viable ruler of his lost kingdom, Lucy became an embarrassment to him. There is no hard evidence for later reports – chiefly emanating from James, Duke of York, in order to smear Monmouth, his rival for the throne – asserting that Lucy descended to living as a common prostitute.

By 1655, Charles saw Lucy as an impediment to his position as a claimant to the throne and promised her a pension of £400 a year to live independently, with her son put in the charge of Henrietta Maria. It seems that Charles either could not or would not keep his bargain. Lucy became dependent upon other male benefactors or lovers to keep body and soul together. By 1658, she was living in Paris, possibly kept by the Earl of Mar's younger brother. Later that year she died, possibly of syphilis, though even the cause of her death is uncertain. She was only twenty-eight.

As for the fabled black box that was said to contain the marriage certificate proving her wedding to Charles, many reports were made of its existence. Lucy was said to have told Bishop Costin of Durham on her deathbed that she and Charles had married. The box was then handed over for safe keeping to the bishop, with whose death in 1671 the trail went cold. Some said they had seen the box, others that they had seen the marriage certificate within. Despite all the stories, none could lay their hand on it. To this day the box remains, like the Holy Grail, ardently sought after but never found.

Did Lucy and Charles get married? It would have been difficult to do so without witnesses who might later come forward to testify to it. Even the place of the supposed wedding was in doubt, with some saying Liège and others Paris. Some said the marriage ceremony had been simple, others that it had been carried out by the Bishop of Lincoln. If the couple had eloped secretly then it is possible that a Dutch Protestant pastor might have carried out a simple ceremony. From what is known, a marriage is unlikely to have taken place. Despite investigations during the Exclusion Crisis, no evidence was found. Lucy's last years were increasingly desperate. .

Monmouth was educated in France until 1663 when, at the age

of thirteen, he went to London at the request of his father. Charles was hugely fond of the boy and arranged a suitable marriage with a wealthy heiress. A few days after his fourteenth birthday, James married Anne Scott, Countess of Buccleuch, praised by John Evelyn for being 'one of the wittiest and craftiest of her sex'. Upon the marriage, Charles awarded James the title of Duke of Monmouth.

When it became evident that his Catholic uncle would inherit the throne, Monmouth took to declaring that his parents had married. His father always denied this. Four months after his father's death, Monmouth returned from exile at the head of an army in the hope of taking the crown from his uncle's head by force. His ramshackle army was beaten at Sedgemoor and he was declared a traitor. Despite pleading for mercy, on 15 July 1685 he was beheaded on Tower Hill. Dependent upon which version of the story one prefers, it took Jack Ketch the executioner between five and eight strokes of the axe to sever his handsome head.

Monmouth had six children by his wife Anne, Countess of Buccleuch, and a further three by his mistress Henrietta, 6th Baroness Wentworth. The title of Duke of Monmouth was forfeited following his execution, but other titles continued via his widow's Scottish family. The novelist Sir Walter Scott was descended through the ancient Buccleuch line. A Scott novel, *Old Mortality*, features Monmouth, while another contains a fanciful version of the novelist's family history.

Among other descendants were Alec Douglas-Home, Lord Home, who was Prime Minister for two years in the 1960s; his younger brother William, the playwright; their nephew Mark Douglas-Home, the journalist and novelist; Jonny Dumfries (Marquis of Bute), the racing driver; the Duke of Gloucester; and Lord Montagu of Beaulieu. Montagu is famous for founding the National Motor Museum on his estate at Beaulieu in Hampshire and for a sex scandal which led to a change in the law on homosexuality. Montagu, who has always been open about his bisexuality, was arrested in 1954 when police swooped on a party in a beach house.[1] He was charged with the incitement of unnatural and indecent acts, the same offence used to convict Oscar Wilde in 1895. Montagu denied the charge but was sentenced to a year in prison. The backlash against such homosexual witch-hunts ultimately led to the decriminalisation of homosexual acts between two consenting adults in private.

Today, Monmouth's other notable descendant is the 10th Duke of Buccleuch, Europe's largest private landowner, with 280,000 acres stretching across southern Scotland. In answer to journalists who questioned such boundless inherited wealth, the current Duke's father once said that one acre of windswept hill was 'worth about as much as the space occupied by a wastepaper basket in a Fleet Street office'.[2]

As for the wonderful Barbara, following Charles's death she took up with an actor named Coronell Goodman, a notorious rake, giving birth to his child at the age of forty-six. In 1705, the Earl of Cleveland died, leaving Barbara free to marry again. She chose a fortune hunter, Robert 'Beau' Fielding, who turned out to be already married. In 1709, Barbara died from dropsy (fluid retention symptomatic of a variety of ailments) at the age of sixty-eight. The little girl who had secretly toasted the king when she was only nine, had lived life to the full and overflowing. She died in her bed at Walpole House, the beautiful home she had bought by the River Thames at Chiswick. She was buried in the local churchyard of St Nicholas, a short walk along the river, where her headstone can be seen to this day.

Of Barbara and Charles's three sons, the eldest, Charles FitzRoy, was raised to the peerage in 1675 with the titles of Baron Newbury, Earl of Chichester and Earl of Southampton. Her second son, Henry, Duke of Grafton, married Isabella Bennet, the daughter of Barbara's former lover, Lord Arlington. In September 1675 Henry died at the age of twenty-seven, fighting for William III in Ireland, but not before he and Isabella had children. The 3rd Duke of Grafton served as Prime Minister in the eighteenth century.

The current duke, Henry Fitzroy, is the most colourful of the lot, having had a career in the music industry. For a time he lived in Nashville where he worked in music management, played in a band called The Squibs and was a part-time radio DJ. After he moved back to Britain he worked as a merchandiser for the Rolling Stones. When his father died in 2009, he moved to Suffolk to manage the family estate of Euston Hall, with its fine grounds designed by, consecutively, John Evelyn, William Kent and Capability Brown.

The youngest of Barbara's three boys, George, received the titles of Baron Pontefract, Viscount Falmouth and Earl of Northumberland. Barbara and Charles also had two daughters, Anne and Charlotte. Charles was so fond of them that £1500 was taken from Secret Service funds to pay for their wedding dresses of gold and silver lace. As we have seen, following her marriage to Thomas Lennard, 14th Lord Dacre, Anne caused a great scandal by having an affair with Hortense Mancini, one of the King's mistresses. Her younger sister married Edward Henry Lee, Earl of Lichfield, and led a quieter life. Patrick Lichfield, the portrait and glamour photographer, is often cited as a descendant, but this line died out and the current version of the title was created for a different family in Victorian times. Sir Anthony Eden, who served as Prime Minister in the 1950s, was a descendant, as were the philosopher Bertrand Russell and the six famous Mitford sisters, who included two fascists (Diana and Unity), one communist (Jessica), and a novelist (Nancy).

Frances Stuart, the beauty who drove Charles mad by saving her virginity for her future husband, found immortality of a sort. At Charles's insistence, following the second Anglo-Dutch war her image was placed on the commemorative medal and also on coins of the realm. Right up to the 1970s she was to be seen in profile, sitting regally, dressed as Britannia, gazing steadfastly ahead on the fifty pence piece. Like her friend and rival, Queen Catherine, she did not have children. There is a sad irony in this, Frances having been promoted by Buckingham and others as the woman who would give Charles an heir if only he would divorce his queen.

Following Charles's death, Louise de Kérouaille, Duchess of Portsmouth, moved gracefully to France and her fortune evaporated. All the Irish lands Charles had given her were taken away either by James or William. She got into debt and was rescued by Louis XIV, who had always kept a watchful eye over her in return for her efforts on his behalf in England. Louis paid her debts and awarded her a pension. Louise had never quite succeeded in helping to turn England into a Catholic state, but she had done her best, befriending its Catholic queen and ensuring its king died a Catholic. It was not her fault James proved unable to hold on to his crown. In 1734, she died in Paris at the grand age of eighty-five.

The Duchess's children were not of particular note. Her firstborn son, Charles Lennox, Duke of Richmond, was a nonentity but the line that descended from his marriage to Anne, daughter of Baron Brudenell, became more interesting – even if it took several generations to do so. The 2nd Duke was notable only as an early exponent of cricket. The 3rd Duke was altogether different, being an early advocate of universal adult male suffrage and of self-government for the colonies. It is said that during a naval review, he sailed his yacht through the fleet in support of American independence. The current 10th Duke presides over Goodwood racecourse and much else besides. His heir, the Earl of March, indulges his interest in racing cars by hosting annual motoring events at the Goodwood estate. Lord Lucan, the runaway playboy earl, is often said to have descended from the same line, though this is not true. Samantha Cameron (wife of Prime Minister David Cameron) is, however, related.

Louise's rival, Hortense, lived on in London after Charles's death, supported by a pension from James II. James's second wife, Mary of Modena, was related to Hortense. Helped by her friendship with Saint-Evremond and, no doubt, by her scandalous reputation, Hortense's artistic salon thrived. She remained a lively figure in London society well into the reign of William and Mary. She died in

1699, aged fifty-three. According to Evelyn, her death was due to over-indulgence in alcohol, though there is speculation that she committed suicide.

Her body was returned to France, where her crazed husband carried it about with him on his travels, just as he had once insisted his young pregnant wife should accompany him many years before. It is tempting to imagine Hortense spinning in her box as she was carted around a procession of dreary garrison towns. Her remains were finally allowed to rest in the Mazarin family tomb.

True to his brother's wishes, James did not let Nell Gwyn starve. He paid off her gambling debts and mortgages and gave her a pension of £1500 a year. She did not live long to enjoy it, dying in 1687, possibly from complications brought on by syphilis, though some sources put her death as due to stroke.

Of Nell's two children by the King, the younger, James, was to predecease his mother, while Charles was made Earl of Burford and Duke of St Albans. The current Duke's heir, Charles Francis Topham de Vere Beauclerk, is an interesting man. As well as writing a biography of Nell Gwyn, he is a leading proponent of what is known as the Oxfordian Theory, which holds that Shakespeare's works were written by the Earl of Oxford, one of Beauclerk's ancestors. The Oxfordian Theory provides scholars the world over with much harmless fun. Besides these achievements, Beauclerk was propelled into the national headlines in 1999 during a debate in the House of Lords over withdrawal of voting rights for hereditary peers. Beauclerk leapt onto the Speaker's seat, the Woolsack, and declared the proposed reforms to be treason. For this he gained the unusual distinction of being banned from the House of Lords for life. Other descendants have sadly not been so colourful, nor so iconoclastic. But they do include the film and television producer Julian Wintle, who produced the cult TV series *The Avengers*.

No work on Charles II and his women would be complete without dealing with the fabulous story – brought to light thanks to the British historian Lord Acton in the nineteenth century – of the boy supposedly fathered by Charles in Jersey after fleeing from England during the Civil War. If such a child existed, he would be the King's first son, born several years before the Duke of Monmouth.

Acton was editor of a newspaper dealing with Roman Catholic affairs called *The Rambler*, later known as *The Home and Foreign Review*. Being widely known for proselytising for the faith, it did not surprise Acton in 1862 when the head librarian of the Order of Jesuits in Rome came to him with extraordinary revelations.

The librarian, Father Boero, brought a packet of documents that purported to show that Charles had an illegitimate son by Marguerite de Carteret, the daughter of the bailiff of Jersey. On the face of it, the story was plausible. As we have seen, Charles very likely did have an affair with Marguerite. Boero showed Acton letters, apparently from Charles, recognising one Jacobus de la Cloche as his son, even though the boy had the surname, de la Cloche, of Marguerite's subsequent husband. This young man had turned up at the Jesuit seminary in Rome seeking to study for holy orders. Acton was excited: 'The facts I have to relate ... clear up whatever remained uncertain about the attachment of Charles II to the Catholic Church.'[3]

According to the documents, de la Cloche was born in 1646. This created a problem: as Charles arrived in Jersey in mid-April 1646, the earliest the child could have been conceived was around late April or early May of that year. This would put any birth date at January 1647 at the earliest.[4] Although the records are incomplete, they show no child named Jacobus born or baptised in Jersey in 1647. The last recorded child born to the de la Cloches is named as Elizabeth, baptised in 1646. There is another good reason to doubt the stories about the child: Clarendon, who was with the Prince throughout this period, mentions no birth of a child in his recollections.

In any event, the trail of Jacobus de la Cloche soon peters out in Italy, either because the imposter could not sustain the pretence or, more unlikely, he forsook the life of the son of a king and pursued the calling of an obscure priest. The amazing thing is that once de la Cloche vanishes from the records, *another* imposter appears in Italy claiming to be the same person. This person also makes lavish claims and demands for financial help, before vanishing. Again, there are disparities in the dates. In a letter (undoubtedly forged) brought by Boero to Acton, Charles II writes from Whitehall in 1665, a date when the royal court had moved from London to Oxford due to the plague. Sadly, we must allow Jacobus, the Pretender, in both his guises, to fade back into the shadows.

Today, several in the royal circle owe their status to Charles's wayward seed. Camilla, Duchess of Cornwall, married to Prince Charles, is descended from the King's illegitimate line via Louise and the Dukes of Lennox. So, too, is Sarah, Duchess of York, formerly the wife of Prince Andrew, who is fifth in line to the throne. But the person the nation has eyes on is not Charles, the immediate heir, but William, Duke of Cambridge, the nation's favourite prince, who just happens to be descended from Charles II. William's descent from Charles comes through his mother, Diana Spencer. Diana's family lineage goes back to not one but two of Charles's mistresses, Barbara Palmer and Louise de Kérouaille. Diana was a direct descendant of Barbara's second son, Henry, 1st Duke of Grafton, and his wife Isabella Bennet, and was also descended from Louise de Kérouaille through her son, Charles Lennox, 1st Duke of Richmond, and his wife Anne.

It is surprising what a few centuries and the odd lucky alliance can do. It can enable a child born on the wrong side of the blanket to jump over and achieve legitimacy. More than that, it can create an heir to the throne. Charles's descendants pepper the upper ranks of British public life not simply because of his virility but because he had a soft spot for his children. He recognised most of them as his own without quibble and bestowed titles and wealth that eased their way into comfortable aristocratic life.

And so it appears that the nation can hardly wait for the coronation of King William V. Meanwhile, William's father stands patiently in the wings waiting to take up the crown as King Charles III. When he does, though he himself is not descended from Charles II, his consort will be – as was his first wife, and as are his heirs.

The King is dead – but his genes live on.

APPENDIX:
SOME ASPECTS OF SEX IN
THE SEVENTEENTH CENTURY

With lovemaking and Charles II so central to this book, some discussion of sexual life in the seventeenth century will not go amiss. In the thinking of the time, the physiologies of men and women were thought of as a mirror image, a reverse, of one another. Thus a woman's reproductive organs were seen as those of a man turned inside out, and vice versa. This idea dated back to Galen, physician to the Roman emperor Marcus Aurelius: 'Turn outward the woman's, turn inward, so to speak, and fold double, the man's, and you will find the same in both in every respect.'[1] Midwives' handbooks of the seventeenth century echoed Galen's thoughts.[2] With anatomical and procreative knowledge still in a state of flux, the exact nature of conception was a subject of debate and conjecture.

What was widely agreed on was that both men and women should take equal enjoyment in sex and that enjoyment by women was necessary for conception.[3] The clitoris had been discovered as a centre of sexual pleasure, which would 'stand or fall as the yard doth, and makes women lustful and take delight in copulation, and were it not for this they would have no desire nor delight, nor would they ever conceive'.[4] Ejaculation of semen was also known to be necessary, but exactly how impregnation then took place was unknown. Both men and women were thought to ejaculate and their intermingling seed to cause conception. In the 1670s the Dutch physician Renier de Graaf got close to one side of the mystery when he wrongly identified ovarian follicles as eggs, not realising they were vesicles in which the ova developed. The nearest anyone got to demystifying the male contribution was the conjecture by the Dutch grocer turned scientific researcher Anton de Leeuwenhoek that semen contained what he called an 'animalcule' or tiny person.[5] To be fair to Leeuwenhoek, it should be pointed out that this astonishing man had many great successes, including the discovery of bacteria and blood cells, about which he wrote to the newly formed Royal Society in London.

Contraception was not widely available in the seventeenth century for the reason that it was not considered as being culturally or economically necessary, nor as being all that effective. The available methods were primitive and involved either withdrawal before ejaculation or a piece of cloth tied around the glans of the penis, a method that had more currency in France than in England.

An important social aspect of seventeenth-century life was that children bestowed status on a woman as much as on a man.[6] When newlywed couples wished to ensure conception took place, they were heedful of the need for arousal by both parties. Foreplay was considered advisable for the woman. According to a medical and sexual handbook for women, before copulation a woman might fondle herself, 'that she may take fire and be inflamed in venery, for so at length the womb will strive and wax fervent with desire of casting forth its own seed, and receiving the man's seed be mixed together therein'.[7] From all this, it would follow that when young lovers like Charles Stuart and Lucy Walter had ecstasy on their minds, children would almost inevitably follow. As a product of such pleasure, they would not necessarily be seen as a burden or an unwanted result of sexual delight, but as a simple fact of life, like sex itself.

Another fact of life was the constant danger of contracting a sexually transmitted disease. In seventeenth-century London, such diseases were rife and were looked upon as a natural hazard.

The most feared was syphilis. In its later stages it could induce dementia and cause severe skin lesions, including the total loss of the nose. The only remedy for such a disfiguring eventuality was the purchase of a false nose, usually made of metal.

There was no proper understanding of the underlying nature of the disease or its causes. In the seventeenth century, despite great advances in physiology and pathology, medicine was still based on the theories of Hippocrates and, later, of the Roman physician, Galen. The belief was that good health was based on the balance of four bodily 'humours' equating to the four universal elements – earth, air, fire and water. A further complication was that gonorrhoea and syphilis were sometimes mistaken for one another, in their initial stages often presenting similar symptoms. Because it could be hard to diagnose correctly, syphilis became known as the 'great pretender'. Despite these drawbacks, some treatments appeared to work.

The eminent royal physician Richard Wiseman wrote a handbook for doctors entitled *Eight Chururgical* [surgical] *Treatises*, dedicated to Charles II. It was the distillation of a lifetime's knowledge. In his section on *lues venerea*, he described it as a 'venomous contagious disease gotten ... from an impure coition'.

So what to do? Wiseman was clear: the humours must be restored: 'Now the known remedies, all or some of which we use in this cure, are Bleeding, Purging, Vomiting, Salivating, Sweating, Cordials and Opiates; to which we may add Dietetical directions, especially Alternative Drinks, and Topics'.

All of this, explained Wiseman, was to evacuate the 'fermenting humours'. The word evacuation is a clue to the horrors to be endured. First, the patient would be cut with a lancet and have several ounces of blood taken off. Next, they would be purged – fed potions to make them retch and excrete. Various concoctions were administered, composed of ingredients such as posset (a hot sweetened milk curdled with wine or spirits), along with senna, rhubarb, sarsaparilla, cream of tartar, tamarind and something Wiseman called manna, which we can presume was not the miraculous food provided for the Israelites in the wilderness. A little gold might be added.

Next, the patient would be wrapped in yards of cloth and blankets and swaddled like a newborn child. Hot bricks would be placed around them to heat them up until the sweat pored out of them. Around London, sweating houses were common, where those afflicted with the pox could hope to sweat their way to a cure. And a cure there would be of a kind, for the initial signs of syphilis tend to disappear in anything from ten to forty days, while the disease lurks on inside, waiting to wreak terrible harm in later years.

There was one further method of ensuring the patient had all bad humours removed – the production of excessive saliva. 'The methods of salivating are divers, but all by mercury,' Wiseman pronounced. When the mercury was amalgamated with gold, both vomiting *and* salivation could be induced. Mercury could indeed cause salivation – it was one of the first signs of mercury poisoning. If enough was taken, worsening symptoms included inflammation and ulcers of the mouth, rotten teeth, bad breath, inflammation of the intestines, increased heart rate, kidney failure and ultimately death. An experienced practitioner like Wiseman would hopefully ensure the later stages were never reached. By now, if all went well with the treatment, the overheated patient would be as dry as kindling, free of fermenting humours, and apparently free of the pox.

Wiseman had further tricks up his sleeve: 'In the case of pain we add a grain or more of laudanum. Mercury thus mixt with purgatives it is from which we must expect our main success. For though the other may purge strongly, they of themselves have not virtue to check the malignity of even the lesser species of this disease.'

The opium would certainly have made the poor benighted patient feel better during the uncomfortable treatment, while the use of gold and mercury smacked alarmingly of the alchemist's laboratory. But the mercury worked wonders, healing the chancres, or skin ulcers, caused by primary syphilis. This effect had been discovered by trial and error. What was not known was how. In fact, what was happening was that, when applied in a dressing or poultice to the ulcers, mercury killed off the localised bacterium causing the disease. It would be 1905 before this bacterium was pinpointed, when the role of the spirochete *treponema pallidum* was discovered. A true cure did not become generally accessible until the 1940s when the use of penicillin became commonplace.

Wiseman pronounced that those physicians who treated the pox without mercury would 'prolong their cure to no purpose, and meet with disgrace at last; it being very sure, that no species of it will be cured without it'. By omitting mercury, 'the Ulcer the while spreading and breaking out fresh in some parts while we were endeavouring to Cure them in others, the Disease becoming more fierce in some of them whilst their bodies were purged with Caharticks without mercury.'

The botanist and apothecary Nicholas Culpepper recommended a different approach. He proposed the treatment of syphilis with a preparation made from heartsease, an English wildflower. Much later it would be discovered that heartsease had an antimicrobial capacity. Culpepper's methods were unlikely to be taken up by those who treated royalty. He was a radical in both his views on politics and the treatment of disease. He fought on the Parliamentary side in the Civil Wars, foretold the death of Charles I by the use of astrology, and argued against what he saw as antediluvian practices such as bloodletting.

The ideas of such a man were unlikely to recommend themselves to the society physicians who treated royalty, for whom remedies involving mercury and gold were reassuringly expensive and exclusive. How many of Wiseman's procedures Charles II and Louise underwent we cannot say for sure, though it is safe to surmise that for such important patients the physician would have used everything in his armamentarium.

LIST OF MAJOR CHARACTERS

HOUSE OF STUART

King Charles I, executed 1649

Henrietta Maria, Charles I's widow

King Charles II, born 1630, reigned 1660–85

Catherine of Braganza, Charles II's queen, daughter of king of Portugal

James, Duke of York, Charles II's brother, reigned as James II 1685–8

Henry, Duke of Gloucester, Charles and James's youngest brother, died 1660

Henrietta Anne (Minette), daughter of Charles I, married the Duke of Orléans

Mary and Anne, daughters of James, Duke of York

William of Orange, nephew of Charles II

MISTRESSES AND LOVERS OF THE KING

Christabella Wyndham, Charles's former wet nurse

Elizabeth Killigrew, dissolute sister of the royalist playwright Thomas Killigrew

Lucy Walter, Charles's bewitching but reviled first love

Eleanor Byron, said to have squeezed a fortune out of Charles

Catherine Pegge, daughter of royalist baronet, had affair with Charles in Bruges

Barbara Villiers, Countess of Castlemaine, Duchess of Cleveland, dominated Charles II for a decade

Frances Teresa Stuart, virginal teenage coquette, eventual royal mistress

Mary (Moll) Davis, actress, paid £200 to retire and become royal mistress

Nell Gwyn, actress, the self-styled 'English whore', whom the people loved

Louise de Kérouaille, Duchess of Portsmouth, French spy, most hated and expensive mistress

Hortense Mancini, ostentatiously bisexual and Charles's last grand passion

COURTIERS

James Croft, Duke of Monmouth, the King's illegitimate and favourite son

George Digby, Earl of Bristol, impeached Clarendon

Henry Jermyn, Earl of St Albans, renowned seducer

Edward Montagu, Cromwellian admiral turned monarchist

Ralph Montagu, ambassador, bedded both Barbara and her daughter

Daniel O'Neill, senior courtier, outraged at treatment of the Queen

Roger Palmer, Earl of Castlemaine, Barbara's cuckolded husband

Philip Stanhope, Earl of Chesterfield, Barbara's first lover

Charles Stuart, Duke of Richmond and Lennox, eloped with 'La Belle Stuart'

Theodore, Viscount Taaffe, Lucy's lover and protector

George Villiers, 2nd Duke of Buckingham, politician, the King's boyhood friend

WOMEN OF THE COURT

Anna, Countess of Shrewsbury, Buckingham's mistress, likened to Messalina

Anne, Countess of Sussex, bisexual daughter of Charles and Barbara

Margaret Cavendish, Duchess of Newcastle, writer and philosopher

Elizabeth Lady Harvey, lesbian society hostess

Anne Hyde, Chancellor's daughter, married James Duke of York

Jane Myddleton, rivalled Hortense Mancini as most beautiful woman in London

Mary Villiers, Duchess of Richmond and Lennox, Barbara's enemy

MINISTERS AND OFFICE HOLDERS

Henry Bennet, Earl of Arlington, Buckingham's rival in Cabal

Sir Charles Berkeley, Keeper of the Privy Purse, Charles's favourite roisterer

James Butler, Earl of Ormond, enemy of Barbara

William Chiffinch, Keeper of the Private Closet, dubbed 'pimpmaster general'

Edward Hyde, Earl of Clarendon, dominating Lord Chancellor

Baptist May, boyhood friend of Charles II, groom of the bedchamber

Sir Edward Nicholas, Secretary of State, Clarendon ally

Thomas Osborne, Earl of Danby, corrupt Lord Treasurer

Sir Henry de Vic, royalist resident in The Hague, wanted to marry Lucy

Henry Wriothesley, Earl of Southampton, Clarendon ally against Barbara

WITS AND OTHER PHILANDERERS

Sir Charles Berkeley – see under Ministers

John Churchill, eighteen-year-old future war hero found in bed with Barbara

Sir George Etherege, bawdy Restoration playwright and court wit

Jacob Hall, handsome acrobat, Barbara's lover

Thomas Killigrew, theatre manager and playwright

Charles Sackville, Lord Buckhurst, later Earl of Dorset, famous for setting up a *ménage à trois* with Nell Gwyn and Sir Charles Sedley

Sir Charles Sedley – see Charles Sackville

John Wilmot, 2nd Earl of Rochester, talented hell-raiser, leader of the 'Merry Gang'

OPPOSITION VOICES

Anthony Ashley Cooper, Earl of Shaftesbury, Whig leader

William Lord Russell, led anti-Catholic campaign, executed
Algernon Sidney, republican, executed for treason

ARTISTS, AND MEN AND WOMEN OF LETTERS
Aphra Behn, writer and spy
Gilbert Burnet, bishop and historian
John Dryden, Poet Laureate
John Evelyn, writer and diarist
Thomas Hobbes, philosopher
Peter Lely, court painter to Charles II
Andrew Marvell, metaphysical poet and royalist MP
Samuel Pepys, government official and diarist
Antony van Dyck, court painter to Charles I
George Villiers, playwright – see also Courtiers
John Wilmot, poet – see also Wits
Christopher Wren, architect and mathematician

POPISH PLOT
Titus Oates, anti-Catholic fabrications had him hailed as saviour of the
    nation
Israel Tonge, architect of the Popish Plot

CROMWELLIANS
Sir John Barkstead, governor of the Tower of London
Oliver Cromwell, Lord Protector
John Lambert, republican general
George Monck, architect of the Restoration
Sir Harry Vane, executed after Charles broke his word

HELPERS IN CHARLES'S ESCAPE FROM WORCESTER
Juliana Coningsby
Jane Lane
Col. John Lane
Henry Lascelles

Hugh Penderel and brothers
Nicholas Tattersall, sea captain
Henry Wilmot, 1st Earl of Rochester
Col. Francis Wyndham

COURT OF FRANCE
Louis XIV
Philippe, Duc d'Orléans, bisexual brother of Louis XIV
Jean-Baptiste Colbert, Louis's chief minister
Charles Colbert de Croissy, ambassador to England
Isabelle-Angelique de Montmorency, Duchesse de Châtillon
Anne-Marie-Louise de Montpensier, also known as La Grande
    Mademoiselle
Cardinal Jules Mazarin, Louis XIV's chief minister, uncle of Hortense
    Mancini
Philippe de Vendôme, Louise's arrogant lover who defied Charles

CHARLES'S ILLEGITIMATE CHILDREN
By Lucy Walter: James Scott, Duke of Monmouth; Mary, at first
    accepted by Charles, but repudiated
By Catherine Pegge: Charles FitzCharles, 1st Earl of Plymouth; Anne
    FitzCharles
By Barbara Palmer: Anne Lennard, Countess of Sussex (some said she
    was the daughter of the Earl of Chesterfield); Charles FitzRoy, 2nd
    Duke of Cleveland, Earl of Southampton; Henry FitzRoy, 1st Duke
    of Grafton; Charlotte Lee, Countess of Lichfield; George FitzRoy, 1st
    Duke of Northumberland; Barbara FitzRoy, possibly the daughter of
    John Churchill, later Duke of Marlborough
By Mary (Moll) Davis: Lady Mary Tudor
By Nell Gwyn: Charles Beauclerk, 1st Duke of St Albans; James, Lord
    Beauclerk
By Louise de Kérouaille: Charles Lennox, 1st Duke of Richmond and
    Lennox

NOTES

1 The Last Soirée

1 John Evelyn, *Diary*, 1818.
2 For details of the layout and state of repair of Whitehall Palace in the reign of Charles II see *Survey of London*, Vol. 13, ed. Montagu Cox and Philip Norman, 1930; and Simon Thurley, *Whitehall Palace, An Architectural History of the Royal Apartments*, 1999.
3 Evelyn, *Diary*.
4 Samuel Pepys, *Diary*, ed. Latham and Matthews, 1970–83.
5 Frank H. Ellis, *Dictionary of National Biography*, 2004; John Aubrey, *Brief Lives*, compiled 1669–93, republished 2000.
6 Pepys, *Diary*.
7 John Evelyn, *Tyrannus, or, the Mode*, 1661.
8 Douglas Chambers, *Dictionary of National Biography*.
9 Sir Raymond Henry Payne Crawfurd, *The Last Days of Charles II*, 1909.
10 Bishop Gilbert Burnet, *A History of My Own Times*, 1724.
11 Evelyn, *Tyrannus*, 1661.
12 Evelyn, *Diary*; Thurley, *Whitehall Palace*.
13 *December, Capricorn: Louis XIV boar hunting in view of the Chateau de Monceau*, designed by Charles Le Brun. Now at the Chateau de Pau in south-west France.
14 Evelyn, *Diary*.
15 Ibid.
16 Ibid.

17 Ibid.
18 Earl of Ailesbury, *Memoirs*, ed. W.E. Buckley, 1890.
19 Crawfurd, *Last Days of Charles II*.

2 The Making of a Prince

1   *Letters of Henrietta Maria*, ed. Everett Green, 1857.
2   M. Newcastle, *The Duke and Duchess of Newcastle*, 1910.
3   Earl of Clarendon, *The History of the Rebellion and Civil Wars in England*, 1717.
4   Hugh Trevor Roper, foreword to *Earl of Clarendon, Selections from the History of the Rebellion and The Life by Himself*, ed. G. Huehns, 1978.
5   Clarendon, *History*.
6   David Cressy, *Dictionary of National Biography*.
7   Clarendon, *History*.
8   Ibid.
9   Clarendon State Papers, IV.
10 Newcastle, *The Duke and Duchess of Newcastle*.
11 John Rushworth, *Historical Collections*, Book 6, 1722; Emanuel Green, 'Siege of Bridgwater', in *Bye-paths of Bath and Somerset History*, 1905.
12 Quoted in Clarendon, *History*.
13 Lord Acton, 'The Secret History of Charles II', in *Historical Essays and Studies*, ed. John Neville Figges and Reginald Vere Laurence, 1907.
14 *The Letters, Speeches and Proclamations of Charles I*, ed. Sir Charles Petrie, 1935.

3 Exile and First Love

1   Fernand Braudel, *Civilization and Capitalism*, Vol. 1, *The Structures of Everyday Life*, English translation 1981.
2   Clarendon, *History*, Book XI.
3   Ibid.
4   Motteville, *Memoirs of Mademoiselle de Monpensier*, Vol. 1, 1848.
5   Ibid.
6   Ibid.
7   Burnet, *History of My Own Times*.
8   Thomas Seccombe in the *Dictionary of National Biography* puts Lucy Walter's birth *c*. 1630.
9   Pepys, *Diary*.

10 John Carswell, *The Porcupine, A Life of Algernon Sidney*, 1989.
11 Ibid.
12 H. Noel Williams, *Rival Sultanas*, 1915.
13 Lord George Scott, *Lucy Walter: Wife or Mistress*, 1947.
14 *Dictionary of National Biography*.
15 Evelyn, *Diary*.
16 Clarendon, *History*.
17 *Lucy Walter*, attributed to Peter Lely, Scolton Manor Museum, Haverfordwest, Pembrokeshire.
18 For a clear exposition of the complex and numerous intricacies of Scottish politics at this time, see Ronald Hutton, *Charles the Second*, 1991.
19 Françoise Bertaut de Motteville, *Memoirs of Mademoiselle de Monpensier*, 1726.
20 Hutton, *Charles the Second*.
21 James Aikman, *Annals of the Persecution in Scotland from the Restoration to the Revolution*, 1844.

4 The Fugitive

1 *An account of the escape of King Charles 2nd from the battle of Worcester till his landing in France dictated to Samuel Pepys Esq*, ed. William Matthews, 1966.
2 *The Boscobel Tracts relating to the escape of Charles 2nd after the battle of Worcester and his subsequent adventures*, ed. John Hughes, 1857.
3 *Memorials of the great civil war in England from 1646 to 1652: edited from original letters in the Bodleian Library*.
4 *The History of his Sacred Majesty's Preservation after the battle of Worcester*, anon, 1660.
5 A.M. Broadley, *The Royal Miracle, a collection of rare tracts, broadsides, letters, prints and ballads concerning the wanderings of Charles 2nd after the Battle of Worcester*, 1912.
6 *An account of the escape of King Charles 2nd*.
7 *The Boscobel Tracts*, ed. J. Hughes, 1858.
8 Clarendon, *History*.
9 Ibid.
10 *An account of the escape of King Charles 2nd*.
11 Ibid.
12 Ibid.
13 Ibid.

14   John Buchan, *A Book of Escapes and Hurried Journeys*, 1922.
15   Clarendon State Papers, 1786, 3.153.

5 The Life of an Exiled King

1   William Cobbett, Cobbett's *Complete Collection of State Trials and Proceedings for High Treason*, 1809, Vol. 5.
2   Eva Scott, *Travels of the King*, 1907.
3   S.R. Gardiner, *History of the Great Civil War*, 1894.
4   Walter Harris, *Clarendon and the English Revolution*, 1983.
5   Marie Catherine Baronne D'Aulnoy, *Memoirs of the Court of England in 1675*.
6   Andrew Kippis, *Biographica Britannia or the Lives of the Most Eminent Persons*, 1793.
7   *Thomas Carte's Collection of Original Papers*.
8   Taaffe letters, 1688, ed. Timothy Crist, 1974.
9   T. Morrice, *Life of Roger Earl of Orrery*, 1743.
10 James Walen, *The House of Cromwell*, 1897.
11 Clarendon State Papers, III, Dom.
12 Thomas Henry Lister, *Life of Clarendon*, 1838.
13 Clarendon State Papers, Venice, Vol. 32.
14 John Jesse, *Memoirs of the Court in England Under the Stuarts*, 1857.
15 Ibid.
16 Thurloe State Papers.
17 Brian Bevan, *James Duke of Monmouth*, 1973.
18 Clarendon, *History*.
19 Bevan, *James Duke of Monmouth*.
20 Clarendon State Papers.
21 D.E. Williams, *The Life and Correspondence of Sir Thomas Lawrence, Kt.*, 1831.

6 Restoration

1   Margaret Gilmour, *The Great Lady*, 1941.
2   G. Steinman, *A Memoir of Barbara Duchess of Cleveland*, 1871; *Letters of Philip, Second Earl of Chesterfield*, 1930.
3   Burnet, *History of My Own Times*.
4   William Cobbett, *The Collected Social and Political Works*, ed. Noel Tompson, 1998.

5 Edmund Burke, *Works*, Vol. 6, 1839.

6 Henri Forneron, *The Court of Charles II*, 1897.

7 Julia Cartwright, *Madame, a life of Henrietta daughter of Charles 1st*, 1894.

8 Evelyn, *Diary*.

9 Clarendon State Papers, Venice.

10 D. Jordan and M. Walsh, *The King's Revenge*, 2012.

11 J. Fitzgerald Molloy, *Royalty Restored*, 1885.

12 Harold Love, *Dictionary of National Biography*.

13 N.H. Keeble, *The Restoration: England in the 1660s*.

14 Cyril Hughes Hartman, *The King's Friend: A Life of Charles Berkeley*, 1951.

15 R.A. Stradling, *Spanish Conspiracy in England 1661–3*, unpublished Ph.D., 2 vols, University of Wales, 1968.

16 Molloy, *Royalty Restored*.

7 The Bride's Price

1 Anthony Hamilton, quoted by Lillias Campbell Davidson in *Catherine of Braganza, Infanta of Portugal*, 1928.

2 *Provas da Historia Genealogica da Casa Real Portuguesa*, given in Davidson, *Catherine of Braganza*.

3 Pepys, *Diary*.

4 *The Letters, Speeches and Declarations of King Charles II*, ed. Sir Arthur Bryant, 1935.

5 Ibid.

6 Sir John Reresby, *Memoirs*, 1734.

7 Burnet, *History of My Own Times*.

8 For descriptions of dress in the 1660s and beyond, see Susan Vincent, *Dressing the Elite*, 2003, and C.W. Cunnington and P. Cunnington, *Handbook of English Costume in 17th Century*.

9 Clarendon, *History*.

10 Ibid.

8 The Dissolute Court

1 Vivian de Sola Pinto, *Restoration Carnival*, 1954.

2 John Aubrey, *A Brief Life of Thomas Hobbes*, 1588–1679, in *Brief Lives*, 1680–93, 1898 edition.

3   Hobbes, *Leviathan*.

4   Hamilton.

5   Laura Gowing, *Common Bodies: Women, Sex and Reproduction in Seventeenth Century England*, 2003.

6   Vivian de Sola Pinto, *Sir Charles Sedley, 1639–1671*, 1927.

7   Clarendon, *Life*.

8   Lorenzo Magalotti, *At the Court of Charles II and Travels*, 1669.

9   Clarendon, *Life*.

10 Ibid.

11 Simon Schama, *History of Britain, Vol. 2, The British Wars 1603–1776*, 2001.

12 David Bergerson, *King James and Letters of Homoerotic Desire*, 1999.

13 Brian Fairfax, *Memoirs of the Life of George Villiers, Duke of Buckingham*, 1758.

14 Reresby, *Memoirs*; Burnet, *History of My Own Times*.

15 John Dryden, *Absalom and Achitophel*, 1681.

16 Sir John Denham, *Directions to a Painter for Describing our Naval Business; in Imitation of Mr Waller*, 1667.

17 Pepys, *Diary*, 17 February 1669.

18 Burnet, *History of My Own Times*.

19 John Wilmot, 'A Satyr on Charles the Second': http://andromeda.rutgers.edu/~jlynch/Texts/charles2.html

9 Married Life

1   Pepys, *Diary*.

2   Lansdowne mss.

3   Matthew Jenkinson, *Culture and Politics at the Court of Charles 2nd*, 2010.

4   Jean Adrien Antoine Jules Jusserand, *A French ambassador at the Court of Charles the Second: Le Comte de Cominges*, 1892.

5   Daniel O'Neill to Ormond, Carte 32, fols 10–11.

6   Jusserand, *A French Ambassador*.

7   Pepys, *Diary*.

8   Molloy, *Royalty Restored*.

9   Hartman, *The King's Friend*.

10 Phillip W. Sergeant, *My Lady Castlemaine*, 1912.

11 Lord Dartmouth's note to Burnet, *History of My Own Times*, Vol. I, p. 436.

10 Illness, Plague and Fire

1 Jusserand, *A French Ambassador*.
2 Pepys, *Diary*.
3 Ibid.
4 Ibid.
5 Reresby, *Memoirs*.
6 Charles Knight, *God's Terrible Voice in the City*, 1667.
7 Pepys, *Diary*.
8 Clarendon State Papers, Venice.
9 Cobbett, *State Trials*.
10 Grace Wharton, *Wits and Beaux of Society*, 1890.
11 Violet Barbour, *Henry Bennet, Earl of Arlington*, 1914.
12 Pepys, *Diary*, 8 February 1664.
13 Jusserand, *A French Ambassador*.
14 Ibid.
15 J. Britton et al., *The Beauties of England and Wales*, 1808.
16 Burnet, *History of My Own Times*.
17 Walter Bell, *The Story of London's Great Fire*, 1929.

11 Rivalry and Betrayal

1 Gramont, *Memoirs*.
2 *Court Beauties*.
3 Ruth Norrington, *My Dearest Minette*, 1996.
4 Clarendon, *History*.
5 J.L. Avey, *An Alternate History of the Netherlands*, 2012.
6 Pepys, *Diary*.
7 PRO, SP 29/205/63.
8 Pepys, *Diary*, 29 July 1667.
9 Burnet, *History of My Own Times*.
10 Pepys, *Diary*, 12 July 1667.
11 Molloy, *Royalty Restored*.
12 Burnet, *History of My Own Times*.
13 Harris, *Clarendon and the English Revolution*.
14 Lister, *Life of Clarendon*.
15 Molloy, *Royalty Restored*.
16 *House of Commons Journal*, Vol. 1, pp. 101–27.

12 Entrances and Exits

1   Pinto, *Restoration Carnival*.
2   *Cambridge History of English and American Literature*, Vol. 8, 1907–21.
3   Roi Cooper Megrue and Walter C. Hackette, *It Pays to Advertise*, 1914.
4   Pinto, *Restoration Carnival*.
5   Samuel Johnson, *Lives of the Most Eminent English Poets*, 1779–81; Pepys, *Diary*, 17 July 1663.
6   Ibid.
7   Cibber, *Lives of the Poets*, 1753.

13 Theatrical Rivals

1   Pepys, *Diary*.
2   Evelyn, *Diary*.
3   Parliamentary Statutes.
4   Charles II, *Letters*.
5   Tim Harris, 'The Bawdy House Riots of 1668', *The Historical Journal*, No. 29, 1986.
6   *Middlesex County Records*, Vol. 4, 1667–88, 1892.
7   Ibid.
8   Ibid.
9   Alfred H. Knight, *The Life of the Law*.
10 F. Braudel, *Civilization and Capitalism, 15th–18th Century*.
11 Aphra Behn, *The Works of Aphra Behn*, ed. Montague Summers, 1915; *The Uncollected Verse of Aphra Behn*, ed. Germaine Greer, 1989.
12 Charles II, *Letters*.
13 Charles Beauclerk, *Nell Gwyn*, 2005.

14 A Secret Pact

1   Colbert to Croissy, ms Affairs Etranger, 20 January 1669.
2   Ibid., 14 September 1668.
3   Louis XIV to Colbert de Croissy, 7 November 1668.
4   Gramont.
5   Pepys, *Diary*, 28 April 1669.
6   Clarendon State Papers, Dom, 1671, 271.
7   Secretary Lionne to Colbert, 20 April 1669.
8   Ibid., 6 August 1667.
9   Montagu to Arlington, 3 May 1669.

10 Ruth Norrington, ed., *My Dearest Minette: Letters of Charles II to his Sister*, 1996.
11 Elizabeth Hamilton, *The Illustrious Lady*, 1928.
12 Charles McCormick, *The Secret History of the Court and Reign of Charles 2nd*, 1792.
13 Julia Cartwright, *Madame: Life of Henrietta, daughter of Charles I*, 1894.
14 Pepys, *Diary*, 20 April 1669.
15 Nancy Nicholls Barker, *Brother to the Sun King*, 1989.
16 British Library, Add. MS. 36916.

15 The French Rival

1 Sergeant, *My Lady Castlemaine*.
2 David C. Hanrahan, *Charles II and the Duke of Buckingham*, 2006.
3 Hartley Coleridge (John Dove), *Life of Andrew Marvell*, 1835.
4 Ibid.
5 B.M. Cook, Parliamentary Research archive.
6 D. Jordan and M. Walsh, *White Cargo*, 2007.
7 Hume and Smollett, *History of England*.
8 Clarendon State Papers, Dom 11.277.
9 Sergeant, *My Lady Castlemaine*.
10 Pope, *Second Satire on the first book of Horace*.
11 Gerard Langbaine, *Account of the English dramatic poets*, 1691.
12 Bulstrode papers, 10 January 1671.
13 Burnet, *History of My Own Times*.
14 John Dryden, 'Upon the three dukes killing a beadle'.
15 Clarendon State Papers, Dom, 11 April 1671.
16 Colbert to Lionne, 10 September 1670.
17 Henri Forneron, *Louise de Kérouaille, Duchess of Portsmouth*, 1886.
18 Ibid.

16 A Spy in the Bed

1 Evelyn, *Memoirs*, Vol. 1.
2 Ibid.
3 Derek Wilson, *All the King's Women*, 2003.
4 Evelyn.
5 Colbert to Louvois, French Ministry, 2 November 1672.
6 Ibid., 20 February 1673.

7   Ibid., 24 December 1672.
8   Reresby, *Memoirs*.
9   Fergus Linnane, *London the Wicked City: 1000 Years of Prostitution*, 2003.
10 Henri Forneron, *Louise de Kérouaille, Duchess of Portsmouth*, 1886.
11 Colbert, dispatch to Pomponne, 23 January 1673.
12 Ibid., 30 January 1673.
13 Letter to Williamson, Clarendon State Papers, Dom, 15 June 1673.
14 Clarendon State Papers, Venice, 1673–5, 305.
15 Ruvigny to Pomponne, 18 May 1674.
16 Courtin to Foreign Minister Louvois, undated.
17 Evelyn, *Diary*.

17 A Sensational Encounter with the Past

1   S. Sorbiere, *Relation d'un Voyage en Angleterre*, 1666.
2   Antonie Pannekoek, *A History of Astronomy*, 1961.
3   Burnet, *History of My Own Times*.
4   *Memoirs of Hortense Mancini and Marie Mancini*, trans. Sarah Nelson, 2008.
5   Madame de Sevigné, quoted in H. Noel Williams, *Rival Sultanas*, 1915.
6   *Memoirs of Hortense Mancini*.
7   Williams, *Rival Sultanas*.
8   Hortense's memoir may have been written with the assistance of her admirer, the historian Cesar Vichard. See Williams, *Rival Sultanas*.
9   This portrait hangs in Broughton House, Northamptonshire, Montagu's French-influenced country mansion.
10 Charles de Saint-Evremond, *The Works of Monsieur de Saint-Evremond, Made English from the French*, etc., ed. and trans. Pierre des Maizeaux, London, 1728.
11 Ibid.
12 Williams, *Rival Sultanas*.
13 E.C. Metzger, 'Ralph Montagu', *Dictionary of National Biography*.
14 Hamilton, *The Illustrious Lady*.
15 Williams, *Rival Sultanas*.
16 Saint-Evremond, *Discourse on Friendship*, in *Works*.
17 Saint-Evremond, *The Character of the Duchess Mazarin*, in *Works*.
18 Barillon, quoted in Forneron, *Louise de Kérouaille*.

19 Rathery and Boutron, *Mademoiselle de Scudery, Sa Vie et Sa Correspondance*, 1873.

18 Plots and Alarms

1   Barillon to Louis XIV, 5 December 1678.
2   Forneron, *Louise de Kérouaille*.
3   Bulstrode Whitelock, *Memorials of English Affairs from the Reign of Charles I to the Reign of Charles II*.
4   Hamilton, *The Illustrious Lady*.
5   *Life of Titus Oates*, 1685.
6   Roger L'Estrange, *History of the Times*, 1687.
7   Roger L'Estrange, *Oates, his Case, Person, Character and Plot*, 1685.
8   Reresby, *Memoirs*.
9   Titus Oates, *A sermon preached at an Anabaptist meeting in Wapping on Sunday the 9th of February by the Rev T.O.*, 1699.
10 British Library, Add. MS. 41/656.
11 *Grey's Debates*, 21 October 1678.
12 Cobbett, *State Trials*, Vol. 11.
13 Bryan Bevan, *Charles II's French Mistress*, 1972.
14 Cobbett, *State Trials*, Vol. 11.
15 Sydney diary, 1 June 1679.
16 *House of Commons Journal*, 28 February 1679.
17 National Archives, c212.
18 Sydney diary.
19 Ibid.
20 Burnet, *History of My Own Times*.
21 *Correspondence Politique*, Vol. CXXVI.
22 Dryden, 'Satire on court ladies'.
23 *Articles of High Treason and other high crimes and misdemeanours against the Duchess of Portsmouth*.
24 French Foreign Affairs archive, 26 July 1679.
25 Quoted in Williams, *Rival Sultanas*.
26 Ibid.
27 Adolphos William Ward, *Cambridge Modern History*.
28 Burnet, *History of My Own Times*.
29 Barrillon to Louis XIV, 18 June 1683.
30 Williams, *Rival Sultanas*.
31 Cobbett, *State Trials*, Vol. 9.

19 Death of the King

1   Sir Charles Scarborough, *Account of the Death of King Charles II*, translation from the Latin MS, published in Crawfurd, *Last Days of Charles II*.
2   Burnet, *History of My Own Times*.
3   Scarborough, *Account of the Death of King Charles II*.
4   Burnet, *History of My Own Times*.
5   *The Life of King James II*, 1816.
6   Letters from Monsieur Barillon to the French court, in *Memoirs of Great Britain and Ireland*, ed. Sir John Dalrymple, 1773.
7   Burnet, *History of My Own Times*.
8   J. Hudleston, *A Brief account of particulars occurring at the happy death of our late Sovereign Lord King Charles the 2nd*, printed in *Original Letters Illustrative of English History including numerous Royal Letters*, 2nd series, Vol. 4, ed. Henry Ellis, 1827.
9   Ibid.
10 Ibid.
11 Paul Barillon d'Amoncourt, *Dispatches to Louis XIV*.
12 Scarborough, *Account of the Death of King Charles II*.
13 Burnet, *History of My Own Times*.
14 Barbara Cartland, *The Private Life of Charles II*, 1959.
15 M.L. Wolbarsht and D.S. Sax, 'Charles II, a Royal Martyr', *Notes and Records of the Royal Society of London*, Vol. 16, November 1961.
16 Frederick Holmes, *The Sickly Stuarts: The Medical Downfall of a Dynasty*, 2003.
17 Anthony Wood, *Aethenae Oxonienses*, 1691–2.
18 Fiona Tucker, 'Kill or Cure: The Osteological evidence of the mercury treatment of syphilis in 17th to 19th century London', *London Archaeologist*, Spring 2007.
19 Crawfurd, *Last Days of Charles II*; 'Nova et Valera', *British Medical Journal*, Vol. 2, 1938.
20 Burnet, *History of My Own Times*.
21 George Savile, Marquis of Halifax, *Character of King Charles II*, 1750.
22 Faramerz Dabhoiwala, *The Origins of Sex*, 2012.
23 Evelyn, *Diary*.
24 Dabhoiwala, op. cit.
25 Alexander Pope, *Essay on Criticism*, 1709.

Postscript: The King's Descendants and their Legacy

1 Lord Montagu, *Wheels within Wheels*, 2001.
2 Obituary, *Daily Telegraph*, 5 September 2007.
3 Acton, 'Secret History of Charles II'.
4 http://www.theislandwiki.org/index.php?title=La_Cloche
   and:
   http://www.theislandwiki.org/index.php/La_Cloche_baptisms_in_St
   Helier_1596-1665

Appendix: Some Aspects of Sex in the Seventeenth Century

1 Galen, quoted in T. Laqueur, *Making Sex, Body and Gender from the Greeks to Freud*, 1990.
2 Jane Sharp, *The Midwives Book*, 1671, ed. Elaine Hobby, 1999.
3 *The Compleat Midwives' Practice*, 1656 (believed to have been written by Thomas Camberlayne).
4 Sharp, *The Midwives Book*.
5 Anton de Leeuwenhoek, *Philosophical Transactions of the Royal Society*.
6 Gowing, *Common Bodies*.
7 John Sadler, *The Sicke Woman's Private Looking Glass*, 1636.

ACKNOWLEDGEMENTS

Books of a factual nature being what they are, many thanks are due to many. We are especially grateful to Tim Whiting at Little, Brown, who steered us towards this project and lent his invaluable support throughout; to Claudia Connal for her clear-sighted editing, always keeping in focus what was necessary, and to Linda Silverman and Iain Hunt. Thanks are also due to Dr Ted Vallance, Reader in Early Modern History at the University of Roehampton, who made many helpful suggestions and observations on the manuscript. The eminent pathologist Professor Sebastian Lucas kindly reviewed the evidence regarding the cause of Charles II's death, and Dr Paul Harlow offered perceptive psychiatric observations on Charles's character. Books like this cannot be written without archives and archivists; we take this opportunity to thank them in general, and more especially those at the British Library and the National Archives. Finally, thanks go to our wives, for their constant, but by no means uncritical, support during the writing of this book.

SELECT BIBLIOGRAPHY

The following is not an exhaustive list of the sources consulted but is intended as a general list of works we found valuable and illuminating. This list only scratches the surface. For a more complete list the reader should refer to the references where a much more comprehensive list, including contemporary sources and journals, will be found.

Acton (Lord), 'The Secret History of Charles II', in *Historical Essays and Studies*, 1907

James Aikman, *Annals of the Persecution in Scotland from the Restoration to the Revolution*, 1844

Ailesbury, Earl of, *Memoirs*, ed. W.E. Buckley, 1890

Augustus Anglicus, *Life and Reign of Charles 2nd*, 1686

Pietro Aretino, *Sonetti Lussurioso*, 1524

John Aubrey, *Brief Lives*, compiled 1669–93, Penguin edition 2000

Aulnoy, Marie Catherine, Baronne D'Aulnoy, *Memoirs of the Court of England in 1675*

J.L. Avey, *An Alternate History of the Netherlands*, 2012

Violet Barbour, *Henry Bennet Earl of Arlington*, 1914

Paul Barillon d'Amoncourt, *Dispatches to Louis XIV*, 1808

Nancy Nicholls Barker, *Brother to the Sun King*, 1989

Charles Beauclerk, *Nell Gwyn*, 2005

Walter Bell, *The Story of London's Great Fire*, 1929

David Bergerson, *King James and Letters of Homoerotic Desire*, 1999

Bryan Bevan, *James Duke of Monmouth*, 1973

—— *Charles II's French Mistress*, 1972

Fernand Braudel, *Civilization and Capitalism 15th–18th Century, Vol. 1, The Structures of Everyday Life*, English translation 1981

J. Britton *et al.*, *The Beauties of England and Wales*, 1808

A.M. Broadley, *The Royal Miracle, A collection of tracts, broadsides, letters etc.*, 1912

Sir Arthur Bryant, ed., *The Letters, Speeches and Declarations of King Charles II*, 1935

John Buchan, *A Book of Escapes and Hurried Journeys*, 1922

Edmund Burke, *Works*, 1839

Gilbert Burnet, *A History of My Own Times*, 1674–85, 1724

H. Carey, *Memorials of the Great Civil War in England from 1646 to 1652: edited from original letters in the Bodlean Library*, 1842

John Carswell, *The Porcupine, A Life of Algernon Sidney*, 1989

Barbara Cartland, *The Private Life of Charles II*, 1959

Julia Cartwright, *Madame: Life of Henrietta, daughter of Charles I*, 1894

T. Chamberlayne, *The Compleat Midwives' Practice*, 1656

Charles I, *Letters, Speeches and Proclamations*, ed. Sir Charles Petrie, 1935

Charles II (with Samuel Pepys), *His Majesty Preserved, an account of the escape of King Charles 2nd from the battle of Worcester till his landing in France dictated to Samuel Pepys Esq.*, 1954

Colley Cibber, *Lives of the Poets*, 1753

Clarendon, Earl of, *The History of the Rebellion and Civil Wars in England*, 1717

William Cobbett, *Cobbett's Complete Collection of State Trials and Proceedings for High Treason*, 1809

Hartley Coleridge (John Dove), *Life of Andrew Marvell*, 1835

Montagu Cox and Philip Norman, eds, *Survey of London*, 1930

Sir Raymond Henry Payne Crawfurd, *The Last Days of Charles II*, 1909

C.W. Cunnington and P. Cunnington, *Handbook of English Costume in 17th Century*, 1972

Faramerz Dabhoiwala, *The Origins of Sex*, 2012

Sir John Dalrymple, ed., *Memoirs of Great Britain and Ireland*, 1773

Lillias Campbell Davidson, *Catherine of Braganza, Infanta of Portugal*, 1928

Sir John Denham, *Directions to a Painter for Describing our Naval Business; in Imitation of Mr Waller*, 1667

John Dryden, *The Major Works*, ed., Keith Walker, 1987

Roger L'Estrange, *History of the Times*, 1687

John Evelyn, *Diaries*, 1818

—— *Tyrannus, or, the Mode*, 1661

Brian Fairfax, *Memoirs of the Life of George Villiers, Duke of Buckingham*, 1758

Henri Forneron, *The Court of Charles II*, 1897

—— *Louise de Kérouaille, Duchess of Portsmouth*, 1886

S.R. Gardiner, *History of the Great Civil War*, 1894

Margaret Gilmour, *The Great Lady*, 1941

Laura Gowing, *Common Bodies: Women, Sex and Reproduction in Seventeenth Century England*, 2003

Emanuel Green, 'Siege of Bridgwater', in *Bye-paths of Bath and Somerset History*, 1905

Elizabeth Hamilton, *The Iillustrious Llady*, 1928

David C. Hanrahan, *Charles II and the Duke of Buckingham*, 2006

Ronald W. Harris, *Clarendon and the English Revolution*, 1983

Tim Harris, *Restoration, Charles II and his Kingdoms*, 2006

—— 'The Bawdy House Riots of 1668', *The Historical Journal*, no. 29, 1986

Letters of Henrietta Maria, ed. Everett Green, 1857

Cyril Hughes Hartman, *The King's Friend, Life of Charles Berkeley*, 1951

Samuel Holford, *Augustus Anglicus, Life and Reign of Charles 2nd*, 1686

Frederick Holmes, *The Sickly Stuarts, The Medical Downfall of a Dynasty*, 2003

J. Hudleston, *A Brief account of particulars occurring at the happy death of our late Sovereign Lord King Charles the 2nd*, printed in *Original Letters Illustrative of English History including numerous Royal Letters*, 2nd series, Vol 4, ed. Henry Ellis, 1844

John Hughes, ed., *The Boscobel tracts relating to the escape of Charles 2nd after the battle of Worcester and his subsequent adventures*, 1857

David Hume and Tobias Smollett, *History of England*, 1822

Ronald Hutton, *Charles the Second*, 1989

James II *et al.*, *The Life of King James II*, 1816

Matthew Jenkinson, *Culture and Politics at the Court of Charles II*, 2010

John Jesse, *Memoirs of the Court in England Under the Stuarts*, 1857

Samuel Johnson, *Lives of the Most Eminent English Poets*, 1800

D. Jordan and M. Walsh, *The King's Revenge*, 2012

—— *White Cargo*, 2007

Jean Adrien Antoine Jules Jusserand, *Le Comte de Cominges, a French ambassador at the court of Charles II*, 1892

N.H. Keeble, *The Restoration: England in the 1660s*, 2004

Andrew Kippis, *Biographica Britannia or the Lives of the Most Eminent Persons*, 1793

Alfred H. Knight, *The Life of the Law*, 1998

Charles Knight, *God's Terrible Voice in the City*, 1667

Gerard Langbaine, *Account of the English Dramatic Poets*, 1691

T. Laqueur, *Making Sex, Body and Gender from the Greeks to Freud*, 1990

Anton de Leeuwenhoek, *Philosophical Transactions of the Royal Society*, 1848

Fergus Linnane, *London the Wicked City: 1000 Years of Prostitution*, 2003

Thomas Henry Lister, *Life of Clarendon*, 1838

Lorenzo Magalotti, *At the Court of Charles II and Travels*, 1669

Charles McCormick, *The Secret History of the Court and Reign of Charles 2nd*, 1792

Roi Cooper Megrue and Walter C. Hackette, *It Pays to Advertise*, 1914

E.C. Metzger, *Ralph Montagu, Dictionary of National Biography*

Thomas Middleton, *A Mad World My Masters*, 1604

J. Fitzgerald Molloy, *Royalty Restored*, 1885

T Morrice, *Life of Roger Earl of Orrery*, 1743

Francois Bertaut De Motteville, *Memoirs of Mademoiselle de Monpensier*, 1848

S. Nelson, trans., *Memoirs of Hortense Mancini and Marie Mancini*, 2008

M. Newcastle, *The Duke and Duchess of Newcastle*, 1910

Ruth Norrington, ed., *My Dearest Minette: Letters of Charles II to his Sister*, 1996

Titus Oates, *Life of Titus Oates*, 1685

—— *A sermon preached at an Anabaptist meeting in Wapping on Sunday the 9th of February by the Rev T.O.*, 1699

Antonie Pannekoek, *A History of Astronomy*, 1961

Samuel Pepys, *Diary*

Vivian de Sola Pinto, *Sir Charles Sedley, 1639–1671*, 1927

—— *Restoration Carnival*, 1954

Alexander Pope, *Essay on Criticism*, 1709

—— *Second Satire on the First Book of Horace*, 1738

E.J.B. Rathery and Boutron, *Mademoiselle de Scudery, Sa Vie et Sa Correspondance*, 1873

Sir John Reresby, *Memoirs*, 1734

John Rushworth, *Historical Collections*, 1708

John Sadler, *The Sicke Woman's Private Looking Glass*, 1636

Charles de Saint-Evremond, *The Works of Monsieur de Saint-Evremond, Made English from the French*, etc., ed. and trans. Pierre des Maizeaux, London, 1728.

George Savile, Marquis of Halifax, *Character of King Charles II*, 1750

Sir Charles Scarborough, *Account of the Death of King Charles II*, 1909

Simon Schama, *History of Britain, Vol. 2, The British Wars 1603–1776*, 2001

Eva Scott, *Travels of the King*, 1907

Phillip W. Sergeant, *My Lady Castlemaine*, 1912

Jane Sharp, *The Midwives Book*, ed. Elaine Hobby, 1671, 1999

S. Sorbière, *Relation d'un Voyage en Angleterre*, 1666

G. Steinman, *A Memoir of Barbara Duchess of Cleveland*, 1871 and *Letters of Philip, Second Earl of Chesterfield*, 1930

R.A. Stradling, *Spanish Conspiracy in England 1661–3* (unpublished Ph.D., 2 vols.)

Robert Talbor, *Pyretologia*, 1672

Robert Talbor and others, *The English Remedy*, 1682

Simon Thurley, *Whitehall Palace, An Architectural History of the Royal Apartments*, 1999

Fiona Tucker, 'Kill or Cure: The osteological evidence of the mercury treatment of syphilis in 17th to 19th century London', *London Archeologist*, Spring 2007

Jenny Uglow, *A Gambling Man*, 2009

George Villiers, 2nd Duke of Buckingham, *The Rehearsal*, performed 1671, first published 1672

Susan Vincent, *Dressing the Elite*, 2003

James Walen, *The House of Cromwell*, 1897

Adolphos William Ward, *Cambridge Modern History*, 1934

Grace Wharton, *Wits and Beaux of Society*, 1890

Bulstrode Whitelock, *Memorials of English Affairs from the Reign of Charles I to the Reign of Charles II*, 1682

D.E. Williams, *The Life and Correspondence of Sir Thomas Lawrence, Kt.*, 1831

H. Noel Williams, *Rival Sultanas*, 1915

John Wilmot, 2nd Earl of Rochester, *Collected Works*, 1926

Derek Wilson, *All the King's Women*, 2003

M.L. Wolbarsht and D.S. Sax, 'Charles II, a Royal Martyr', *Notes and Records of the Royal Society of London*, Vol. 16, November 1961

Anthony Wood, *Aethenae Oxonienses*, 1691–2

INDEX

abortion, 66
Acton, Lord, 26, 298–9, 300
Albemarle, 2nd Duke of, 216
Alberti, Girolamo, 230
America, 76, 172
Anglican Church, 15, 26, 34, 93–4,
   98–9, 177, 225, 228, 235, 261;
   Book of Common Prayer, 104;
   Great Ejection, 122
Anglo-Dutch war, second
   (1665–7), 114, 136, 140, 142,
   149–53, 158, 171–2, 196–7; Dutch
   navy's Medway attack, 7, 152–4,
   160, 170
Anglo-Dutch war, third (1672–4),
   227–8, 233, 235
Anne, Duchess of York (Anne
   Hyde), 78–80, 97, 106, 126, 155,
   225, 228
Anne of Austria (widow of Louis
   XIII), 29, 31, 200
Anne-Marie Louise d'Orléans ('La
   Grande Mademoiselle'), 16,
   31–3, 39, 60
Aretino, Pietro, 7*
Argyll, Marquis of, 40–1

Arlington, Countess of, 208, 217,
   219–20, 221
Arlington, Henry Bennet, Earl of:
   Buckingham and, 132, 151, 155,
   159, 196, 229; in Castlemaine
   circle, 138, 139, 140; character
   of, 85, 104, 105, 132, 159;
   Clarendon and, 85, 105, 138,
   156; as a court wit, 108, 111, 112;
   France and, 177, 196, 198, 221,
   252; Louise de Kérouaille and,
   208, 217, 218, 219–20, 221, 227,
   229–30; Hortense Mancini and,
   247; marriage of daughter
   Isabella, 222, 295; political
   career, 59, 100, 103, 104, 105,
   139, 159–60, 177, 196, 202,
   229–30; as rumoured lover of
   Lucy Walter, 58, 59
Arundel, Lord, 202
astronomy, 235–6
Aubigny (French crown property),
   226–7
Aubrey, John, 163
Audley End House, 190
Augustus Anglicus, 75

ABOUT THE AUTHORS

Don Jordan is a writer and filmmaker who has won, among other awards, two Blue Ribbons at the New York Film and Television Festival. He has worked widely in television current affairs, documentaries and drama. He co-wrote and co-produced the award-winning feature film, *Love is the Devil*, about the painter Francis Bacon.

Michael Walsh is a writer and filmmaker. After twelve years as a reporter/presenter on the ITV series *World in Action*, he worked on many other programmes, most recently a documentary on the Holocaust. His programmes have won six national and international awards.

Together they have written three books, including *White Cargo*, acclaimed by Nobel Laureate Toni Morrison as 'an extraordinary book'.